# THE ILLUSTRATED ENCYCLOPEDIA OF
# HOUSE PLANTS

ISBN 0-7063-5819-8

# THE ILLUSTRATED ENCYCLOPEDIA OF
# HOUSE PLANTS

Jud Arnold

**WARD LOCK LIMITED · LONDON**

# Contents

# Introduction

A home without house plants is drab and uninteresting. House plants can give your home a lush green sub-tropical appearance, providing greenery all year-round. Or, they can simply add a splash of colour to the dark, dark days of winter. But more than anything, they provide you with the opportunity to satisfy the urge to grow plants.

During the past 15 years or so, radical changes in our way of living—central heating is no longer a luxury reserved for the rich, the perils of town gas have receded and our houses are much better insulated and less draughty—have led to greatly improved growing conditions for plants. So much so that your choice of house plants has increased from a few dozen 'easy' ones to literally hundreds of different species. For the beginner, there's a wide selection of charming plants including *Araucaria excelsa* Norfolk Island Pine, *Beloperone guttata* Shrimp Plant, *Ficus elastica* Rubber Plant, *Monstera deliciosa* Swiss Cheese Plant, *Neanthe bella* Parlour Palm and *Sansevieria trifasciata laurentii* Mother-in-Law's Tongue. The more experienced gardener can try his hand at growing plants like *Codiaeum pennick* Blood Red Croton, and *Platycerium alcicorne* Stagshorn Fern. And for the enthusiast, there's a huge range of delicate plants which need lots of care and attention and carefully controlled growing conditions—*Begonia rex* Fan Plant, *Dieffenbachia* Dumb Cane and *Maranta tricolor* Red Herringbone are a few of the most popular examples.

This book has been specially designed and written to help you, the indoor gardener, choose, buy and cultivate healthy and beautiful house plants.

The main part of this book looks at over 175 house plants, in turn, giving all the essential details about temperature requirements, humidity, light, watering, feeding, potting compost and hints for successful growing. If you do run into trouble—a Rubber Plant dropping its leaves, for example—there's a section for each plant telling you what has gone wrong and how to deal with it. For those people interested in increasing their stock of plants—for themselves or presents for their friends—there's information on the best way to propagate each plant. But, probably more important than anything else, each plant has been clearly photographed or illustrated making it easy for you to identify those plants you already have and to plan which ones you would like to own. If you've ever wondered where a plant originally came from, what its native environment is like, how it was brought to this country and how it has been further developed, then the answer is here. Each plant has its own historical and background profile.

The second part of this book goes into more detail about how you can achieve the levels of humidity needed, how to make your own potting compost, how to supply the water and food for your plants and how you can make the most of your available light and improve on it by using artificial lights. This part also has a number of special sections from which you will learn about the ancient oriental art of bonsai, how to grow plants in a terrarium and the techniques of the new hydroculture—growing plants in water. Finally this book tells you how you can put all your plants together to form living-room decorations and gives hints to overcome that problem time for house plants—when you go away for your summer holidays.

All the house plants are indexed by both common and botanical names to make it easy for you to find the answers to your problem. Botanical names may be a bit of a mouthful to pronounce and more difficult to remember than the more descriptive common names, but it's worth the time and trouble to get to know plants by them. Botanical names are the only sure way to identify plants.

Part One
Encyclopedia

# ABUTILON
*Flowering Maple, Weeping Chinese Maple*

The name "parlor plant" always conjures up a certain nostalgia of the wood and coal stove days. The Parlor Maple (Flowering Maple) is one such plant that never quite disappeared after that era and is now experiencing a well-deserved return to popularity as a small indoor tree as well as a tender plant for the patio and outside.

## Origin

Genus Abutilon is a member of the Mallow family (Malvaceae) with approximately 150 species native to the tropical and semi-tropical areas, especially Central and South America.

## Description

This tender, soft wooded shrub has slender stems, up to 15 feet, with soft haired, long stemmed, green, sometimes variegated leaves that are mostly palmate or maple shaped with 3, 5 or 7 lobes. Drooping flowers, somewhat similar to partly opened Hollyhocks, are borne freely from the leaf axils. They are bell shaped with 5 petals in yellow, orange or reddish purple and often strikingly veined. The principal species that are grown include:
*A. hybridum*, Flowering Maple, a collection of varieties developed by plant breeders, usually grows to 5 feet with flowers in various shades of white, red, yellow and orange.
*A. insigne*, one of the originals from Colombia and Venezuela, grows to 4 feet with whitish to rose colored flowers. It was reportedly introduced into Europe around 1851 by Lucien Linden.
*A. megapotamicum variegatum* is a trailing variety from South Brazil, growing 2 to 6 feet with arrow shaped, modestly lobed leaves and red flowers. This plant, with pruning, is widely used for hanging baskets.
*A. pictum*, from Brazil, grows to 15 feet with 3, 5 or 7 lobed leaves. Flowers are yellowish with crimson veins.
There are several varieties with variegated leaves.

## Cultivation

Locate plant in a sunny to semi-sunny spot to encourage and maintain flowering over winter. Average home temperature and humidity are suitable for Abutilon. Regular pinch pruning will produce bushy plants and more flowers since they are produced from fresh terminal growth. Plants are often grown in the outside border during the frost-free months. Such plants may be cut back in autumn, lifted and potted for growth indoors during the winter months. Avoid crowding the plant and treat it as a specimen for room decoration.

## Potting

Use a rich friable soil mixture such as equal parts loam, coarse builders' sand, peat moss, rotted or dried manure or leafmould. Cover the drainage hole with a generous layer of broken crock, crushed stone or pea gravel. Repotting should be undertaken in early spring. Once a plant has reached the determined final pot size, a root bound condition may be alleviated by supplementary feeding or by turning the plant out of the pot and cutting away a one-third slice of the root ball and returning it to the same pot using fresh potting soil in the open space.

## Watering

Moisture loss from the large soft foliage may be considerable, thus the soil must be kept evenly moist at all times.

## Feeding

Since the plant will grow and flower the year round, supplementary feeding, especially for pot bound plants, should be given on a 10 to 14 day schedule with a water soluble general fertilizer.

*Abutilon hybridum*

## Propagation

Readily from seeds which are available from most seed houses, sown in winter or early spring. Cuttings 4 to 6 inches in length, from terminal growth, will readily root in moist sand or vermiculite. Dip the cut ends in rooting hormone powder to accelerate this process. Enclose the rooting bed in a clear plastic bag to reduce leaf wilting during the rooting phase. Keep out of direct sun.

## Special Problems

Aphids are fond of the soft juicy growth. They are readily controlled with malathion spray.

# ACALYPHA hispida

*Chenille Plant, Red Hot Cattail, Foxtail*

Acalypha is commonly called Chenille Plant, Red Hot Cattail, Foxtail, because of the bright flowers that grow in long drooping tails.

## Origin

*Acalypha hispida* is one of over 400 species of genus Acalypha —all are members of the Spurge Family (Euphorbiaceae).

## Description

Chenille Plant is a shrub growing to 15 feet in its native habitat of Malaya. The heart shaped leaves are about 9 inches long and the red to purple pendant flower spikes may reach 18 inches and 1 inch in diameter.

## Cultivation

Grow in semi-sun except during winter when full sun is desirable. Average room temperature is satisfactory with a night temperature of 18°C. (65°F.). It takes many years to grow large specimens.

## Potting

Use a rich friable soil mixture of equal parts loam, coarse builders' sand, peat moss and rotted or dried manure or compost. For prompt drainage use a generous layer of pebbles or pea gravel over the drainage hole.

## Watering

Keep evenly moist at all times. Place the plant over a humidity tray and mist spray the foliage with clear tepid water.

## Feeding

Use a water soluble general fertilizer on a two week schedule during the growing and flowering period, spring through summer.

## Propagation

Cuttings from mature wood taken at any time of the year. Use a rooting hormone powder on the cut ends and place in moist sand or peat moss. Bottom heat will accelerate rooting.

## Special Problems

Excessive dryness can destroy the plant. Control red spider and mealy bugs with malathion insecticide.

*Acalypha hispida*

# ACIDANTHERA

One of the outstanding features of this late-summer flowering corm is the exotic sweet perfume of the flowers.

## Origin

Acidanthera is a member of the Iris family (Iridaceae) and is a native of tropical South Africa.

## Description

This plant is a herbaceous perennial growing from a gladiolus-like corm. The foliage appears blade-like and ribbed and on initial inspection, one might think the plant is a gladiolus. The blades of foliage reach a height of 30 inches and are a pleasant medium green. Each plant bears one spike with about 12 flowers. Only one flower is in full bloom at any one time. For this reason, the best effect is achieved by planting in clumps. Individual flowers are orchid-like in appearance, creamy white with a dark purplish-red blotch in the throat. Each blossom is on a long 4-inch tube which removes it from the stiff floral formality of the gladiolus. Flowers are 4 inches across and have a total of 6 petals. The flower spike eventually grows 4 feet high. The flowering period extends well into October.

## Cultivation

In late May, plant at least 10 corms in a low, wide pot or tub using a potting mixture of equal parts coarse builders' sand, peat moss and rotted or dried manure. Plant about one inch deep and water thoroughly. In about a week sprouts will begin to show and the planting should be moved into the bright light of a sunny window or out of doors in a sunny location. Plants grown outdoors must be moved indoors well before the first frost. A growing temperature of 15 to 18°C. (60 to 65°F.) is ideal.

Promptly after flowering, cut off the tops and harvest the corms from the soil and dry in a warm ventilated area. Pack in paper bags and store in a cool dark place as with gladiolus. Replant again the following spring.

## Potting

In late May, plant at least 10 corms one inch deep in a low wide pot using a mixture of equal parts coarse builders' sand, peat moss, and rotted or dried manure. Make certain the drainage hole is open and well covered with broken shard or pea gravel.

## Watering

Keep the soil evenly moist at all times.

## Feeding

Use a water soluble general fertilizer on a 10 to 14 day schedule throughout the growing and flowering period.

## Propagation

From seeds or the numerous cormels that are around the corm.

## Special problems

No special problems.

*Acidanthera*

# AGAPANTHUS africanus

*Lily-of-the-Nile, Blue African Lily*

Easy to grow, this plant produces beautiful indigo flowers from late spring to autumn.

## Origin

Commonly known as Lily of the Nile, Blue African Lily, *Agapanthus africanus* of the Lily family (Liliaceae), is native to the Cape of Good Hope. It is reported that plants introduced by the Dutch were grown in Europe well before 1629.

## Description

This plant grows from a tuberous root stock and is classed as half-hardy. It flowers from late spring to autumn, but mostly during the summer months. Each established plant may provide up to 30 flowering stalks, each topped with a cluster of 20 to 30 individual, trumpet-shaped flowers colored porcelain blue. The strap-shaped foliage is dark green, about half an inch wide with some individual leaves as long as 24 inches. The toal height of a plant in bloom is 30 to 36 inches.

## Cultivation

This plant is usually kept dormant during winter with only enough water and light to keep the leaves from falling. Beginning in the spring, give full light with some sun and keep the soil constantly moist. This plant will tolerate average house humidity and cool temperatures, preferably not over 21°C. (72°F.) in winter.

After blooming, watering and feeding should be reduced and the plant should be stored in a cool shaded location—as low as 7°C. (45°F.) is ideal. Don't allow the plant to become bone dry during this period. Normally, heavier watering should be started up again in March to have the plant in active growth for summer bloom. For spring blooming, start heavier watering during January.

## Potting

The potting soil should be a mixture of equal parts rich loam, coarse builders' sand, peat moss and well rotted or dried manure. Make certain that the pot has good drainage by placing a layer of pea gravel or broken pottery over the drainage hole. This plant is normally grown in a fairly large pot or wooden tub. The roots are so strong they sometimes break a clay pot.

Plant the growing end of the root just level with the surface of the soil. Soak the pot after planting and keep moist. Place in a sunny location. Frequent repotting is not conducive to free flowering and it is better to treat a pot bound condition with generous feeding during the active growing and blooming period. However, once a decline in vigor is noted, repotting should be undertaken during March in time for the new growth period.

With care, the tuberous roots will last for many years.

*Agapanthus africanus*

## Watering

Keep soil constantly moist after the winter dormancy period.

## Feeding

This plant requires rich soil and continuous feeding as well as watering. Use a water soluble general fertilizer mixed to manufacturer's directions, often and generously.

## Propagation

Usually by division of the roots rather than from seeds. Division should take place in early spring.

## Special Problems

Essentially trouble-free.

# AGAVE
*Century Plant, Thread Plant*

*Agave attenuata*

A truly magnificent group of plants of economic importance particularly to Mexico. The leaves are used for cattle feed, while the fibers of the leaves (sisal hemp) are formed into thread, cord and ropes. The sap of some species is fermented to yield Mexican Pulque. Distilled, it becomes mescal and tequila. The pulp is used for making soap.

## Origin

Native to the hot, arid deserts in America. There are well over 300 species of Mexican origin that have been identified and described. Agave is a member of the Agave family (Agavaceae).

## Description

These are truly handsome plants with long, stiff, grey-green evergreen leaves that are formed in clumps or rosettes, which in some species can be over 6 to 8 feet in diameter with a flowering spike 30 feet high. Some species are armored with hard sharp teeth along the leaves and a thorn-like tip. Most species grow so large that they are useful as house plants only during their early years. Eventually they become tub plants which, with care, can be kept somewhat dwarfed. *A. attenuata* is a medium size species with soft grey-green rosettes that are totally unarmed. In nature a mature plant has a four foot trunk with leaves 6 inches wide and 30 inches long. The flower spike often reaches 10 feet. *A. americana*, is probably the most widely known because of its immense size. On the mature plants leaves may be 8 inches wide and as long as 80 inches. The leaves are heavily armed with an end spike and teeth along the edges. The fact that this plant was rarely observed in bloom gave rise to the belief that it flowered once in a hundred years (Century Plant) which of course is erroneous since mature plants in their native habitat will bloom after only ten years.

## Cultivation

Plants need good light throughout the year and they may be summered outside during the frost-free months. Over winter, as with cacti, they should have a light cool location with a temperature of 10 to 15°C. (50 to 60°F.). Large tub size specimens may be stored in a cool greenhouse over winter at 4°C. (40°F.).

## Potting

Move plants to larger size pots only when the root ball has become thoroughly compacted. Tub specimen plants may be held to container size by removing the plant and pruning away a slice of the root ball from one side, returning to the tub and adding soil mix to replace the cut away portion. Allow the roots to heal for a week before watering. Potting soil can be two parts loam and one part coarse builders' sand or equal parts coarse builders' sand, peat moss and rotted or dried manure. It is important that the drainage holes be well covered with sand or gravel.

## Watering

Only when the top of the soil becomes dry to touch then soak and drain thoroughly and allow the soil to become dry before watering again.

## Feeding

Growth will be accelerated with supplementary feeding during the summer growing period. Water soluble general fertilizer may be used on a 14 day schedule. Plants may be kept smaller with less feeding.

## Propagation

Older plants of *A. americana* produce may off-shoots which may be separated with a sharp knife. Allow cut

*Agave americana variegata*

ends to heal in the open air for a few days before rooting in coarse damp builders' sand.

## Special Problems

Over-watering can induce rot.

# AGLAONEMA modestum

*Chinese Evergreen*

One answer to the apartment dweller's prayers is *Aglaonema modestum,* otherwise known as Chinese Evergreen. This plant, as with Aspidistra, can really take it.

## Origin

Native to tropical Asia, Aglaonema is a member of the Arum or Calla family (Araceae). This evergreen genus of plants has about 50 species that grow from rhizome-type roots, usually in tropical forests in damp air and low light.

## Description

Aglaonema species *modestum* has lance-shaped, erect leaves 8 to 10 inches long and 4 inches wide. The foliage is an attractive glossy-green. When carefully grown, the plant produces light green calla-like flowers followed by orange berries. In nature, *modestum* is found from South China into North Thailand. Young plants are often used in terrarium plantings because of the slow growth habit.

## Cultivation

Chinese Evergreen will prosper in semi-shady to shady locations in average room temperature and humidity. Leaves should be wiped occasionally with a soft cloth and clear water to keep them bright and shiny.

## Potting

Use a mixture of equal parts loam, builders' sand and peat moss and plant in wide, low azalea or bulb pots. Cover the drainage holes with a generous amount of shard or gravel. Plants will also survive for a long time in a dish of water. Add pieces of activated charcoal to keep the water sweet.

## Watering

Water freely during the growing season and keep just moist over winter.

## Feeding

During the growing period, March to August, use water soluble general fertilizer on a 14 day schedule.

## Propagation

Stem cuttings will root in water or moist sand.

## Special Problems

Essentially trouble-free. Invasions of mealy bugs or spider mites should be treated with malathion spray.

*Aglaonema modestum*

15

# ALOCASIA

*Elephant's Ear Plant*

These exotic foliage plants make an outstanding tropical display.

## Origin

Genus Alocasia with about 70 species is a member of Arum or Calla family (Araceae). They are native to South Asia and the East Indies.

## Description

Sometimes called the Elephant's Ear Plant, these plants are notable for their large ornamental foliage. The leaves are remarkable for their various shapes and sizes as well as the coloring and marking. Some of them have a rich metallic color, while others are green, or green and white with prominent veining and maroon purple beneath. Plants grow from rhizomatous type roots. Species fall into two classes, one evergreen, the other which takes a rest period each year during which leaves are shed. Commonly grown evergreen species include:

*A. cuprea* from Borneo with two foot stems and broadening oval, wavy leaves up to 18 inches wide and 24 inches long. The upper leaf surface is dark metallic green with a darker rib and veins, the underside is a rich purple.

*A. longiloba* from Malaya and Indonesia has one foot stems bearing green leaves on both sides, up to 30 inches in length and triangular in shape.

*A. watsoniana* also from Malaya and Indonesia has egg shaped leaves to 3 feet in length and 2 feet wide, with the upper surface dark olive and a pale green mid rib. Edges are ivory white and the underside red-purple. These are borne on stems up to 3 feet in length.

## Cultivation

Place in a semi-sunny spot where the temperature never drops below (16°C.) (60°F.). High humidity is required in the 50% range which calls for a humidity tray and frequent mist spraying of the foliage with clear water.

## Potting

Use a potting mix of one part fibrous loam, two parts peat moss and one part of a mixture of activated charcoal and perlite or vermiculite. Cover the drainage holes with a generous layer of pebbles or pea gravel. Large plants will require a 10 to 12-inch size pot. Repot only when absolutely necessary by trimming the root ball and returning to the pot with fresh potting soil.

## Watering

Keep evenly moist at all times.

## Feeding

Use water soluble general fertilizer on a two week schedule throughout the year.

## Propagation

From basal offshoots or rhizome cuttings planted in 4-inch pots during the month of March. Also from seeds planted during the same time.

## Special Problems

Drafts and temperature below 16°C. (60°F.) will cause edges of leaves to brown.

*Alocasia cuprea*

# ALOE

Known through the ages as a medicinal plant grown by the Greeks and Romans as a pot plant, Aloes continue to be popular house plants.

## Origin

The genus Aloe is a member of the Lily family (Liliaceae) that has over 200 species, mostly native to Africa's tropic region. It is reported that the Spaniards introduced the plant into Mexico and Southern California for medicinal purposes.

## Description

The thick, lance-like leaves of this succulent are arranged in rosettes that give an appearance somewhat like the Agave for which it is sometimes mistaken. However, the soft pulpy leaves of the Aloe readily distinguish it from the tough, fibrous leaves of the Agave. The members of this genus vary in height from 2 to 3 inches to tree-like shrubs, 15 feet or more in height. While the Aloe is much admired for its leaves and form, it also excels as a flowering plant. In its native Southern Hemisphere, the Aloe blooms in spring and summer which means flowers are produced during autumn and winter in the north. The easiest and most popular of the potted plant types are: *Aloe brevifolia*, a 2 to 3½-inch diameter rosette type that sends up an 18-inch flowering spike. The 1¾-inch tubular flowers are red with greenish markings. This plant is widely used in dish gardens. *Aloe variegata* (Partridge Breast Aloe or Tiger Aloe) is widely known for its attractive markings overlapping leaves. The erect, and triangular, V-shaped leaves eventually reach 9 to 12 inches and are dark green, generously marbled and margined with white.

The 12-inch flower spike bears red flowers with green veins. *Aloe vara vulgaris* reaches 18 to 24 inches with spreading lance-like leaves gradually narrowing from a 2 to 3-inch base to 12 to 18 inches in length, usually mottled white. The edges of the leaves are armored with soft widely spaced teeth. The flower spike reaches 2 to 3 feet and bears simple 1 inch long yellow flowers. This plant is widely grown in pots and is commonly called "the first aid plant" since the juice from a broken leaf is often used to treat minor burns, sunburn and insect bites. It is a handy plant to have beside the pool and barbecue grill or in the kitchen.

*Aloe variegata*

## Cultivation

Place in a window that provides sunny to semi-sunny light. Use a south window in the winter and east or west window in summer. Avoid temperatures over 23°C. (75°F.). During winter this plant will succeed in a temperature as low as 6°C. (43°F.) In the frost-free months, plants may be summered on a patio or located in a border with the pot sunk into the ground.

When flowering and active growth ceases, allow the plant to go dormant by placing in a cool, light spot, 7 to 15°C. (45 to 60°F.) and water only enough to prevent shriveling. This plant as with Christmas Cactus, is programmed for southern hemisphere culture.

## Potting

A loose friable soil is best suited to this plant and a mixture of equal parts rich loam, coarse builders' sand and peat moss is ideal. Drainage is considered to be even more important than the soil mixture. Young plants should be repotted only when the root ball fills the container. Older, mature plants will keep healthy for several years in the same pot and produce lots of flowers.

## Watering

Very little water is required except during periods of active growth at which time the plant should be watered thoroughly and allowed to approach dryness before watering again. Average home humidity is satisfactory. The plant will thrive in dry air.

## Feeding

Feed sparingly with half strength water

*Aloe brevifolia*

soluble general fertilizer once a month during the growing period.

## Propagation

Readily from seeds but will not reproduce true to type. Best method is from offsets and suckers around the base of the plant. Leaf cuttings should be dusted with powdered charcoal and allowed to dry for a few days, preferably in the sun, before inserting in coarse damp builders' sand. Very little water is required during the rooting.

## Special Problems

Over-watering will kill the plant. Aloes are essentially pest-free.

# ANANAS comosus
*Pineapple*

Barbecue a ham, garnish with fresh ripe pineapple, and save the top to start a free new plant. An ecological recycle maybe—but in any event a lot of fun.

## Origin

Contrary to popular belief, the pineapple is native to the American tropics, principally Brazil, from whence it has been introduced around the world.

Introduction into England was in the latter part of the 18th century.

## Description

Pineapple *(Ananas comosus)* is one of the Bromeliaceae that grows in soil, thus is designated as terrestrial.

Most bromeliads are epiphytes like orchids, growing in the branches and crotches of trees where roots are formed mainly to hold such plants in position to be nourished by moist tropical air.

Plants in the wild may produce a rosette of stiff spiked, green leaves up to 6 feet in diameter. When the plant matures in six months to three years, it sends up a 3 to 4 foot stock bearing a purple flowered inflorescence that is crowned with a tuft of green leaves. This becomes the fleshy fruit. For cultivation, plants with smaller rosettes have been developed to take less space in the fields.

There are also dwarf forms, many with white edged leaves and a rosette no more than 12 inches in diameter used as decorative plants which you have probably seen at the local florist or nursery.

---

## Cultivation

For starting a pineapple see Propagation.

Place the planting in a bright, warm spot out of direct sun. Water the soil regularly, but let the soil become somewhat dry between waterings to promote root formation. Mist-spray the leaves. Once roots have formed, grow the plant in a sunny to partly sunny location and mist spray often to help keep the humidity above 30%.

Sometimes, not always, after two or three years, a plant will come into flower again and produce a new fruit.

## Potting

See Propagation for starting and potting.

## Watering

Water freely during summer but avoid wet soggy soil conditions that can induce rot. Discard any water that accumulates in the saucer.

## Feeding

During the growing period, use water soluble general fertilizer on a two-week schedule.

## Propagation

For a free pineapple plant, select a fruit that is ripe with a nice green top. Slice off the top with about one inch of fruit attached. Carefully trim away the fruit flesh with a sharp knife or tweezers to the hard stringy center. It is important to remove the soft flesh to prevent rot and mold.

Bare the lower part of the stem by peeling off the lowest small leaves and set the top aside for two or three days in a cool dry location. During this period, scar tissue will form.

Prepare a 4 or 6-inch pot for planting by covering the drainage hole with a generous layer of pea gravel or small crushed stone. Fill to within half an inch of the top with a mixture of equal parts builders' sand, pea gravel or crushed stone, rotted or dried manure or leafmould, and garden loam. Moisten thoroughly.

Center the top of the pineapple with the bare end projecting into the soil mixture. Now surround the top with thin bamboo sticks to keep the top upright. Tie the top to the sticks if it proves to be the least bit wobbly. A wobbly top takes much longer to root and if it is too unstable it may not root at all if newly-formed roots are constantly broken.

## Special Problems

As with most bromeliads, the tough foliage is essentially trouble-free. During the winter, locate where the night time temperature remains above 15°C. (60°F.).

*Ananas comosus*

# ANTHURIUM

*Flamingo Flower, Pigtail Plant / Oilcloth Flower*

This unusual tropical plant is well-suited to large terrariums. The red type with its bright red, heart-shaped, high-gloss spathe (special leaf) and bright yellow tail (spadex) is often featured in florists' windows.

## Origin

The genus, Anthurium, has over 600 species and is a member of the Arum or Calla family (Araceae). It is native to the rain forests of Central and South America.

## Description

*Anthurium scherzerianum*, the Flamingo Flower, is native to Costa Rica, where it is known as the Pigtail Plant because of its spirally twisted spadix. The brightly colored, heart-shaped spathe is the attention getter of this plant and it comes in intense red, rose, salmon, variegated and white. The plant grows up to 15 inches in height with shiny, dark green, stemmed leaves. The flowers are long lasting and a well-grown plant will produce throughout the year. *Anthurium andraeanum*, the Oilcloth Flower, is native to Columbia and its many hybrids offer 6-inch heart-shaped, waxy flower spathes above shining, deep green, stemmed leaves that are 12 to 16 inches in length. Spathes (petal-like bracts) can be shades of red, rose, pink or white. This plant is somewhat larger than *A. scherzerianum*. Anthurium flowers are long lasting and are often used as cut flowers.

## Cultivation

This evergreen plant is very tolerant of light and does well in a semi-shady location away from direct sunlight. Care must be taken to ensure that the soil and air temperatures do not drop below 18°C. (65°F.).

## Potting

Use a potting mix that is very loose and open. A mixture of osmunda fiber, leaf-mould, unmilled sphagnum moss and activated charcoal is ideal. The bottom of the pot should be covered with two to three inches of pea gravel to ensure thorough drainage.

The roots of offsets, when they appear, should be covered with sphagnum moss. Repot in early spring and only when the plant has outgrown its container. Keep the potting mixture evenly moist throughout the year.

## Watering

Keep evenly moist. Humidity is important, as much as 50% is ideal. Grow plants over a humidity tray and spray frequently with lukewarm water from a mister or discarded window spray bottle.

## Feeding

Fertilize on a 10 to 14 day schedule with a water soluble general fertilizer prepared to the manufacturer's instructions.

## Propagation

Propagation is readily achieved by separating and potting up the offshoots that develop. Plants may be propagated from seed that will take at least 30 days to germinate and two years or so to develop good-sized plants.

*Anthurium andraeanum*

## Special Problems

Problems arise mainly from excessively dry air and direct sunlight; otherwise, the plant is trouble-free.

# APHELANDRA

*Zebra Plant*

Sooner or later most indoor gardeners become seduced by the exotic Zebra Plant with its prominent white veining on dark green leaves. Then when the plant does what comes naturally—drops leaves in protest at growing conditions—disillusionment follows.

## Origin

Aphelandra (Zebra Plant) is native to the hot moist Brazilian jungle and is a genus of the Acanthus family (Acanthaceae).

## Description

A tropical 3-foot flowering shrub with 6 to 9-inch leaves marked with prominent white veins producing terminal flowers which may appear on any size plant. They shoot out from the top two leaves in a cockade that is somewhat cone shaped. When the yellow, orange or scarlet flowers fade they are replaced with two new stems. While the flowers are attractive, the foliage is really the outstanding feature. Species *A. squarrosa 'Louisae'* with its showy yellow flowers is the most commonly grown. This plant flowers usually during autumn and winter.

## Cultivation

Locate the plant in a warm, light location with no direct sun since in nature it thrives in the hot, moist jungle in diffused light. Humidity is very important and the pot should be placed above water level in a humidity tray of pebbles and water. Frequent misting of the foliage with clear tepid water should be practiced to keep relative humidity above 30%. Since most homes cannot provide an even hot temperature and high humidity, the plant drops its lower leaves and becomes leggy. When the plant is not on display it may be kept in a clear plastic bag, pot and all. Seal the bag with a tie and you have a miniature green house or terrarium. A decorative terrarium with its high humidity and constant temperature is an ideal way to grow the Zebra plant.

## Potting

Aphelandra must be grown in a rich friable soil mixture that is easy to keep moist and yet will drain off all excess water. A mixture of equal parts builders' sand, peat moss and well rotted manure is ideal and regular feeding with water soluble general fertilizer solution will provide the correct nutrient balance. Make certain that the drainage hole is open and cover it with a generous amount of shard or pea gravel.

## Watering

Maintain generous watering with tepid water to keep the soil evenly moist.

## Feeding

With water soluble general fertilizer during spring and summer on a 10 day schedule. Apply only to pre-moistened soil.

## Propagation

Propagation is a must if you are going to maintain decent looking plants and may be undertaken at any season using half ripened wood or new growth that

*Aphelandra squarrosa*

has a small heel from the old stem. Rooting must take place in a temperature of 24 to 27°C. (75 to 80°F.). Use a hormone rooting powder to accelerate root formation and root in sand, vermiculite or perlite.

## Special Problems

Leaf drop results from a dried out root ball and cold drafts.

# ARAUCARIA heterophylla

*Norfolk Island Pine*

The Norfolk Island Pine provides a definite, indoor living Christmas tree and specimen plants are available in one to six-foot sizes during the holiday season.

## Origin

Norfolk Island Pine, *Araucaria heterophylla (excelsa)*, is a member of the Araucaria family (Araucariaceae) and is native to the island from which it takes its name. This island is a tiny speck of land east of Australia and north-west of New Zealand. This pine is one of the most ancient and primitive of the conifers.

## Description

The Norfolk Island Pine is one of the best known and most attractive of the conifers. In nature it grows to 200 feet, has stiff needles and woody cones. The symmetrical branches grow in whorls and the needles are bright green. The tree shape is somewhat formal and triangular, much like the balsam fir. Outdoor planting is popular in Southern California and Hawaii. This is a slow growing plant that will, at most, add only one or two tiers per year.

## Cultivation

Grown as a pot plant in the north, the Norfolk Island Pine should be kept in a semi-sunny location protected from hot sun. Put it in a west window over winter and an east or north window during summer. Since the plant will tolerate low humidity it is a good candidate for apartment gardening. Growing temperatures should be on the cool side and preferably not above 21°C. (70°F.).

After danger of frost, the plant may be placed outside in a semi-shade location, under a tree or near a north wall. Sink the pot into the ground to within one inch of the top of the rim.

## Potting

Use a friable open potting mix of equal parts loam, builders' sand, peat moss and leafmould, or rotted or dried manure. This mixture, along with a generous layer of broken shard or pea gravel over the drainage hole will provide prompt drainage and aeration of the root system. Repotting is required only when the container is crammed with roots. Check for this condition by tipping the plant out of its pot.

## Watering

Keep evenly moist at all times. Avoid soggy waterlogged conditions which can mean death to the root system.

## Feeding

During the summer growing season with a regular 10 to 14 day application of water soluble general fertilizer.

## Propagation

The plant grows readily from seed, but the most shapely plants are grown from cuttings of the leader growth of young plants. Specimens that have outgrown available space should be treated in this manner. Treat the cut end with a hormone rooting powder and place in moist sand or vermiculite.

*Araucaria heterophylla (excelsa)*

Enclose in a clear plastic bag, out of direct sun, until roots have formed, then pot up in the potting mixture described previously. Cuttings from the side branches do not produce well shaped plants.

## Special Problems

Mealy bugs and spider mites can be held at bay by regular spraying with malathion. Regular mist spraying of the foliage with clear water also discourages spider mites that are partial to hot drying conditions.

# ARISTOLOCHIA elegans

*Calico Flower*

This plant is a vine with unusual odd shaped flowers.

## Origin

Genus Aristolochia is a member of the Birthwort family (Aristolochiaceae) and is one of five genera. It has over 300 species native mostly to the tropical and warm temperate regions of the world.

## Description

*Aristolochia elegans* is native to Brazil. It is a slender, evergreen climber, growing 8 to 10 feet, with long stems and heart-shaped leaves. Solitary flowers are borne on the new pendulous growth. The 1½-inch flower tube is yellow-green with a 3-inch heart-shaped face, blotched in purple and white. Flowering occurs in late spring and summer. Most species have a strong unpleasant odor to attract insects, but A. *elegans* is free of this unpleasant characteristic.

## Cultivation

Locate in semi-sun to semi-shade and protect from strong sun during the summer. Plants will grow in average home temperature but strongest plants are produced in a temperature around 16°C. (60°F.).

## Potting

Use a rich friable soil mixture of equal parts loam, coarse builders' sand, peat moss and rotted or dried manure or compost. Place a generous layer of small pebbles or pea gravel over the drainage hole. Move young plants on to the next size container as soon as the root ball fills the pot. Young plants can reach a 9 to 10-inch pot size in 9 months. Practice root pruning when plants reach terminal pot size.

## Watering

Keep plants moist at all times, use slightly less water during the winter rest period. Above average humidity is required, use a humidity tray and mist spray foliage with clear tepid water.

## Feeding

During the growing period, late February to August, apply water soluble general fertilizer on a 14 day schedule. This plant is a vigorous grower and selective pinch pruning should be practiced.

## Propagation

Cuttings of well matured wood root readily in moist sand or peat moss. Use rooting hormone powder on the cut ends. January cuttings may be in flower the following summer. Seeds available from specialty seed houses germinate readily and flower within 12 months.

*Aristolochia elegans*

## Special Problems

Red spider mites, scale, aphids and mealy bugs can be controlled with insecticide malathion. Use a cotton swab dipped in rubbing alcohol for removing individual pests.

# ARTHROPODIUM
*Rock Lily*

This plant is a welcome addition for any indoor gardener.

## Origin

Genus Arthropodium is a member of the Lily family (Liliaceae) and is native to New Zealand and Australia. There are about ten species.

## Description

These perennial plants grow from fibrous, fleshy roots. Long leaves grow from the crown of the plant and white to purplish flowers are borne on a branching flower stem. Two species are available:

*A. candidum* has narrow, basal 10-inch leaves about 1/4 inch wide. Small, simple white flowers are produced on an unbranched flower stem. The plant reaches 12 to 14 inches in height.

*A. cirrhatum* grows to 3 feet with long fleshy leaves up to 24 inches in length and 2 inches wide. White 1-inch flowers are borne on a 12-inch branching flower stem.

## Cultivation

Grow in a semi-sun location in average room temperature.

## Potting

Use a rich friable soil mixture of equal parts loam, coarse builders' sand, peat moss and rotted or dried manure or compost. Provide for adequate drainage with a generous amount of pebbles or pea gravel over the drainage hole. Repot when root ball becomes compacted.

## Watering

Water freely during the flowering period, keep evenly moist at other times. Normal room humidity is adequate.

## Feeding

Use water soluble general fertilizer on a two week schedule during the bud forming and flowering period.

## Propagation

Readily by division or seeds.

## Special Problems

Essentially trouble-free.

*Arthropodium cirrhatum*

# ASPARAGUS
*Asparagus Fern*

Widely used as greens by commercial florists, Asparagus Fern provides a useful alternative for apartment dwellers with low humidity problems and consistent failures with true ferns.

## Origin

While Asparagus Fern is a member of the Lily family (Liliaceae), along with hardy garden asparagus *(officonalis)* from Europe, it is a native of South Africa. Records show introduction by Thomas Cooper from his South African field trip around 1860.

## Description

Mostly climbers with lacy needle-like foliage, these plants have found wide usage in the commercial trade as a delicate, green foil for bouquets and corsages.

While not true ferns, the resemblance is close enough to satisfy most fern lovers.

The popular species grown are: *A. setaceus ('Sprengeri'),* sometimes called Emerald Feather, has long feathery branches reaching up to 6 feet, covered with rich green, flat, needle-like leaves, 1/2 to 1 inch long. Flowering usually occurs in May to June. The small whitish-pink flowers are followed by red berries that ripen around Christmastime. The roots are white, elliptic tubers that eventually fill the pot and force the plant out, signaling the time for repotting. *A. densiflorus (plumosus)* with shamrock-green, feathery foliage is generally a tall woody vine.

Two dwarf varieties, compactus and nanus, are usually grown in areas of limited space. The numerous, fine, needle-like leaves are no more than one-quarter inch in length.

A newer variety, 'Meyers,' produces many base-branching, plumed fronds that are erect and arching. Each frond is densely covered with tight clusters of fine light green foliage.

## Cultivation

Plants are grown without a rest period in normal room temperature. They like a semi-sunny location, but will tolerate a light shade. However, a dark location away from a window will result in weak foliage that will invite aphids. Plants used outside during the summer should be moved indoors well before frost.

## Potting

Use rich friable soil mix such as equal parts loam, builders' sand, peat moss and dried or rotted manure or leafmould. Provide ample drainage with a generous layer of pea gravel or broken shard at the bottom of the pot. Move on to a larger sized container as soon as the root ball becomes compacted.

## Watering

Keep the root ball evenly moist at all times. This plant is tolerant of dry air, but enjoys an occasional mist spray of clear water.

## Feeding

Use water soluble general fertilizer on a 10 to 14 day schedule, one tablespoon to one gallon of water. Flush away excess salt build-up with clear water every few months.

## Propagation

By division, which may be undertaken in spring or autumn. This plant readily reproduces from seed which takes about 30 days for germination in a warm moist condition.

## Special Problems

Loss of vigor will result from allowing the root ball to become dry. A dark growing location will produce weak growth and attacks from aphids. Control aphids with a malathion spray.

*Asparagus setaceus*

# ASPIDISTRA

*Cast-Iron Plant*

This foliage plant withstands heat, dust, poor soil and dim light—a gem among plants for the difficult corner where nothing else will grow. It was an outstanding favorite during Victorian England and no sitting room was complete without at least one jardinière of this "parlor palm."

## Origin

A member of the Lily family (Liliaceae) native to Himalaya, China and Japan with very few species.

## Description

This thick rooted perennial has stiff, glossy evergreen leaves, usually 1½ feet long. It is grown exclusively for the foliage effect since the flowers are inconspicuous, dark colored and borne close to the soil, which means they are hidden by the foliage and thus usually go completely un-noticed. *Aspidistra elatior*, commonly known as the Cast-Iron Plant, is the principal species. The cut foliage has outstanding lasting qualities and it is raised commercially and sold to florists for cut flower arrangements. *A. elatior* 'Variegata' has leaves striped green and white. However, if and when any green leaves appear they must be cut out immediately to ensure continuance of the variegated foliage.

Some authorities maintain that use of rich potting soil will also cause the plant to lose its variegation.

## Cultivation

To grow the biggest Aspidistra in the world (as the song says) the plant must be well nourished, watered and tended. It resents direct sun and soggy roots. Keep in cool temperatures preferably not over 23°C. (75°F.) in winter.

## Potting

Potting soil made from a mixture of equal parts coarse builders' sand, peat moss and leafmould or well rotted manure, will provide the nourishment and drainage required for specimen plants. While the plant will survive for years without repotting, it is best to completely repot every second year with a partial replacement of the upper soil in the pot every other year. Make sure the drainage hole is open and well covered with a layer of shard or pea gravel.

## Watering

Watering technique calls for soaking and allowing the soil to approach dryness before soaking again. If the plant is being grown or placed in a fancy jardinière keep a close check to ensure there is no accumulation of excess water that will eventually drown the roots.

## Feeding

Supplementary feeding, especially during spring and summer, may be undertaken on a 10 to 14 day schedule with water soluble general fertilizer.

## Propagation

Propagation is achieved by division of the thick roots especially from March to September. Each piece of the root (rhizome) should have a few fine roots attached as well as two or three leaves. Pot up in the soil mixture discussed under potting, maintaining the same planting depth. Water thoroughly and place in a warm shaded spot for a few days until new root activity begins.

## Special Problems

Aspidistra has no significant disease or insect problem—it is a cast iron plant.

*Aspidistra elatior*

# ASPLENIUM nidus

*Bird's Nest Fern*

Bird's Nest Fern with its bright green shiny leaves has always been a popular house plant.

## Origin

*Asplenium nidus* is a member of the Fern family (Polypodiaceae) and is one of 700 species of the genus Asplenium. It is native to Southeast Asia.

## Description

*Aspleniun nidus* is a large epiphytic plant that grows in trees in the tropical rain forest. The bright green, shiny leaves arise from a deep funnel shaped rosette and may reach 4 feet in length and 8 inches in width.

## Cultivation

Locate in a semi-sunny, to semi-shady spot in average room temperature. Nighttime temperature should not go below 16°C. (60°F.).

## Potting

This plant, being epiphytic, may be grown attached to a piece of dead branch or fern tree root. Wrap the base of the plant in sphagnum moss and wire in position with thin copper wire. For pot culture use a mixture of loam, peat moss and builders' sand with the pot one-half filled with small pebbles or pea gravel which will not only provide drainage but provide weight for balancing large size plants.

## Watering

During summer, maintain water in the center of the plant. Normally the funnel is allowed to go dry over the resting period to prevent rotting. However, in a warm location, a small amount of water in the funnel is an advantage. Mist spray the leaves with clear tepid water.

## Feeding

Use only a very weak solution of water soluble general fertilizer during the summer months.

## Propagation

Use basal offsets from the parent plant.

## Special Problems

Strong sun and cool temperatures below 16°C. (60°F.) may brown the leaf edges.

*Asplenium nidus*

# AUCUBA japonica variegata

*Gold-Dust Plant, Spotted Laurel*

This small evergreen tree grows to 15 feet.

## Origin

Genus Aucuba, with seven species, is a member of the Dogwood family (Cornaceae) and is mostly native to Japan.

## Description

*A. japonica variegata*, Gold Dust Plant, is a small evergreen tree growing to 15 feet with glossy, green leaves mottled in chrome yellow. The oblong, toothed leaves can grow to 7 inches.

## Cultivation

Grow in sun or semi-sun (south, west or east window). Average room temperature is suitable. Preferred winter temperature is around 13°C. (55°F.).

## Potting

Use a soil mixture of equal parts loam, coarse builders' sand, peat moss and rotted or dried manure or compost. Provide for drainage with shard, pebbles or pea gravel over the drainage hole.

## Watering

Soak, then allow to approach dryness before soaking again during the spring and summer season. Less water is needed over winter. This plant tolerates average room humidity.

## Feeding

During the growing period spring to autumn, use water soluble general fertilizer on a 14 day schedule.

## Propagation

Use cuttings of half ripened wood. Dip cut ends in rooting hormone powder and insert in moist sand or vermiculite.

## Special Problems

High temperature over winter may promote insect attacks. Control with malathion insecticide.

*Aucuba japonica variegata*

# AZALEA

What to do with the gift Azalea received at Christmas, Valentine's Day, Easter or even as late as Mother's Day is a situation faced by many. In an overheated, dry house, there is not much alternative but to discard the plant after flowers have faded. With a cool sunny window and a spot for outdoor growing during summer, you can save the plant to bloom again.

## Origin

Azaleas are classified as Rhododendrons of which there are over 300 species distributed in the temperate and cold regions of the northern hemisphere. Gardeners consider Azaleas distinct from Rhododendrons and treat them as a separate group. The genus is a member of the Heath family (Ericaceae).

## Description

Azaleas are flowering shrubs ranging in size from dwarf plants 1 foot high to tall bushes of 20 feet. They are often grouped as evergreen, semi-evergreen or deciduous. The common hardy types drop their leaves in the autumn or at best are semi-evergreen. *Azalea canadenises* is a native deciduous type that grows to a height of 1 to 3 feet in the damp areas from Labrador through Quebec into the New England area. The rose-purple flowers come into bloom in April to May before the new foliage appears. The Azalea pot plants from the florist are not hardy in cold areas and must never be exposed to frost, even a light frost.
*Azalea indica* is the most widely grown in the florist trade since it is evergreen with large single or double flowers. *Azalea xKurume* is used for forcing. They are evergreen as well with much smaller flowers. The flowers are produced in great profusion and often completely obscure the foliage at the height of the blooming period. 'Coral Bells' is a favorite variety of this hybrid.
There are many varieties that cover a color range from white, pink to crimson.

## Cultivation

Once the plant has finished blooming, it should continue growing in a bright, cool window, sunny if possible, with a temperature around 15°C. (60°F.). The plant must be kept uniformly moist, and mist spraying of the leaves with clear water will help maintain the moist cool condition that promotes the best and strongest growth.

After the last spring frost, the plant is best summered outside by sinking the pot into the ground in a bright sunny area or, at most, light shade. Before the first frost, move the plant inside since the slightest touch of frost will destroy the new flower buds. To have the Azalea bloom for Christmas it will need four weeks of cool storage starting October 1st at a temperature no higher than 10°C. (50°F.). During this period the plant must continue to have light, otherwise it will start to shed leaves. On November 1st, bring the plant to a warmer temperature, 15 to 18°C. (60 to 65°F.) in a sunny location and it should come into flower for the holiday season.

## Potting

Repotting will be necessary every two or three years to accommodate the increase in size. For best appearance use Azalea pots that are three-quarters as deep and wide as regular pots. Add a potting mixture consisting mostly of peat moss and a small amount of coarse builders' sand for porosity. A generous amount of pea gravel or small stones over the drainage hole ensures prompt drainage and proper aeration of the roots.

## Watering

Keep the plant well watered at all times especially during summer.

## Feeding

This plant is a heavy feeder and should receive supplementary feeding with a water soluble fertilizer on a two week schedule. Use water soluble general fertilizer.
Azaleas are acid soil plants and to maintain this condition they should be treated once or twice during the season with a solution of one ounce of aluminum sulphate or ammonium sulphate to a gallon of water.

## Propagation

Usually relegated to the professional. For the venturesome, use $2\frac{1}{2}$ to $3\frac{1}{2}$-inch cuttings of well hardened (July to November) stems of current season growth. Remove bottom leaves, treat with rooting hormone and place in moist packed sand. Shade from direct sun. Propagation from seed is difficult and is usually undertaken in April in a screened mixture of coarse sand and oak leafmould. Germination takes 14 to 30 days.

## Special Problems

To prevent yellowing of the leaves, supplement fertilizing with an iron chelate solution.

*Azalea indica*

# BAMBUSA glaucescens

*Bamboo*

Bamboo makes an exotic tub plant with an oriental flavor.

## Origin

Genus Bambusa is a member of the Grass family (Gramineae) with around 100 species mostly native to tropical and sub-tropical Asia.

## Description

While many species are grown for food and timber, there are a few that make excellent ornamentals. Most species are tender and stems are produced in clumps from spreading underground rhizomes. In nature some species reach a height of over 100 feet with a diameter of 12 inches. The jointed green to yellow stems are as much a feature as the light airy foliage. Dwarf species are used in pots for patio and indoor culture. The most common species used is:

*B. glaucescens* sometimes identified as *B. multiplex nana.* This plant is native to China and Japan and grows 3 to 10 feet in height. Thick clumps of thin, hollow canes grow from a rhizome-like root stock. The light green, long and thin leaves are spaced evenly along the canes.

## Cultivation

Locate in bright, indirect and filtered sun, any exposure except north. Average room temperature is suitable with 16°C (60°F.) night temperature where possible.

## Potting

A rich friable soil mixture is required. Use equal parts loam, coarse builders' sand, peat moss, rotted or dried manure and leafmould. Small pebbles or pea gravel should be used over the drainage holes to ensure prompt drainage.

## Water

Keep evenly moist at all times. Average house humidity is adequate.

## Feeding

Feed during spring and summer with water soluble general fertilizer on a 10 day schedule.

## Propagation

Divide the rhizome clumps in early spring when new growth commences.

## Special Problems

Plants may go dormant between November and May and drop leaves because of short daylight. New growth will appear in the spring as the days lengthen. Aphids and red spider mites that thrive on low humidity may be controlled with malathion insecticide spray. Mist spraying with clear water will discourage mites.

*Bambusa glaucescens*

# BEAUCARNEA recurvata

*Pony-Tail, Bottle Palm, Elephant Foot Tree*

This spectacular plant is sometimes called Pony Tail.

## Origin

Beaucarnea is a genus of the Agave family (Agavaceae) and has about six species mostly native to Texas and Mexico.

## Description

*Beaucarnea recurvata* is a tree-like plant with a tall trunk that can reach 30 feet outside but rarely more than 4 to 6 feet in-doors. The top of the trunk carries a rosette of evergreen, long, narrow, tough cascading leaves. The base of the trunk is large and swollen, thus the name Elephant Foot Tree.

## Cultivation

Plants need good light throughout the year and they may be summered outside during the frost-free months. Over winter, as with cacti, they should have a light, cool location in a temperature of 10 to 15°C. (50 to 60°F.).

## Potting

Move plants to larger size pots only when the root ball has become thoroughly compact. Tub specimen plants may be held to container size by removing the plant and pruning away a slice of the root ball from one side, returning to the tub and adding soil mixture to replace the cut away portion. Allow the roots to heal for a week before watering. Potting soil can be two parts loam and one part coarse builders' sand or equal parts coarse builders' sand, peat moss and rotted or dried manure. It is important that drainage holes be covered with small pebbles or gravel.

## Watering

Water only when the top of the soil becomes dry to touch, then soak and drain thoroughly and allow the soil to become dry before watering again.

## Feeding

Growth will be accelerated with supplementary feeding during the summer growing periods. Water soluble general fertilizer may be used on a 14 day schedule. Plants may be kept smaller with less feeding.

## Propagation

Older plants will produce basal off-shoots which may be separated with a sharp knife or razor blade. Allow cut ends to heal in the open air for a few days before rooting in coarse damp sand.

*Beaucarnea recurvata*

## Special Problems

Over-watering can induce rot. Attacks of mealy bugs should be controlled with insecticide malathion spray.

# BEGONIA

## Origin

The original discovery, according to record, was in the West Indies, although the Begonia family (Begoniaceae) is most abundant in Mexico, Central and South America. The genus was named in honor of Michel Begon (1638-1710), a French naval officer who served successively as intendant of the French West Indies, of Canada, Rochesfort and LaRochelle. He was celebrated for his love of science in botany.

While the genus has over 750 species, there are more than 1,000 varieties of which 100 make outstanding house plants.

## Description

Begonias are tender plants, somewhat succulent in characteristic. The proliferation of hybrids and names can be somewhat confusing and for pratical purposes it is best to consider only the three major groupings that are commonly cultivated.

### Tuberous Begonias

Tuberous Begonias are undoubtedly the most beautiful of all the summer flowering tubers and bulbs. With improvements in colors and shapes in recent years, it is possible to have the rose shaped types producing flowers 8 to 9 inches in diameter. The trailing habit of the pendulant varieties makes them ideal subjects for hanging baskets and window boxes. Male and female flowers are borne separately on the same plant. Pinch pruning of the female flowers will result in even larger male flowers, which are usually double. Being a summer flowering plant, it must have long day treatment which means over 13 to 14 hours of light a day to keep flowers in full production. Natural long days occur between mid-April and mid-August after which supplemental light is required to lengthen the day artificially to maintain indoor blossoming.

The growing of tuberous begonias is relatively simple when you start with tubers. The Fibrous Rooted Begonia group is probably the most widely planted of all Begonias being useful as house plants as well as landscape accents where dramatic masses of color or design are desired.

### Begonia semperflorens (Wax Begonia)

*Begonia semperflorens*, commonly called Wax Begonia, is the most valuable of the group. The plant is dwarf and erect with smooth leaves that may be green, red or bronze, with color intensity responding to the amount of sunlight. This plant has outstanding "flower power." It blooms all summer long and may be lifted in the autumn for indoors where flowering continues uninterrupted all winter. Flowers are mostly single and range from white to pink to various shades of red. The golden stamens stand out in the small flower clusters that cover the mound shaped plant. If you have never grown Begonias this is the one to start with, you will not be disappointed.

Varieties are available that grow in heights from 4 to 6 inches up to 9 to 10 inches. Plants grown indoors may tend to become leggy but pinch pruning will correct this and keep the plant tidy and well branched Plants lifted from the garden in the autumn for the

## Cultivation

Inside, grow in bright light, east or west window in summer, south in mid-winter except for Rex Begonias. Outside, place in semi-shade away from hot mid-day sun.

Begonias are readily available as mature plants, seedlings, seeds and dormant tubers in the case of Tuberous Begonias. In late February or early March, place dormant tubers, dimple or cup side facing up on a bed of rooting mix that is equal parts coarse builders' sand and peat moss. Keep moist and around 18°C. (65°F.) until its pink sprouts begin to show, then cover the tubers completely with the sand/peat moss mix to a depth of one-half to three-quarters of an inch. Continue growing at a temperature of 18°C. (65°F.) and water only enough to keep uniformly moist. As soon as leaves start to appear, place the plants in bright light. In about 40 to 45 days the plants will have developed sufficient roots and leaves to be lifted and placed in individual pots. Each pot should have a generous layer of crushed stone or broken crockery over the drainage hole and the potting soil should be a mixture of equal parts loam, coarse builders' sand, peat moss and humus (compost or rotted manure).

After 10 days, start a regular supplementary feeding program with water soluble general fertilizer.

After danger of frost, the plants may be planted outside for the summer or grown on a bright windowsill indoors. At the end of summer when the outside plants begin to fade and well before frost, lift them and place in a cool dry place until the foliage and stems wither. Remove the withered material and store the tubers in dry peat moss or sand at a temperature of 7 to 10°C. (45 to 50°F.).

## Potting

All types need a rich friable potting mix such as equal parts loam, coarse builders' sand, peat moss and rotted or dried manure. Provide for ample drainage with shard or pea gravel over the drainage hole. Repotting should be undertaken only when the roots have completely outgrown the existing pot.

## Watering

Keep evenly moist year around. If excessive dryness results, soak in tepid water and drain thoroughly. Hot dry air may cause browning of leaf edges and dropping of buds and flowers. Place plants in a humidity tray filled with stones and water. Keep the bottom of the pot above the water level. Mist spray the foliage with care so as not to produce excessive humidity.

## Feeding

From April to September, provide supplementary feeding on a two week schedule with water soluble general fertilizer.

## Propagation

All Begonias propagate readily from leaf and stem cuttings placed in coarse moist sand or a glass of water with a bit of activated charcoal.

Tuberous Begonias may also be multiplied by dividing the tubers. Once sprouts have appeared, divide the tuber with a sharp knife allowing one or two sprouts for each section. Cut surfaces should be treated with dusting sulphur to prevent development of rot.

All types of Begonias may be grown from seed which is usually as fine as dust and requires special care and extra time. Besides the challenge, there is the possibility of finding exciting new shapes and colors from the seedlings. This following procedure is used by professional hybridizers in developing and selecting new plants for commerce. Newly planted seed germinates in 10 to 14 days at 18°C. (65°F.) and at the end of two months the first true leaves will be visible.

For the seed bed, use a flat or pot of a size to suit the scope of the plant. Screen a well drained organic soil mix of equal parts loam, coarse builders' sand and leafmould or other humus through a one-quarter inch wire cloth. Since the seed bed must be sterile, the soil mix should be heated in the oven at 82°C. (180°F.) and held at this temperature for 30 to 40 minutes. After cooling, fill the flat or pot and firm to within an inch of the top. Reserve some of the sterilized soil mix. Moisten the seed bed thoroughly and

house are usually cut back to 3 inches to assist settling into the changed growing conditions. If you venture outside the dwarf sizes you will find fibrous varieties that will grow up to 10 feet tall. Such varieties are referred to as cane or Angel-Wing types.

Notable in this group are *Begonia 'Corallina'* which grows 8 to 10 feet with dark glossy green leaves and large pendant clusters of coral red flowers. This variety is usually trained to a pillar, drooped over rafters, or used as a feature on a free standing cupboard.

*'Lucerna,'* so named because it originated in Lucerne around 1900, grows 2 to 6 feet high, with wing shaped leaves spotted white. The long pendulous clusters of pink summer flowers are often 12 inches in diameter.

Also notable among recent introductions is *Rieger'* which was developed in Germany as a house plant. This plant grows about 10 to 12 inches and is somewhat pendulous. It blooms virtually year round. Flower size is closer to that of the tuberous rather than the fibrous rooted types. This variety is very showy and it is protected by patent.

### Rhizomatous Begonia (Rex Begonia)

Begonia, group Rhizomatous is grown mainly for the handsome foliage. This group is characterized by thick root stocks that grow near the surface of the soil from which arise long stemmed ornate leaves. They are mostly hairy with rich metallic shades of maroon, lilac, rose, green and silver grey, blended in stripes, bands and mottlings. While the group is fairly extensive with creeping, trailing and climbing types, it is the low, compact Rex Begonia and its variations that are the most familiar and most often grown.

Rex Begonias were first introduced into England around 1850. Since that time they have not suffered from lack of attention from hybridizers and hundreds of varieties have been named and introduced.

The plant originally came from the Forest of Assam, India where the climate, although tropical, is cool and extremely moist. The regular hot season of India is absent in the area because of the nearby hill ranges and excessive rainfall. Like all other Begonias, they do flower and produce seeds but these characteristics are overshadowed by the ornamental nature of the leaves.

*Begonia rhizomatous (Rex Begonia)*

---

allow the excess water to drain away. Sprinkle a small amount of the dry reserve mix over the moist compacted surface to provide an open texture for the fine Begonia seed that you now scatter over the surface.

Place the planted seed bed in a clear plastic bag and pull the bag tightly over the rim of the flat or pot. Hold it in place with a cord or rubber band so that the plastic never touches the surface of the seed bed.

Place in bright light but don't allow the sun to shine directly on the seed bed otherwise the seedlings might be destroyed by excessive heat.

Normally no further watering will be necessary for two months at which time the plastic is removed. Shortly after this period and before crowding takes place, the seedlings should be transferred to other flats for more space, or to individual pots. From this point on , treat the plants the same as if you had started from tubers. Try to keep the plants growing unchecked for the best results. They will grow well in 13 to 18°C. (55 to 65°F.) temperature in a bright window light sheltered from direct hot sunshine.

## Special Problems

In the event of an attack of leaf mildew or stem rotting, isolate affected plants immediately and treat with a fungicide.

*Begonia 'Rieger'*

# BILLBERGIA
*Living-Vase Plant, Queen's Tears*

A plant of easy culture and unusual flowers.

## Origin

Genus Billbergia is a member of the Pineapple family (Bromeliaceae). There are over 50 species mostly native to Brazil.

## Description

These epiphytic plants generally form tall, tubular, slender rosettes of leaves and are much admired for the color combinations of the flowers. Some of the species grown are:

*B. amoena* has a medium tubular rosette growing to 2 feet. Leaves are green and the flower bract is rose colored. The flowers are pale green with lavender blue ends.
*B. amoena* variety *rubra* has red leaves spotted with white and yellow.
*B. iridifolia* grows to 18 inches with fresh green wavy leaves covered with grey scurf. Leaf margins have scattered spines. Flowers are yellow with a pale pink flower bract.
*B. nutans* is one of the commonest species grown and is called Queen's Tears. It grows to 18 inches with narrow arching leaves forming a somewhat open rosette. The graceful and drooping flower stem has a bright rose flower bract with one-inch sepals, reddish and yellow-green marked in blue.
*B. venezuelana* is a big tubular species growing to 3 feet. The leaves are mottled and banded in chocolate brown and silver. The flower stalk is equally bold and laden with pink flower bracts and purple petals. It is native to Venezuela.
*B. zebrina* grows to 3 feet with broad 3-inch bracts, tubular grey-green foliage banded with silver. The drooping flower stem carries large pink bracts and yellowish-green to golden flowers.

## Cultivation

Grow in a sunny to semi-sunny location in average room temperature.

## Potting

Plants may be grown on driftwood or old branches by wrapping the base with sphagnum moss and wiring into position. For pot culture use osmunda fiber, ground bark or very coarse, loose leaf mold.

## Watering

Keep the rosette vase filled with water. Average house humidity is acceptable. Occasional mist spraying with clear water is beneficial. If grown in pots, water the pot only occasionally.

## Feeding

Feed very little, possibly once during the summer with one-quarter strength of water soluble general fertilizer.

## Propagation

From basal offsets of the parent plant. Remove with a sharp knife when large enough to handle. After flowering, the parent plant will wither and die, thus it is best to leave at least one offset for replacement.

## Special Problems

A trouble-free plant when grown properly.

*Billbergia nutans*

# BOUGAINVILLEA
*Paper Flower*

Most Northerners return from visits to sub-tropical areas completely enthralled with the spectacular, breathtaking display of Bougainvillea with its rosy red and magenta bracts that enclose the inconspicuous flowers.

## Origin
Named after the French Navigator, Louis Antoine de Bougainville, this plant, of the Four O'Clock family (Nyctaginaceae), is a native of South America and grows readily throughout the Caribbean, Florida, Central America and California.

## Description
Almost anywhere you look in the frost-free areas, this perennial vine is climbing over a roof top, spilling over a fence and even climbing into a tree, 20 to 30 feet high or more. The principal species are *Bougainvillea glabra* with magenta color bracts and *Bougainvillea spectavilis*, a more rampant grower with deep, rose colored bracts.

## Cultivation
During February and early spring small flowering size plants are available from the nursery and florist. Such young plants may be set out in the garden for the summer in full sun and then lifted and potted in the autumn. However, earlier blooming plants result when the plants are kept in pots that are sunk in the ground over the summer.

In autumn the plants must be lifted before frost and since this is the start of the natural rest period, water is gradually reduced. The plants should be stored cool at 10°C. (50°F.) in bright light and the potting soil kept barely damp. After mid-January prune out all the weak growth, top dress the potting soil, and if necessary repot. Begin regular watering and place the plant in a sunny warm spot with a minimum temperature of 15°C. (60°F.). With this treatment the plant will produce flowers for Easter. In May, after the last frost, set the plant out in the garden in a sunny location, move inside in the autumn, rest and repeat the growing procedure.

Since the plant blooms well at a small size, it may be kept under control with regular pinch pruning. When growing larger size plants (6 to 8-inch pot), the growth may be trained over a balloon shaped wire cage made of chicken wire. With patience Bougainvillea can be trained as a standard, much the same as with Fuchsia or Geranium.

## Potting
Use a rich friable mixture such as equal parts garden loam, coarse builders sand, peat moss and well rotted compost or manure. Make certain the drainage hole is open and well covered with broken shard or pea gravel.

*Bougainvillea spectavilis*

## Watering
The best technique is to soak, then allow the soil to become almost dry before soaking again. Discard excess water in the saucer.

## Feeding
During the active growing periods supplementary feeding with water soluble general fertilizer should be undertaken on a 10 to 14 day schedule, especially for those plants that have filled their containers with roots.

## Propagation
Use 6 to 12-inch cuttings of half ripened wood or young shoots. Dip cut ends in rooting hormone powder and place in moist sand or vermiculite at a temperature of 21°C. (70°F.).

## Special Problems
This plant is essentially trouble-free.

# BRASSAIA actinophylla

*Umbrella Tree*

With its rise in popularity, this plant is now available in just about any size from 6-inch to 6 foot specimens.

## Origin

Genus Brassaia with its 50 species is often included in Genus Schefflera with 150 species. Both are members of the Ginseng family (Araliaceae). Both genera are tropical and sub-tropical evergreens, many of which are epiphytic shrubs and climbers, only a few are terrestrial or become trees. The native habitat covers an extensive area of the South Pacific from India to Australia.

## Description

Within the last few years, *Brassaia actinophylla*, (often identified as *Schefflera actinophylla)*, has become a popular pot and tub plant for the home, office and indoor public areas. This plant is a tree in its native habitat, growing 40 to 100 feet in height. The foliage is decorative and graceful, with medium green glossy leaflets grouped like fingers at the top of the stems forming, in a way, a small umbrella. The individual leaflets are clustered in groups of 6 to 16, depending upon the age of the plant. Individually they grow up to 12 inches in length and 4 inches wide at the broadest point. Older plants produce purplish red flowers. Several stems are normally grown in a pot.

## Cultivation

Umbrella Tree adapts to average home conditions of temperature and humidity quite readily, and prospers best in good light without much sun in an east or west window location.

## Potting

As with other tropical plants, the Umbrella Tree requires a porous potting soil that will drain thoroughly. Use a mixture of equal parts of loam, coarse builders' sand, peat moss and rotted or dried manure along with 2 or 3 inches of pea gravel over the drainage hole. Repotting may be delayed for several years with a regular program of supplementary feeding.

## Watering

Watering calls for thorough soaking and allowing the soil to approach dryness before soaking again. Do not allow the plant to become too dry since this will cause leaf drop.

## Feeding

On a regular 10 to 14 day schedule with water soluble general fertilizer during the periods of active growth.

## Propagation

From fresh seeds that germinate in about 20 days in moist warm conditions, 23 to 27°C. (75 to 80°F.). Plants that have reached the ceiling may be rescued by rooting the top section by air layering. Once roots have formed and the section is cut away for potting,

*Brassaia actinophylla*

the main stem may be pruned back to 6 to 12 inches high. New growth will form on the stub at the old leaf nodes.

## Special Problems

The plant is essentially pest-free. However, if an invasion does occur, a few treatments with malathion will get things back in order. Individual bugs may always be removed with a cotton swab moistened with rubbing alcohol. For topnotch appearance, the leaves should be washed regularly under the shower or with a soft cloth dampened with tepid water. This will clean off any dust and grime as well as any mealy bugs and spider mites that might be congregating for an invasion.

# BROMELIADS

Apartment dwellers with plant growing problems should not overlook the Bromeliads. These plants have amazing adaptability and will survive despite dim light, too little water, no humidity and general neglect. However, given reasonable care they can be the delight of the indoor gardener.

## Origin

Bromeliads are native to the Western Hemisphere with some species found in the southern United States, Mexico and Central America but the majority are from South America particularly Brazil. The family name Bromeliaceae is from the genus Bromelia named in honor of Oleus Bromela a Swedish botanist. The family has 40 genera and about 1,000 species.

## Description

In their natural state Bromeliads are mostly tree dwellers and are true epiphytes, or "air plants." They grow high up in the tree tops in partial shade using the rough bark of the tree for anchorage because of their sparse root system. As with orchids this plant is not a parasite; it merely uses its host tree for support in a favorable growing location. This plant combines toughness with bold, spectacular foliage and exotic flowers. It has been a much favored house plant in Europe for many years; in fact many of the plants offered at retail originate from growers in Holland rather than from the south. Foliage of Bromeliads is tough, somewhat leathery and except in rare instances is typified by a rosette of leaves often with sharp teeth and serrations at the edges. Because of the rosette formation most Bromeliads end up with a water type funnel in the center. This vase or bowl formation will hold water, sometimes as much as a full cup. In mature plants this receptacle collects not only water but organic matter, insects and small frogs. Because of this water collecting characteristic, history records that at the time of the Panama Canal construction, the Bromeliads in the area had to be destroyed as part of the sanitation program since they were providing a convenient breeding spot for malaria mosquito.

While most of the Bromeliads are air plants, a few are terrestrial meaning their roots grow in the ground in soil. Notable in this group is the one familiar to all, the Pineapple (*Ananas comosus*).

Genus *Aechmea* species *fasciata* is readily available and is usually the novice's first introduction to this family of plants. It has 24-inch leaves mottled and striped in silver, and blooms in summer with bright rose bracts and blue flowers. Other notable genera include *Billbergia*, *Gravisia*, *Tillandsia*.

*Vriesea*

## Cultivation

Grow the plants in an airy location in semi-sun or filtered sun. Average house temperature suits Bromeliads, daytime 21 to 26°C. (70 to 80°F.) with a nighttime temperature of 13 to 18°C. (55 to 65°F.). When humidity drops below 30%, misting the foliage will be beneficial. After the danger of frost is past in warm areas, hang or fasten your plants in a tree or on a wall where they can enjoy the air and filtered light for the summer.

Flowers may be red, pink, lavender, blue, white, yellow or green while varying in size from microscopic to the size of 3 inches. While the individual blooms last for a few days at the most, the floral bracts and berries continue their attractive exotic appearance for months.

Sometimes it becomes necessary to force a reluctant plant into bloom and there are two methods of persuasion. The first calls for placing the plant in a large clear plastic bag with a ripe apple. The bag is sealed and the setup is placed in a bright location for five days. Usually within a couple of months a spike will begin to show. Ripe apples give off ethylene gas which stimulates bloom in mature Bromeliads.

The second procedure in forcing a plant is to make a solution of 1/4 ounce of calcium carbide in one quart of water. Empty the plant cup or vase and refill with this solution and allow to stand for 24 hours. At the end of this period empty the cup and wash it out with water and then fill with fresh clean water. Genera such as *Aechmea* and *Billbergia* will come into flower in one to three months.

## Potting

Plant in pot with a porous potting mixture of peat moss, sphagnum moss, osmunda fiber or ground fern bark. Make certain the drainage hole is open and well covered with broken shard or pea gravel.

## Watering

Bromeliads do not have an extensive root system and as long as the vase holds water they will live a long time. Attached to a piece of bark or driftwood they can survive being dry for many weeks. When planted in pots with a porous potting mixture of peat moss, sphagnum moss, osmunda fiber or ground fern bark, they will develop larger root systems. Under such conditions they require water at the roots once a week as well as in the vase which really should never be empty of water.

## Feeding

In nature, leaves and debris decompose in the vase providing nutrients and nourishment required for full development. Under cultivation it is desirable to replace this phenomenon with a

*Tillandsia*

weak solution of water soluble general fertilizer applied into the leaf vase every 14 days during the active periods of growth, spring and summer.

## Propagation

Once the flowering cycle is complete the rosette will die but not before sending out a couple of basal offshoots (as many as 12) at the base of the rosette. These may be separated from the mother plant when six months old or when they have at least three good size leaves. Use a sterile knife and make a sharp clean cut. Pot immediately in the coarse potting mixture previously described and fill the cup with water. In general, the offshoot plants will flower in one to two years.

## Special Problems

This plant is essentially trouble-free.

# BUXUS microphylla japonica

*Boxwood*

Boxwood is a favorite outdoor shrub in the milder regions. Indoors the dwarf forms make interesting green accents in and amongst other potted plants.

## Origin

Genus Buxus of the Boxwood family (Buxaceae) has about 30 species mostly native to the tropical and sub-tropical regions of the Mediterranean, East Africa, West Indies and Central America.

## Description

*Buxus microphylla japonica,* a native of China and Japan is a small evergreen shrub growing to about 6 feet. The leaves are bright, shiny green, ovate in shape and 1/2 to 1 1/4 inches in length. It responds well to shearing for maintenance of shape and height and grows very slowly.

## Cultivation

Locate in semi-sun to semi-shade in a cool location, 16 to 18°C. (60 to 65°F.).

## Potting

Use a rich friable soil mixture of equal parts loam, coarse builders' sand, peat moss and rotted or dried manure or compost. Place a generous layer of pebbles or pea gravel over the drainage hole. Repot only when the root ball is compacted.

## Watering

Keep evenly moist at all times. Mist spray occasionally with clear water.

## Feeding

Feed with care about once every six months with water soluble general fertilizer.

## Propagation

By division or cuttings of mature wood, dipped in rooting hormone powder and placed in coarse moist sand.

## Special Problems

Forced soft growth may be attacked by aphids. Control with malathion insecticide spray.

*Buxus microphylla japonica*

# CALATHEA makoyana

*Peacock Plant*

The Peacock Plant is prized for its decorative green leaves, marked or striped with other colors.

## Origin

Genus Calathea, with around 100 species, is a member of the Arrowroot family (Maran-taceae) and all are native to tropical America.

## Description

Native to Brazil, *Calathea makoyana*, Peacock Plant, is a perennial foliage plant, 1 to 4 feet, with 20-inch leaves arising from a crown. The leaves are ovate and somewhat pointed. The upper surface is olive green or cream colored with dark green blotches, while the underside is similarly marked in red. The leaf stems are purplish red.

## Cultivation

Grow in shade to semi-shade. Strong sun can damage the delicately textured leaves. Average room temperature that doesn't drop below 18°C. (65°F.) is suitable.

## Potting

Use a mixture of equal parts loam, coarse builders' sand, peat moss, rotted or dried manure and leafmould. Soil stagnation must be avoided so cover the drainage hole with pebbles, crock or pea gravel up to one-third. Repot each spring.

## Watering

Keep thoroughly moistened and provide high humidity. Frequent mist spraying of the foliage will help.

## Feeding

Use water soluble general fertilizer on a 14 day schedule during spring and summer.

## Propagation

From suckers that are freely formed or by division of the crown.

## Special Problems

Excessive cold and low humidity can inhibit growth and damage the foliage.

*Calathea makoyana*

# CAMELLIA

It is generally agreed that the Camellia makes an aristocratic house plant with its waxy flowers and polished dark green leaves.

## Origin

Camellia is a member of the Tea family (Theaceae). Camellias are evergreen shrubs that are Asiatic in origin and found on the Indochina mainland north to Korea and of course Japan from whence introduction came to England and subsequently to the United States in the 18th century.

## Description

*Camellia japonica* is the hardiest member of the family and can be grown out of doors in all parts of the country. Other camellias may need the shelter of a wall. They quickly make good specimens and are much admired for their floral display from late autumn to winter. Attractive small specimens may be grown in pots as house plants. The evergreen leaves are 3 to 3½ inches in length with short leaf stalks, alternating in location. The leaves have a fine tooth edge. A three year old plant will be about 24 inches in height and may bear up to 30 buds which will develop into double button-like flowers up to 3½ inches in diameter. Individual flowers often have eight petals or more. The plant is slow growing but will eventually reach tub size and a height of 3 to 4 feet.

## Cultivation

Camellias are not difficult to grow if strict attention is given to their particular cultural requirements. They require semi-sunlight year round and, if possible, should be moved outdoors in summer to the balcony or patio with protection from hot, dry winds. Indoors, keep the plant as cool as possible, 10 to 12°C. (50 to 55°F.). They like cool nighttime temperatures even as low as 5 to 10°C. (40 to 50°F.).

## Potting

Provide good drainage by covering the hole of the pot with broken shard and pea gravel. This is an acid soil plant (pH 4.0 to 5.5), that requires a potting mix of two parts peat moss, one part coarse builders' sand and one part rotted or dried manure. Mature plants usually require repotting every three years and should never be overpotted. When repotting is called for, do it immediately after flowering. At the same time, prune out excessive shoots and cut back any maverick growth so as to maintain a tidy compact plant. Flower buds develop during the summer on new growths.

## Watering

Watering is very critical and dryness of the roots for only a brief period will result in bud drop and thus no flowers. Never let the soil dry out and maintain high humidity by wetting the foliage from the hose outside or a mister while inside.

## Feeding

Enhance the soil acidity about four times a year with a solution of one teaspoon of sulphate of ammonia or sulphate of iron to one gallon of water. March to September maintain a regular 10 to 14 day feeding schedule with water soluble general fertilizer once the spring and summer growth period

*Camellia japonica*

commences immediately after blooming.

## Propagation

Propagation is very easy from cuttings rooted in a mixture of one part peat moss and two parts coarse builders' sand at a temperature of 22°C. (72°F.). Cuttings may be 3 to 6 inches long with four to six leaf nodes. Remove the lower leaves. Enclose the rooting bed in clear plastic to maintain humidity during the three-month rooting period. Locate in bright light away from direct sun.

## Special Problems

Dryness of the roots will result in bud drop and, therefore, no flowers.

# CAMPANULA isophylla
*Star-of-Bethlehem, Italian Bellflower*

An old time perennial for hanging baskets.

## Origin

Genus Campanula, with over 300 species, is a member of the Bell Flower family (Campanulaceae), all native to the Northern Hemisphere.

## Description

Star-of-Bethlehem, *Campanula isophylla alba*, is a perennial from Italy with trailing stems and long stemmed, grey-green, toothed leaves about $1^1/2$ inches long with white flowers. Variety 'Mayii' has larger blue flowers. Both flower in summer.

## Cultivation

Grow cool in bright light. This alpine plant will tolerate normal room temperature but grows best on a sun porch where the temperature is 10 to 13°C. (50 to 55°F.).

## Potting

Use a mixture of loam, coarse builders' sand, peat moss and rotted or dried manure. Incorporate a modicum of ground limestone. Drainage is important; use a generous layer of shard, pebbles or pea gravel. Repot when roots become compacted.

## Watering

Keep evenly moist during spring and summer, less in winter. In dry locations mist spray the foliage with clear water. Small young plants may be grown over a humidity tray.

## Feeding

Use water soluble general fertilizer on a 10 day schedule during spring and early summer.

## Propagation

From seeds sown in March in a 16°C. (60°F.) temperature and by division of plants at the time of repotting or by stem cuttings taken in spring.

## Special Problems

Wet soggy conditions will lead to root rot. Control aphids and green fly with malathion insecticide.

*Campanula isophylla alba*

# CARISSA grandiflora
*Natal Plum*

The edible, red fruits, resemble cranberry in flavor.

## Origin

Genus Carissa, with over 30 species, is a member of the Dogbane family (Apocynaceae). All are from the tropics of the Eastern Hemisphere.

## Description

*Carissa grandiflora*, Natal Plum, is a heavily spined shrub growing 12 to 15 feet. The oval shaped leaves are glossy, and dark green. White 2-inch flowers are produced followed by red, berry shaped half inch fruits that are used in jellies.

## Cultivation

Grow in a semi-sunny location in average room temperature.

## Potting

Use a soil mixture of equal parts loam, coarse builders' sand, peat moss and rotted or dried manure. Provide drainage with a layer of pebbles or pea gravel over the drainage hole. Repot when roots become compacted.

## Watering

Keep evenly moist. Average room humidity is acceptable.

## Feeding

Use water soluble general fertilizer during spring and summer.

## Propagation

From seeds at any time. From stem cuttings of mature wood taken in spring and rooted in moist sand or vermiculite.

## Special Problems

Use gloves when handling for protection against the 2-inch spines. Control insect pests with malathion insecticide.

*Carissa grandiflora*

# CATOPSIS

These interesting durable plants for table decoration are not widely grown but are becoming more readily available.

## Origin

Genus Catopsis is a member of the Pineapple family (Bromeliaceae) of which there are around 20 species native to the West Indies and Southern Mexico to Peru.

## Description

These epiphytic (air) plants have smooth leaves in a basal rosette that form a vase or container for holding water and decaying vegetation. Available species include:

*C. berteroniana,* forms a rigid symmetrical rosette 1½ to 3 feet high. The leaves are concave and spreading. The stout erect flower stalk bears overlapping white flowers with pale green bracts.

*C. floribunda* from West Indies and Central America grows to 2½ feet with a small stiff rosette of pea green leaves, 16 inches long and 1¼ inches wide, tapering to a sharp point. White flowers are borne on a branch flower spike during spring.

*C. morriniana* from South Mexico, Guatemala in Central America, forms a small rosette with 4 to 8-inch, strap-like, glossy green leaves. The small white flowers have yellow bracts.

*C. mutans* from West Indies, Central and South America, grows only 7 to 16 inches with open, broad pointed 1 inch wide leaves, green above and somewhat whitish below. The pendulous flower spike produces small bright yellow flowers.

## Cultivation

Grow in a sunny to semi-sunny location in average room temperature.

## Potting

Plants may be grown on driftwood or old branches by wrapping the base with sphagnum moss and wiring into position. For pot culture use osmunda fiber, ground bark or very coarse loose leafmould.

## Watering

Keep the rosette vase filled with water. Average house humidity is acceptable, occasional mist spraying with clear water is beneficial. If grown in pots, water the pot only occasionally.

## Feeding

Very little, possibly once during the summer with one-quarter strength of water soluble general fertilizer.

## Propagation

From basal offsets of the parent plant. Remove with a sharp knife when large enough to handle. After flowering, the plant will wither and die, thus it is best to leave at least one offset for replacement.

## Special Problems

This is a trouble-free plant when grown properly.

*Catopsis morriniana*

# CEROPEGIA woodii

*String-of-Hearts, Rosary Vine*

A plant for the windowsill or hanging basket.

## Origin

Genus Ceropegia, with over 100 species, is a member of the Milkweed family (Asclepiadaceae) mostly native to tropical Asia and Africa.

## Description

*Ceropegia woodii*, String-of-Hearts, from South Rhodesia, has one-inch, dark green, mottled white, heart-shaped leaves, along pendulous thread-like stems. The one-inch purplish flower tubes have an inflated rounded base. The plant grows from a corm-like root.

## Cultivation

Grow in semi-sun in average room temperature.

## Potting

Use a soil mixture of equal parts loam, coarse builders' sand, peat moss and rotted or dried manure or compost. Provide for good drainage with a generous amount of broken crock, pebbles or pea gravel. Repot only when roots and tubers fill the container.

## Watering

Water as with other succulents by soaking, then allowing the soil to approach a dry condition before soaking again. Average room humidity is suitable.

## Feeding

During the period spring to August, use one-half strength water soluble general fertilizer on a 14 day schedule.

## Propagation

Stem cuttings in moist sand or vermiculite. Allow the cut end to dry for a day or so. From tubers that are freely found in the soil and available at the time of repotting and from seeds when available.

## Special Problems

Essentially none.

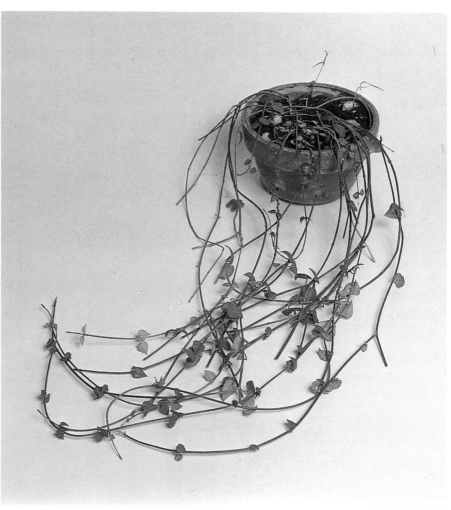

*Ceropegia woodii*

# CESTRUM nocturnum
*Night Jessamine*

Plant for nighttime fragrance.

## Origin
Genus Cestrum, with about 150 species, is a member of the Nightshade family (Solanaceae) from the American tropics.

## Description
*Cestrum nocturnum*, Night Jessamine, is a spreading shrub growing up to 12 feet and is native to the West Indies. Greenish, white to cream white flowers resembling those of Jasmine appear over a long period through late spring and summer. They are especially fragrant at night.

## Cultivation
Grow in full sun in winter with some shade during spring and summer. Average room temperature is suitable. Shape plants by pinch pruning to encourage bushiness.

## Potting
Use a mixture of equal parts loam, coarse builders' sand, peat moss and rotted or dried manure or compost. Cover the drainage hole with shard, pebbles and pea gravel. Spring rooted cuttings should reach 6-inch pot size by September. Repot older plants only when the root ball becomes compacted.

## Watering
Keep evenly moist. Average room humidity with occasional mist spraying will discourage red spider mites.

## Feeding
Apply water soluble general fertilizer on a 14 day schedule during spring and summer.

## Propagation
Five to 6-inch stem cuttings root readily in spring with warmth. Use moist sand or vermiculite.

## Special Problems
Red spider mites, scale and mealy bugs can be controlled with insecticide spray malathion.

*Cestrum nocturnum*

# CHLOROPHYTUM elatum vittatum

*Spider Plant*

This easily grown plant *Chlorophytum elatum vittatum* is a must for all indoor gardeners, new or experienced alike. The graceful, distinctive flowering stems develop spider-like plantlets.

## Origin

The Spider Plant is a member of the Lily family (Liliaceae) and has 60 or more species that are native to the warm areas of Asia, Africa and the Americas. The most commonly grown varieties originate from South America.

## Description

This plant has a tuberous root system that sends up narrow, white striped leaves 10 to 16 inches long. During spring and summer the plant produces small, insignificant flowers on two to three foot stems. The flowers are soon followed by clusters of leaves that weigh down the stems causing them to arch into an attractive waterfall effect. This trailing habit makes Spider Plants ideal for hanging baskets, a high shelf or inside an old bird cage.

## Cultivation

Best growth is in a sunny, east, west or south window. However, the plant will tolerate partial shade. Average room temperature and humidity is satisfactory. After danger of frost, plants may be summered outside in a protected, bright location.

## Potting

While this plant is relatively undemanding, it grows best in a rich friable potting soil such as equal parts loam, coarse builders' sand, peat moss and rotted or dried manure. Growth is rapid and repotting should occur when the tuberous roots become cramped and start pushing out of the soil. Spring is the best time for repotting.

## Watering

Keep the soil evenly moist and water freely during the summer growing period. Mist spraying of the foliage is always beneficial.

## Feeding

During the growing period, apply water soluble general fertilizer on a 10 to 14 day schedule. Make certain the soil is well moistened before applying the fertilizer solution.

## Propagation

This is readily accomplished by removing the aerial plantlets that form on the cascading flower stems. Plant in the soil mixture described previously and water thoroughly. Enclose the plant in a clear plastic bag for the first few weeks, out of direct sun. This hastens root development. Older plants may be divided. Make certain each section has leaves along with the roots.

## Special Problems

Browning of the tips of the leaves is usually an indication of lack of moisture and drying out of the root ball. Green flies and aphids may be controlled with malathion.

*Chlorophytum elatum vittatum*

# CHRYSANTHEMUM morifolium

*Florist's Mum, Mum*

Widely grown in the garden as well as a favorite pot plant.

## Origin

Genus Chrysanthemum is a member of the Anthmis tribe of the Composite family (Compositae) which is reportedly the world's largest plant family.

## Description

Florist's Mum is considered to be a hybrid evolving from *C. indicum* and *C. japonense*, of Chinese origin and cultivated in China and Japan for 3,000 years. This perennial plant may be 2 to 4 feet or more in height, branched, with strong scented, lobed leaves. The terminal flowers come in almost any color except blue and have been developed into many forms, pom-pom, single, incurved, spider, etc.

## Cultivation

While they are best grown in the field and potted up in late summer, they may be grown in pots in a bright sunny window in a cool room. However, since they are a light sensitive plant (short day bloom), provision should be made to assure no indoor lighting after sunset as with the Poinsettia. Young plants should be pinch pruned up until the first week of July.

## Potting

Use a rich friable soil mixture of equal parts loam, builders' sand, peat moss and rotted or dried manure. Cover the drainage hole with pebbles or pea gravel. Rooted cuttings in 3-inch pots should be moved up in size as soon as the roots fill the pots. Plants may be flowered in a 6-inch pot. Plants lifted from the garden in late summer should be handled carefully to assure minimum disturbance to the roots, and then placed in an adequate size pot.

## Watering

This is a thirsty plant that requires lots of water especially in a warm room. Average room humidity is adequate.

## Feeding

Feed regularly on a two week schedule with water soluble general fertilizer.

## Propagation

Two to three-inch offsets from the root clump root readily in moist sand or vermiculite.

## Special Problems

Excessive heat and long periods of light at flowering time can prevent formation of buds and flowers. Control aphids and other pests with malathion insecticide spray.

*Chrysanthemum morifolium*

# CISSUS antarctica
*Kangaroo Vine*

These climbers are among the easiest vines to grow.

## Origin
Genus Cissus, with 350 species, is a member of the Grape family (Vitaceae).

## Description
*Cissus antarctica*, Kangaroo Vine, is a woody tendril climber from New South Wales. The oblong, glossy green leaves are undivided and up to 5 inches in length.

## Cultivation
Grow in shade in average room temperature.

## Potting
Use a soil mix of equal parts loam, coarse builders' sand, rotted or dried manure, leafmould or compost, (omit peat moss), add a modicum of bone meal. Repot when roots become compacted. Drainage is critical—use a generous layer of shard, pebbles, or pea gravel.

## Watering
Keep evenly moist. Never allow the plant to stand in excess water. Average room humidity is suitable.

## Feeding
Feed during spring and summer with water soluble general fertilizer on a two week schedule.

## Propagation
Readily from stem cuttings at any time.

## Special Problems
Soggy wet conditions can destroy the plant. Hot sun will disfigure the foliage. Spray or dust occasionally with an insecticide/fungicide spray.

*Cissus antarctica*

# CISSUS rhombifolia

*Grape Ivy*

Many plants will grow on a shelf, on top of a free standing cupboard or suspended from the ceiling in a hanging pot. Grape Ivy is an undemanding work horse of a plant that can either climb or cascade to suit a decoration.

## Origin

Grape Ivy *(Cissus rhombifolia)* is a member of the Grape family (Vitaceae) and is native to northern South America and the West Indies.

## Description

Grape Ivy takes to indoor cultivation more readily than the regular Ivy *(Hedera helix)*. It requires a minimum of care and in many ways is much more adaptable for indoor decoration in that it is less stiff and formal with its three leaflets on each leaf stalk. The deep green leaves have tooth edges and are about 3 inches long and 2 inches wide. They are produced in abundance on the many trailing or climbing stems of the plant. New leaves have a slight reddish tint and growing tips have a silvery down which appears reddish brown further back on the stems before disappearing altogether.

## Cultivation

Grow in bright light, semi-sunny to semi-shady. Average house temperatures are suitable; night temperatures should not drop below 15°C. (60°F.). Humidity in the 25 to 30% range is desirable and mist spraying of the foliage with clear water is always beneficial. With judicious pruning the plant will become very branched and it is often seen growing up a framework of string between a planter and the ceiling.

## Potting

Use a friable soil mixture commercially available as tropical plant soil or make your own using equal parts garden loam builders' sand, peat moss and rotted or dried manure, or leafmould. The mix should always be slightly moist at the time of potting so as not to dehydrate tender white roots. As soon as the roots of small plants fill the pot move up to the next size until a 10-inch size pot is reached. At each move separate any loose soil from the root ball and place the plant in a pot that has a generous amount of crushed stone or broken pottery over the drainage holes.

## Watering

Keep the soil slightly moist and err on the dry side.

## Feeding

Supplementary feeding at two week intervals with water soluble general fertilizer will produce luxurious growth.

## Propagation

Grape Ivy propagates readily from cuttings that may be rooted either in water or moist sand. Use of hormone rooting powder will speed up the time of root formation.

## Special Problems

This plant is essentially trouble-free and will last for many years.

*Cissus rhombifolia*

# CITRUS
*Lemon/Lime/Orange Trees*

You can become a grower of citrus fruits—outside in the summer and inside in the winter. Regardless of where you live, enjoy these remarkable dwarf trees by growing them in a container and have tree ripened fruit, exotic perfumed blossoms and glossy leaves almost any time of the year.

## Origin

Citrus is a native of tropical and sub-tropical Asia and is a member of the Rue family (Rutaceae). It was first used as a tub plant in the Mediterranean regions in the early 14th century.

## Description

*Citrus aurantifolia* (Dwarf Persian Lime) grows up to 2 feet with lots of limes for food and drinks. *Citrus limonia meyeri* (Meyer Lemon) under ideal conditions could become 8 feet tall but, grown in a container, it can easily be restrained to 2 or 3 feet for years. Soft tip pruning is the technique to follow. This will keep the tree free from aphids. *Citrus limonia ponderosa* (American Wonder Lemon) is only 2 feet tall and bears large lemons up to a two-pound size. With good growing conditions the tree will have lemons in all stages of maturity all year round as well as flowers that resemble orange blossoms. The fruit is slightly larger than the fruit of a store lemon and, even when fully ripe, is tart enough for thirst quenching lemonade. It also makes delicious pies. *Citrus mitis* (Calamondin Orange) is a native of the Philippines and is widely cultivated in Hawaii. Pinch pruning in spring and summer will maintain the plant under a height of 2 feet. Although botanists are not certain, there is a strong feeling that *Citrus taitensis* (Otaheite or Tahiti Orange) came from China rather than from Tahiti. It is a bright broad leaf evergreen plant that favors night temperatures of 10°C. (50°F.). It sends out a constant supply of sweet scented flowers plus, of course, clusters of small oranges. The oranges are very tart and not very edible. However, along with a few leaves they do make an outstanding garnish atop a vanilla butter icing on a chocolate cake—a gourmet touch on the birthday cake for the dinner party pièce-de-résistance.

## Cultivation

Light is important for the production of flowers and fruit. Indoors use a south or southwest window since as much sun as possible is desirable. During the summer months keep the tree outside in a sunny location. It is not necessary to repot every year. Once the tree has reached the large container size you can comfortably accommodate it without moving out of house and home, or if the size of the tree has to be held down, the technique to use is to remove the whole plant and root ball out of the container with a sharp knock and remove a one inch slice from the root ball, one side only, with a long sharp knife. Return the tree to the container and replace the sliced portion with enriched soil mixture discussed under potting. It is also permissible, during the growing season, to remove some of the soil on top with a spoon or small trowel and replace with the enriched mixture. Always maintain the trunk at the original soil level.

## Potting

The oxygen requirements of citrus fruits is high so, while the soil around the roots should be moist, under no circumstances should it be allowed to become soggy. This is best controlled by starting off with the proper soil mix—one that is open and friable and allows excess water to drain through promptly. Use a mix of equal parts coarse builders' sand, peat moss and rotted or dried manure. A pH of 6.5 (slightly acid) is best for Citrus so the soil mix should not receive lime. Make a mix and moisten with water. Set the tree in a container of the same height as it was growing in at the nursery. Make certain there is an adequate drainage hole in the container. Cover with coarse material such as shard or pea gravel.

## Watering

Water thoroughly after planting and then on demand, maybe up to twice a week. While Citrus enjoys becoming somewhat dry between waterings it will take some experience and observation to determine the exact point where withholding water will cause the tree to wilt and start to drop its leaves. While a small indiscretion in this matter will not be fatal to the tree, the health and appearance will be affected. The exact amount of moisture required is of course dependent upon the soil, the location (inside or outside), the humidity of the air, the size and age of the tree, etc. If the air is abnormally dry as in winter, more watering will be required. The tree will also benefit from wiping the leaves with a soft moist cloth, mist spraying with clear water, or placing above the water line in a humidity tray filled with stones and water.

## Feeding

During growing periods provide supplementary feeding with water soluble general fertilizer on a 10 to 14 day schedule. This will keep the tree healthy and productive. A well grown Citrus will have flowers, green fruit

*Citrus limonia ponderosa*

and ripe fruit in almost continuous production.

## Propagation

From cuttings of half ripened wood, during spring and summer. Cut ends and apply rooting hormone and place in coarse builders' sand or vermiculite and keep moist.

## Special Problems

Fortunately, Citrus is relatively free of pests. A routine spraying with malathion keeps a healthy growing condition. Follow the manufacturer's directions for application.

# CLERODENDRUM

*Glory-Bower, Bleeding Heart Vine*

Magnificent shrubs and climbers with limited use as house plants.

## Origin

Genus Clerodendron, with over 425 species, is a member of the Verbena family (Verbenaceae), mostly native to the tropics of Asia and East Africa.

## Description

*C. fragrans* is a 5 to 8 foot shrub with fragrant white flowers, native to East Asia. *C. bungei* from China grows to 6 feet and has strong scented rose-red upright flower clusters.

*C. speciosissimum* forms an erect shrub up to 12 feet with bright scarlet flowers. It is native to Java.

*C. thomsoniae*, commonly known as Glory-Bower or Bleeding Heart Vine is a climber from West Africa growing to 12 feet. It produces white and scarlet flowers.

## Cultivation

Grow in a sunny to semi-sunny location. Average room temperature is suitable during the growing period. Coolness around 13 to 16°C. (55 to 60°F.) is desirable during the resting period of October to January. Plants should be pruned after flowering.

## Potting

Use a rich friable soil mixture of equal parts loam, coarse builders' sand, peat moss, rotted or dried manure and coarse leafmould. Cover drainage hole with a generous layer of pebbles or pea gravel. Plants will flower in 6-inch size pots. Repot when roots become compacted. Move up to a larger size pot or tub to increase plant size.

## Watering

Keep evenly moist except during the resting period when less water is required. Mist spray with clear water to maintain higher than normal humidity especially during spring and summer.

## Feeding

Use water soluble general fertilizer on a 10 day schedule from early spring through summer.

## Propagation

Use 6-inch cuttings of half ripened wood. Dip ends in rooting hormone powder and place in moist sand or vermiculite with bottom heat 21 to 24°C. (70 to 75°F.). Maintain humidity by mist spraying or enclose in a clear plastic bag. Seeds sown in February will germinate at 21 to 24°C. (70 to 75°F.) and produce flowering size

*Clerodendrum thomsoniae*

plants in 12 months. Start rooted cuttings and seedlings in 3-inch pots.

## Special Problems

Control white fly, mealy bugs and aphids by spraying regularly with insecticide malathion.

# CLIVIA miniata
*Kafir Lily*

The Kafir Lily is a close relative of the Amaryllis. It has much of the same beauty plus the advantage of being evergreen and retaining attractive foliage year round.

## Origin
Native to Natal, Clivia is a member of the Amaryllis family (Amaryllidaceae) along with Hippeastrum, etc.

## Description
The deep green foliage is sword shaped, up to 18 inches long and 2 to 4½ inches wide. There are usually about 16 leaves on a plant at any one time. The flowering 12-inch spike which rises above the foliage may produce up to 20 long, tubular, orange or red, yellow-centered flowers in an outstanding cluster that lasts for several weeks. The plant is a half hardy perennial and is an undemanding plant for indoors. *Clivia miniata* is the species commonly grown.

## Cultivation
The plant thrives in a cool growing temperature, 12 to 18°C. (55 to 65°F.), and enjoys bright light as in an east window. Strong sun will tend to scorch the foliage and should be avoided. Occasional sponging of the long foliage will keep it glossy and attractive.

## Potting
The thick fleshy roots which resemble those of Agapanthus, enjoy a pot bound condition and for this reason, repotting should always be delayed as long as possible and undertaken only after several years. In view of this, the potting soil should be of a durable lasting nature, one that will stay sweet and well drained. A mixture of equal parts coarse builders' sand, peat moss and well rotted or dried manure will give the desired characteristics. Place a generous amount of crushed stone, pea gravel or broken shard at the bottom of the pot over the drainage hole to facilitate full drainage. Use a 7 or 10-inch pot, whichever accommodates the roots in comfort.

## Watering
During the growing period, which is normally early spring to September, the soil should be kept evenly moist. In late autumn the watering should be reduced somewhat, but not to the point of allowing the foliage to wilt and wither. Over-watering at this time will encourage production of leaves at the expense of flowers. When new growth starts at the turn of the year, top dress with some fresh potting soil and increase the watering.

## Feeding
During the period of active growth, provide supplementary feeding with water soluble general fertilizer solution on a 10 to 14 day schedule. Make certain that the soil is water moistened

*Clivia miniata*

before the application of the fertilizer solution.

## Propagation
This plant may be propagated from seeds sown at room temperature, 21°C. (70°F.). Germination takes about thirty days. This is a slow method since it takes three to four years to produce blooming size plants. The best and fastest procedure is by root division. After flowering has finished in late spring, select an old root-bound plant, remove it from the pot and divide the entire plant into pieces. Trim the roots and place the divisions in small pots. Keep them moist and warm to stimulate new root growth. Move up to a 7-inch size pot as rapidly as possible in pace with the root development.

## Special Problems
If mealy bugs become a problem, use a contact spray such as malathion or a small soft brush dipped in rubbing alcohol to remove individual pests.

# CODIAEUM variegatum

*Croton*

*Codiaeum variegatum pictum*

Indoor gardeners seeking an exotic and challenging plant will find all this and more in Croton. While plant breeding and selection has done much to develop more resilience in Croton, it still remains a somewhat demanding plant.

## Origin

Native to the tropics—Polynesia, Malaysia, Ceylon, Java and India—the first recorded introduction of the Croton in Europe is from the 1864 plant expedition to Australia and the South Pacific by John Gould Veitch. It is a member of the Spurge family (Euphorbiaceae).

## Description

The main feature of this tropical shrub is the glossy, leathery, multi-colored leaves. Variegated with striking combinations of green, white, yellow, orange, pink, red, crimson and brown, they are highly prized in their native lands where they are used for decoration during ceremonial events as well as for head wreaths.

The shrub is classed as an evergreen and it has leaves of various shapes, some narrow, some wide and some even oak and spiral shaped. Specimen plants often grow 6 feet in height.

It is generally conceded that *C. variegatum pictum* is the originating species of hundreds of varieties that have been named and catalogued i.e., *C. variegatum pictum* 'Jungle Queen' with oval, deep green and yellow, red-veined leaves often 15 inches long.

## Cultivation

Poor light will result in the brightly variegated foliage turning green. Locate the plant in a brightly lit to a filtered sunlit spot, away from drafts and especially away from the air conditioner. Normal house temperature will suit this plant, but winter temperature that falls below 15°C. (60°F.) will result in a dramatic shedding of leaves and bare lower stems. During a very warm summer, plants may be kept outside in a sheltered location out of direct, hot sun. The flowers produced in late winter and early spring are inconspicuous and of little interest.

## Potting

Use a potting soil of equal parts loam, builders' sand, peat moss, and rotted or dried manure or leafmould. A generous layer of crushed stone or pea gravel over the drainage holes will ensure the prompt drainage that is essential for good health.

## Watering

Keep the soil evenly moist. Drying out of the root ball is followed by leaf drop. Humidity should be maintained above 30% with the aid of a humidity tray filled with gravel and water. Regular mist spraying of the foliage and stems with clear water is also beneficial.

## Feeding

During the period of active growth, spring to autumn, use a water soluble general fertilizer on a two-week schedule. Take care that the root ball is well moistened before applying the fertilizer solution.

## Propagation

Propagate from stem cuttings.

## Special Problems

While modern day hybrids are tougher

*Codiaeum variegatum delicatissimum*

and more tolerant of drafts, temperature and humidity changes, neglect for even a short period may result in a bare-stemmed plant.

Red spider mites are particularly fond of Croton and the hot dry air of winter favors their rapid spread. Keep the humidity high with regular mist spraying with clear water and protect by spraying routinely with malathion.

# COFFEA arabica
*Arabian Coffee Tree*

Indoors, Coffea makes a superior pot or tub plant.

## Origin

Genus Coffea is a member of the Madder family (Rubiaceae) along with Gardenia. There are about 40 species mostly native to tropical Africa and Asia.

## Description

*Coffea arabica* is the principal species grown and it is widely cultivated in Latin America. The plant is a woody shrub growing to 15 feet, with young plants having one main trunk or stem. Grown indoors as an ornamental it rarely reaches 6 feet. The dark green, glossy leaves are evergreen, elliptic in shape and about 6 inches long. The small pure white, star-like flowers are borne at the three year old leaf axils, during summer, followed by fleshy red, 1½ inch long berries containing two seeds from which coffee is made.

## Cultivation

Rotate in bright light, semi-sun with a bit more light during the winter months. Average room temperature is adequate but never below 16°C. (60°F.).

## Potting

This plant requires a rich friable soil mixture of equal parts loam, coarse builders' sand, peat moss, rotted or dried manure or compost. Drainage is important and a generous layer of small pebbles or pea gravel should be used over the drainage hole. Repot in early spring when the root ball becomes compacted.

## Watering

Water frequently during the summer growing and flowering period, less during the autumn/winter resting period but sufficient that the root ball never dries out. Don't allow the pot to sit in water. Average room humidity is adequate with some mist spraying of the leaves during the resting period. Plants may be summered on the patio in a sheltered semi-shaded location during the frost-free months.

## Feeding

Water soluble general fertilizer on a 10 day schedule should be used during the growing period.

## Propagation

From seeds available from many seed houses. The seed bed should be kept in full light at a temperature of 24 to 27°C. (75 to 80°F.). Germination may take up to 50 days. Cuttings of mature wood taken in late spring require moist warm conditions for rooting.

## Special Problems

Scale may be controlled with a cotton swab dipped in rubbing alcohol or an insecticide spray such as malathion. Avoid the use of systemics if the beans are to be harvested and used for beverage.

*Coffea arabica*

54

# COLEUS blumei
*Painted Leaf Plant, Flame Nettle*

A rainbow of color is about the only way you can describe the Coleus plant, even though the blue portion of the spectrum is missing. But the greens through yellows, golds, reds, pinks, maroon and their combinations give a wealth of possibility not only in color but in size and shape of the leaves.

## Origin

There are more than 150 species of Coleus in the tropics of Africa, India and East Indies. Genus Coleus is a member of the Mint family (Labiatae) along with rosemary, thyme, marjoram, lavender, etc.

## Description

*Coleus blumei* is the most commonly grown species and is a native of Java. Growing in the range of one to three feet high this plant is available in a widening range of color and leaf shapes that now include long slender sword shapes as well as a deeply cut oak leaf type. Spikes of light blue flowers are borne chiefly in summer. These are best pinched and pruned away as soon as they form so as to maintain a compact leafy plant. While Coleus is a perennial, it is best to replace plants on a yearly basis either from cuttings or seed. The really nice plants can be saved from year to year by taking cuttings before frost.

## Cultivation

Coleus makes a colorful winter standby when few plants are in bloom. It is an ideal house plant for the apartment or home and is most frequently used as an outdoor bedding plant. Bright light is needed to maintain intensity and depth of color in the leaves. Locate in a south, west or east window. As the plant is somewhat sensitive to cold, it does not thrive much below 15°C. (60°F.) and at 7°C. (45°F.) it will sulk and die.

## Potting

Use a mixture of equal parts loam, coarse builders' sand, peat moss and rotted or dried manure or compost. Avoid the use of lime as plants thrive best in slightly acidic soil. Use a generous layer of broken shard or pea gravel over the drainage hole.

## Watering

Keep the root ball evenly moist with tepid water. Frequently, dryness and wilting can result in premature leaf drop. It is fairly tolerant of dry air. However, for best results, place pots above the water line in a humidity tray filled with gravel and water.

## Feeding

Use water soluble general fertilizer on a 14 day schedule during periods of active growth.

## Propagation

**Seeds**—There are about 100,000 seeds in an ounce, which gives some idea of their fineness and the care that must be taken in planting. A mixed packet of Coleus seed will provide a fascinating variety of plants. Because of the fineness of the seed, extra care must be taken in planting by merely pressing it into the soil rather than covering. It is important to use a sterilized seeding mix to prevent damp off. This fungus disease attacks seedlings at the soil line and is quite final. Most garden centers sell a sterile seeding mix but you can make your own by mixing equal parts of vermiculite, perlite and milled sphagnum moss; or use a mixture of equal parts peat moss and builders' sand or equal parts vermiculite and perlite. A simple container can be made from a milk carton by cutting away one side or you can use an aluminum loaf tin. Punch many holes in the bottom to insure full drainage. Flower pots or wooden flats also make adequate, conventional seed beds. Fill the container to within half an inch of the top and place in a pan of lukewarm water and allow the mix to become completely saturated. Remove, drain thoroughly and sow the seed by pressing onto the surface. Germination at 21 to 26°C. (70 to 80°F) requires about two weeks. Cover the top of the container with a piece of clear plastic, stretched so that it remains above the seedling mix. Place the container in bright light or under fluorescent light, since light is required to achieve full germination. This is as important as keeping the seedling mix uniformly moist with lukewarm water. As soon as the first seedling leaves appear, remove the plastic and place in the direct sun; if under fluorescent lights, place within six inches of the lights. When the second set of leaves appear start feeding from below with a water soluble fertilizer mixed to a strength suitable for tender seedlings as given in the manufacturer's directions. When the seedlings develop more leaves and are about one inch or so high they should be transplanted into individual peat pots. Use a rich soil mix such as equal parts builders' sand, peat moss, rotted or dried manure or leafmould. Keep in bright light to insure compact plants. It is generally considered that the slow growing seedlings develop into the most colorful plants, so do not throw them out. Seeds are normally sown from February through to the first of April.

**Cuttings**—Cuttings taken at leaf

*Coleus blumei*

joints or even between leaf joints, root readily in water or moist sand, almost in a matter of days. Well rooted cuttings should be potted in the soil mix discussed previously. Do not overpot; plan to move the plant on as soon as the root ball fills the container. This treatment develops bushy specimen plants.

## Special Problems

Aphids, white flies and mealy bugs are very fond of the juices of the Coleus plants. Spray regularly with malathion solution—don't wait until the pests take over. Unshapely plants can be controlled by cutting back and regular pinch pruning of the growing tips.

# COLOCASIA esculenta

*Elephant's Ears, Taro, Dasheen, Kalo, Eddo*

Elephant's Ears is a tuberous rooted, tropical plant sometimes incorrectly identified as Caladium because of the enormous arrow-heart-shaped leaves resembling those of the Caladium.

## Origin

*Colocasia esculenta* is a member of the Arum family (Araceae) and is grown as a food staple in tropical America, Jamaica, China, Tahiti, the Philippines and Hawaii. It is known by many names: Taro, Dasheen, Kalo, Eddo and Elephant's Ears.

## Description

The dark green, sometimes mottled leaves may reach a size of 3 feet and are often carried on stems up to 6 feet long. The general effect of this plant is lush and tropical. In the past, Elephant's Ears was often used as a focal point of large formal planting beds. The edible parts of this plant are the roots (tubers) and the young shoots. The shoots are harvested after spring planting or forced during winter in a warm cellar with the tubers planted near the surface of a moist sand bed. It is reported that the tubers are more starchy than potatoes and a bit richer in protein. Even though the sugar content is only about half that of the sweet potato, the somewhat sweet, nut-like flavor keeps it in good favor with those who use it as a diet staple. The young shoots are cut and used like asparagus, the flavor being somewhat earthy and mushroom-like. Before they open, young leaves are used as greens, cooked with fat meat or a pinch of baking soda to destroy the acrid tang. It takes about seven months to raise a crop. Farming of this plant is pretty much confined to very warm climates.

## Cultivation

In the south, Elephant's Ears is raised for the decorative foliage by planting the tubers in a rich soil, in February in a shaded, warm greenhouse. The tubers may be grown in individual pots that may be kept on the windowsill in bright light or moved outside in June and sunk into the ground, all set for a hasty retreat when early frost threatens.

## Potting

Plant one tuber in a 6-inch pot using a loose friable soil mix of equal parts builders' sand, peat moss and well rotted or dried manure.

## Watering

This plant needs lots of water so make certain that the soil never dries out.

## Feeding

Apply a solution of water soluble general fertilizer every seven days during active growth.

## Propagation

Usually from the small side tubers and the offshoots of the parent plant.

## Special Problems

This plant is essentially problem-free.

*Colocasia esculenta*

# COLUMNEA

A long trailing epiphyte, well suited to the hanging garden.

## Origin

Genus Columnea, with over 100 species, is a member of the Gesneriad family (Gesneriaceae) and is mostly native to the American tropics with many originating from Costa Rica.

## Description

Mostly pendant, these trailing plants have small, hairy offset leaves with large showy flowers originating from the leaf axils, particularly from vigorous leaves near the end of the stems. The tubular, open mouth flowers are readily fertilized by humming birds. Some of the species cultivated include:

*C. arguta* from Panama with yellow throated, orange-red flowers.
*C. gloriosa* from Costa Rica with yellow throated scarlet flowers.
*C. hirta* from Costa Rica with vermilion flowers.
*C. microphylla* from Costa Rica with scarlet flowers that have a yellow patch in the throat as well as at the base of the lower lip.

## Cultivation

Place in a semi-sunny location in average room temperature where night temperature remains at 16 to 18°C. (60 to 65°F.). Avoid drafts. Cut back after flowering to encourage more shoots for next year's flowering.

## Potting

Use a fibrous soil mix that drains readily—equal parts loam, coarse builders' sand, sphagnum moss, rotted or dried manure and coarse leafmould. Avoid stagnant conditions by using a generous layer of pebbles or pea gravel over the drainage hole or at the bottom of a hanging basket.

## Watering

Keep well moistened during the growing and summer flowering season. Use slightly less water during the dormant time. Humidity at 50% is ideal for this plant.

## Feeding

Use water soluble general fertilizer on a two week schedule during spring to summer.

## Propagation

Three-inch cuttings of firm growth will root readily from spring through summer. Rooting hormone and bottom heat will hasten the process.

## Special Problems

Drafts will cause leaf drop. Stagnant soil conditions will cause root rot. Control mealy bug and scale with malathion spray.

*Columnea microphylla*

# CORDYLINE terminalis
*Ti-Plant*

This tree-like plant is ideal for that empty corner.

## Origin

Genus Cordyline has about 20 species and is a member of the Agave family (Agavaceae). At one time it was classified under the Lily family. It originates mostly from South Asia into Australia.

## Description

*Cordyline terminalis*, Ti-Plant, is a tree-like plant growing to 10 feet. The short stem leaves can be 30 inches long and about 5 inches wide, plain green or with markings and stripes of rose, white, yellow or pink.

Some of the variegated forms offered include:
*C. terminalis* 'anabilis' with glossy deep green leaves spotted with rose and white.
*C. terminalis* 'Tricolor' has variegations in red, pink and green over bright green.

## Cultivation

Cordyline does not have to be grown in a window—it will prosper in a semi-shady to shady location. However, during the dark days of winter, it will enjoy being a bit closer to the window. Average room temperature is suitable for this plant.

## Potting

This plant does not require an overly large pot. In fact a 7 foot specimen can readily be grown in a 6 to 8-inch pot. Like all tropical plants, Cordyline requires a light, friable rich soil. Use a mixture of equal parts sharp sand, peat moss and well rotted manure or compost. This will give the proper texture, drainage and moisture retention. Each year, remove all the soil from the top of the pot of older plants. Use a pointed stick for this operation. Replace this lost soil with fresh potting soil.

## Watering

Keeping the soil just moist at all times produces the best and most luxurious plants. Dusting the leaves with a damp cloth keeps them at their best appearance. Average room humidity is suitable for this plant.

## Feeding

During spring and summer apply supplementary feeding using water soluble general fertilizer solution.

## Propagation

When the plant outgrows the ceiling, you can air layer the top growth and when roots are in good supply cut it away from the main trunk and plant in a new pot. The trunk can be cut to a height of your choice and in a few weeks side shoots will start to grow. The portion of the trunk that you have pruned away may be used for propagation by cutting it into 1 to 2-inch pieces and burying them in moist sand. Place each piece on its side. Keep the sand evenly moist and warm—covering with a clear plastic will help maintain a moist atmosphere. When new growth appears, the young plants may be moved into 3-inch pots using the soil mixture discussed under Potting.

*Cordyline terminalis*

## Special Problems

Essentially a trouble-free plant.

# CRASSULA argentea

*Jade Plant*

This plant is a member of the most fascinating and complex group of plants in the world—"succulents." Such plants have adapted to drought and have the ability to collect and store a large volume of water in their fleshy stems, branches and leaves.

## Origin

*Crassula argentea* is a member of the Stonecrop family (Crassulaceae). It is one of the more than 200 species of the Crassula genus and of the visible branching stem group, it is the largest. It is a native of Natal, South Africa and appeared as a house plant in England prior to 1836.

## Description

Jade Plant is a free branching succulent that grows to 10 feet. Careful pruning of the branching, forking stems, exposes an attractive architectural plant form. The leaves are thick, fleshy and spatulate in shape, up to 2 inches long and 1 inch at the widest point. The lower surface is flat and the upper surface rounded, jade green in color and glossy. Older plants bear clusters of small, star-like, pinkish white flowers. All in all a tough attractive house plant.

## Cultivation

Locate in a sunny spot in average room temperature. The Jade Plant will tolerate low humidity. During frost-free months, plants may be used on the patio or balcony. The growing period is March to September, and after flowering in autumn, the resting period extends into February. It is during this resting period that the plant prospers best in cooler temperatures down to 10°C. (50°F.).

## Potting

Almost any container will do for a Jade Plant as long as full and efficient drainage is assured. Selection should be made with an eye to form and color. In general, the pot should be half as wide as the height of the plant above the soil level. Obviously it will take two or three moves to reach the final size container where it may be held by root as well as top pruning. The potting soil should be one part coarse builders' sand, one part rich garden loam and one part well rotted leaf-mould, rotted or dried manure or compost, with a sprinkling of bone meal, bearing in mind the basic needs are perfect drainage and good aeration. Since succulents are very susceptible to rot from excessive moisture in the soil, especially when the roots have been disturbed or pruned, it is considered prudent to plant not only in a dry pot but in dry soil as well, and to leave the plant dry for several days. Place a generous amount of broken crockery or pea gravel over the drainage hole, then a layer of dry soil. Center the plant over this material and add more material around the roots until the container is half full. Tamp or bump the pot to compact the soil (you can continue filling the container), tamp and compact leaving reasonable room at the top for watering. Bury the roots and stems to the same depth as before. If the roots are sparse it may be necessary to support the plant with a small stake and tie until roots have developed sufficiently to anchor into the soil. After several healing days, water sparsely for thirty days or so to allow the roots to return to healthy vigor. Don't use a saucer under the container unless it is first filled with crushed stone.

## Watering

Plants making fresh growth in the spring or summer can be watered as often as the soil dries out. In autumn or winter water only enough to keep the plant from shriveling because during the resting period the plant will use water mainly from its own tissues. When water is indicated, it is preferable to water heavily to remove the stale air around the roots. The plant may go without water for two weeks to a month depending upon size, location and time of year. There is no set rule—experience will guide.

## Feeding

One or twice during the growing season with water soluble general fertilizer.

## Propagation

Roots readily from stems and individual leaves, even parts that fall to the earth. Make cuts with a sharp knife and allow the moist ends to dry before inserting in moist sand or vermiculite. Fastest rooting occurs during springtime.

## Special Problems

The Jade Plant is essentially free of pests. If aphids or mealy bugs make an appearance, spray with malathion mixed to the manufacturer's directions.

*Crassula argentea*

# CROCUS

Each winter we all look forward to the harbingers of spring, the Crocus and the robins. While we can't do much to control the habits of the robin, we can enjoy the Crocus long before it appears in the garden. The bright yellows, blues and whites are all found in a variety suitable for indoor forcing.

## Origin

These stemless plants originated in the Mediterranean area and the corms we buy today are the result of over 400 years of hybridizing by the Dutch. Crocus is a member of the Iris family (Iridaceae).

## Description

The low 3 to 4-inch flowers with grass-like leaves are grown from corms rather than true bulbs. Gladiolus also grow from corms which are different than bulbs in that they are solid rather than being composed of overlapping layers as with a lily or hyacinth bulb. Each year the old corm is replaced by a new one which develops above it. The new corm becomes ripe as the old one below it shrivels and dies. Varieties suitable for forcing include; 'Sky Blue,' 'Yellow Mammoth,' 'Jeanne d'Arc,' *Crocus perpureus grandiflorus.*

## Cultivation

Use 4-inch pots to accommodate about six corms. Mix equal parts of light garden soil, builders' sand and peat moss and place in a pot prepared with a half inch layer of pea gravel or small stones covering the drainage holes. Tap the soil to settle it and then place the corms so that only the tips show. The final soil level should be about half an inch below the rim of the pot. All nutrients are already present in the corm for full growth and flowering. The soil mixture provides the corm with a coarse rooting medium that will hold moisture and provide it as required by the root system. Each pot should be submerged in water up to the rim and allowed to stand fifteen minutes or so and then removed for complete drainage. The next important step in growing Crocus indoors is keeping the corms in a cold location while root formation takes place. The cooling period is from 8 to 12 weeks at near freezing temperature. This duplicates the condition of corms planted in the garden. The simplest method is to set the pots in an outdoor trench in the garden to duplicate the normal conditions. The trench should be at least 6 inches deeper than the pot height plus 3 to 4 inches to accommodate a layer of pebbles or crushed stone to drain away excess water. After placing the pots in the trench cover them with sand or peat moss to at least 3 inches over the tops of the pots. This will allow the shoots to grow with ease. The coarse layer should be covered with a deep layer of leaves and held in place with branches or boards. Mark the outline of the trench with tall bamboo stakes for ease of location in case there is deep snow cover. (In locations where the temperature may go below freezing, the corms and pots should be protected with a generous amount of mulch.)

Storage may also be undertaken in a basement, root cellar, garden shed, refrigerator or garage, if care is taken

*Crocus*

not to let the pots dry out. The pots should be placed in boxes and covered to maintain darkness. Regular watering will probably be necessary.

Good root development occurs at a constant temperature around 4°C. (40°F.). After the rooting period (8 to 12 weeks), the corms should show signs of sprouting with roots probably extending beyond the drainage holes in the pot. At this point you may start bringing some pots into a warmer location to start forcing the flowers. A location that is well ventilated, dark and 16°C. (60°F.) is ideal. In about 7 to 14 days the shoots will have developed leaves and buds will be visible. At this point move the plants to a well lighted area with the temperature 15 to 18°C. (60 to 65°F.). Try to keep the plants cool so the flowers may be enjoyed for a longer period.

## Potting

See Cultivation.

## Watering

Constant moisture during the period when roots are forming and after growth begins is vitally necessary.

## Feeding

No supplementary feeding is necessary.

## Propagation

From newly purchased corms or from ones already planted.

## Special Problems

There are no special problems.

# CROSSANDRA infundibuliformis

*Firecracker Flower*

This splendid indoor plant is becoming very popular.

## Origin

Genus Crossandra is a member of the Acanthus family (Acanthaceae) and has about 50 species, mostly from India and tropical Africa.

## Description

*C. infundibuliformis*, commonly known as the Firecracker Flower, is an evergreen shrub growing to 3 feet in native India and Ceylon. The short stem, 5-inch ovate leaves are a bright, glossy green. One inch rich orange, tubular flowers are borne on a green bracted stem that grows to 6 inches.

## Cultivation

Place in a semi-sunny location in average room temperature. Nighttime temperature should not drop below 16°C. (60°F.). Pinch prune young plants to encourage bushiness. Cut back older plants.

## Potting

Use a rich friable potting soil of equal parts loam, coarse builders' sand, peat moss and rotted or dried manure or compost. Cover drainage hole with a generous layer of pebbles or pea gravel. Repot only when the root ball becomes compacted.

## Watering

Keep evenly moist at all times and place the plant over a humidity tray to maintain above average humidity. Mist spray with clear water.

## Feeding

Feed on a two week schedule with water soluble general fertilizer during the growing season. Well grown plants are almost ever-blooming.

## Propagation

Use tip cuttings dipped in rooting hormone powder and place in moist sand or vermiculite. A lot of heat is required, up to 27°C. (80°F.).

## Special Problems

Avoid low humidity that may encourage insect attacks. Control white fly and red spider mites with malathion spray.

*Crossandra infundibuliformis*

61

# CRYPTANTHUS

*Earth Stars / Rainbow Star / Zebra Plant*

The rosetted leaves make this plant worthwhile.

## Origin

Genus Cryptanthus, with 20 species, is a member of the Pineapple family (Bromeliaceae). All are native to Brazil.

## Description

This group of plants is ground growing (terrestrial) and valued for their multi-colored foliage. Several species are of interest:

*C. acaulis*, Earth Stars, grows to about 5 inches across with a flat rosette. Leaves are medium green with a pale grey scurf. Small white flowers grow low in the center.

*C. minor*, has a small star-like rosette. It is greyish green with two reddish pink bands.

*C. bromelioides tricolor*, Rainbow Star, is a larger plant with pointed up-right leaves about 12 inches long. They are striped lengthwise with ivory white and green overlayed with rose.

*C. zonatus*, Zebra Plant, has a small, attached spreading rosette of wavy, lance-shaped leaves with irregular cross bands of brownish green and irregular silver markings.

## Cultivation

Grow in a sunny to semi-sunny location in average room temperature.

## Potting

Use a potting mixture of equal parts loam, coarse builders' sand, sphagnum moss and leafmould. Grow in small size pots. Repotting is rarely required.

## Watering

Keep the pot barely moist and mist spray foliage during spring and summer. This plant is tolerant of average room humidity.

## Feeding

Apply a very weak solution of water soluble general fertilizer by mist spraying onto the leaves, two or three times during the growing season.

## Propagation

Use small offsets when large enough to handle. Pot up in the potting mixture described under Potting.

## Special Problems

A trouble-free plant.

*Cryptanthus bromelioides*

# CYCLAMEN

Cyclamen is a truly spectacular plant with brightly colored flowers poised like butterflies about to light. With flowers ranging from red, rose, purple to white, sometimes blotched, sometimes ruffled, Cyclamen continues to be a popular gift house plant, despite maintenance difficulties arising from central heating.

## Origin

Cyclamen is a member of the Primrose family (Primulaceae) and is the only one that produces and grows from a cormlike tuber. *Cyclamen persicum* is native to the Mediterranean region from Greece to Syria and is the source of modern day hybrids.

## Description

A well grown Cyclamen with perfect leaves, one overlapping the other just a bit, is a beautiful plant, even without flowers. The elliptical shaped leaves are borne on 6 to 7-inch stems and are marbled or variegated with white. Flowers are held well above the foliage on individual stems reaching 10 to 12 inches. They are scentless and the petals are completely reflexed over the stem, giving a somewhat inside out appearance. *Cyclamen persicum giganteum* is the principal species grown and is the result of years of cultivation, breeding and selection.

## Cultivation

A plant located in a warm room in full sun soon wilts from heat rather than from lack of water. Locate the plant in a cool spot 12 to 15°C. (55 to 60°F.) in a semi-sun location. Faded flower stems and dying leaves should be pulled from the corm rather than cut.

When flowering has finished, usually by early March, prune away a few of the older, outside leaves and remove the plant from its pot. Carefully remove most of the soil and all dead roots. Prune back, just a bit, the heavy healthy roots and repot in a one size smaller pot, keeping the corm half in, half out of the potting soil. Keep just moist in semi-shade at a temperature of 10 to 12°C. (50 to 55°F.). New growth will begin to show in four to five weeks. When the root ball fills the pot move on to the next larger size pot. After spring frost, plants may be summered outside by sinking the pot in the ground to within one inch of the rim. Protect from excessive heat by locating in a semi-shaded place. Return inside before frost.

## Potting

Use a rich humusy soil mix of equal parts rich loam, coarse builders' sand, peat moss, leafmould and rotted or dried manure. A generous layer of broken shard or pea gravel over the drainage hole will insure adequate drainage.

## Watering

During the flowering season, autumn and winter, and after growth periods, the soil should be kept evenly moist at all times. Since it is desirable to keep the water away from the corm which is usually half in and half out of the soil, watering is best accomplished by partial submersion of the pot in a pan of water at room temperature. Excess water should be removed from the saucer to avoid root damage. A large size plant in a warm room, with lots of

*Cyclamen persicum*

flowers and leaves may require watering two or three times a day.

A relative hymidity of at least 50% is ideal for Cyclamens. Dry air will soon finish off the best of plants. Place the plant in a humidity tray filled with gravel and water. Keep the bottom of the pot above water level. Frequent mist spraying of the leaves is also helpful, but avoid wetting the flowers and buds.

## Feeding

Use water soluble general fertilizer on a 10 to 14 day schedule during periods of active growth and flowering. Apply only after watering.

## Propagation

From seed planted in July or August. Germination takes up to 50 days in a temperature of 12 to 15°C. (55 to 60°F.). Plants reach blooming size in about 18 months.

## Special Problems

Mostly arise from low humidity and too high a temperature. Green flies and aphids can be controlled with malathion. Plants showing signs of bacteria soft rot of the stem or corm or the fungus disease stunt, should be completely destroyed. Use sterilized soil to protect against these maladies.

# CYPERUS alternifolius

*Umbrella Plant*

Umbrella Plant thrives under wet soggy conditions and is an ideal plant for the window garden.

## Origin

The Umbrella Plant is a native of Madagascar and a member of the Sedge family, (Cyperaceae), a group of about 900 species of perennial grass-like plants found in marshes and bogs.

## Description

This plant is grown for its foliage which is borne on 2 to 3-foot, bare triangular stems. Each stem is crowned with up to 15 individual grass-like leaves, 8 inches in length and half an inch wide at the broadest point. The leaves droop gracefully giving the appearance of the framework of an umbrella. Stems and leaves start off light green in color and gradually darken to a medium shade. Small, brown, inconspicuous flowers are borne at the center of the crown of the long stems. While the Umbrella Plant is a perennial, it is not hardy in the northern climate. However, it adapts perfectly to indoor tradition and makes an ideal addition to the window garden for the apartment dweller as well as the home.

## Cultivation

Locate the plant in a semi-sunny location as in an east or west window. Over winter, the plant will do best in a temperature of 10°C. (50°F.) and in bright light. However, it will tolerate over 20°C. (68°F.) if the foliage is misted occasionally with clear water. While it is not necessary, the plant enjoys summering outside especially in a lily pond where it may be submerged to the rim at the shallow end during the frost-free months. A few of the older, longer stems often fall over into the water and in a short time roots form and a new plant is underway.

## Potting

For potting and repotting use a mixture of equal parts loam, peat moss and rotted or dried manure. Add a touch of bone meal or super phosphate to the finished mix. Failing this, use a good brand of prepackaged potting soil from the local garden store. This plant needs repotting at least once a year. Browning of the leaf tips is a signal that repotting time has been neglected.

## Watering

This plant must always have its roots in water. Keeping a saucer filled with water can be a bit of a chore so place the pot inside a water tight ceramic jardinière along with some activated charcoal and keep the water level three-quarters the height of the pot.

## Feeding

During the growing season, April to September, feed the plant water soluble fertilizer using about a tablespoon to one gallon of water.

## Propagation

New plants may be rooted by cutting off a top with a 2-inch piece of stem and rooted either in water or in wet sand. Make certain that the crown makes contact with the water or the wet sand. Division of the root clump at the time of repotting is also a favorite method.

## Special Problems

Normally the Umbrella Plant is fairly free of pests. However, hot dry conditions will sometimes bring on an invasion of aphids and spider mites. Wash away the pests with a strong spray of water or sponge away with a soft cloth in a mild soapy water or spray with malathion.

*Cyperus alternifolius*

# CYRTOMIUM falcatum

*Holly Fern*

This handsome, robust plant can survive in those dark corners.

## Origin

Genus Cyrtomium with 10 species is a member of the Fern family (Polypodiaceae) and is mostly of Asiatic origin.

## Description

Holly Fern, *Cyrtomium falcatum*, has glossy dark green foliage. The compound leaves are stiff and erect and more than 18 inches. The leaflets are slightly wavy and up to 4 inches long. Variety 'Rochfordianum,' Holly Fern, is usually favored by most growers because of the coarsely fringed leaf margins.

## Cultivation

This plant can survive in fairly dark corners. However, semi-shade is the best choice. Average room temperature is suitable during most of the year with cooler conditions from November through January, 16°C. (60°F.) and lower, for strongest growth.

## Potting

Use a mixture of loam, builders' sand and peat moss. Incorporate chopped activated charcoal and a modicum of bone meal. Repotting should be undertaken in spring.

## Watering

Keep soil moist at all times. Discard excess water in saucers to avoid rot. Mist spray with clear water especially during spring and summer.

## Feeding

Use one-half strength solution of water soluble general fertilizer during the spring and summer.

## Propagation

From ripe spores caught in sphagnum or peat moss and germinated under humid warm conditions. Also from leaf stems with a small section of root stock attached.

## Special Problems

Essentially pest-free. Excessive heat and dryness can destroy the plant.

*Cyrtomium falcatum*

# DATURA
*Angel's Trumpet / Cornucopia / Thorn Apple or Jimson Weed*

This unusual exotic house plant produces immense lily-like, trumpet shaped blooms in 6 to 10 months from seed.

## Origin

Mostly from the tropical and sub-tropical areas of South America, Datura has about 15 species and is a member of the Nightshade family (Solanaceae) which includes other distinguished members such as peppers, tomatoes and potatoes. It is widely grown throughout the Caribbean and Central Americas.

## Description

Datura has both annual and perennial plants, shrubs and small trees to 15 feet or so. Some are grown as pot and tub plants for the large soft foliage as well as the long pendulous trumpet-like flowers which are often 12 inches in length—others are grown as border plants. The better known species include: *D. suaveolens*, described as the Great White Angel Trumpet is a tree-like shrub 10 to 15 feet high with many pendulous, fragrant snowy white trumpets up to one foot long. The oval, oblong leaves are 6 to 12 inches long and 2 to 4 inches wide. It is native to Mexico and Central America. *D. arborea*, sometimes described as Brugmansia, (Angel's Trumpet) produces a small tree 2 to 5 feet in height and is native to Peru and Chili. *D. fastuosa* (Cornucopia) is an annual growing 4 to 5 feet high. The 6½ to 7-inch flowers are violet outside and whitish within. It is native to India. *D. stramonium*, com-

monly called Thorn Apple or Jimson Weed, is a tropical annual growing to 4 feet with white flowers. It has become naturalized over many cooler parts of the world and is listed among the common weeds of Canada. It is recorded that early settlers of Jamestown, Virginia, U.S.A., ate the fruit of this plant with curious results and mad antics. The priests of Delphi and Peru also used the seed to produce forensic ravings of a supposedly prophetic nature. Actually the plant is classed as being narcotic and poisonous. Small doses of stramonium extract have been used in the treatment of mania, convulsions, epilepsy, etc. but naturally, under prescription; thus any plant grown must be treated with full respect.

## Cultivation

Grow in bright light in an east or south window. Normal room temperature is desirable during the growing and flowering period March to September. At other times keep on the cool side in a semi-dormant state. With care, the woody types may be stored in a cool basement over winter. After flowering, growth should be pruned back to the main branches. Plants may be summered outside during the frost-free months.

## Potting

Use a rich potting mixture of equal parts rich loam, coarse builders' sand, peat moss and rotted or dried manure and moisten before use. Cover drainage holes with 2 or 3 inches of pea gravel or broken shard. This plant needs plenty of room for the large spreading roots and the root ball will reach a 12 to 14-inch pot size fairly rapidly. Repot plants annually in the spring. Remove loose soil and a 2 to 3-inch slice of roots from one side of the root ball before returning to the pot and add fresh soil mix.

## Watering

Roots are large and spreading and require a constant supply of water during the growing period. During the winter less moisture is required.

## Feeding

Use water soluble general fertilizer solution on a 10 day schedule during period of growth. Check that the root ball is moist before application, then thoroughly saturate with the feeding solution.

*Datura arborea*

## Propagation

From cuttings during spring and early summer or from seeds. Plant two or three seeds in peat pellets. Germination takes about two weeks. At the three leaf stage thin to one plant per pellet. When roots begin to show outside the pellet, place in a 4-inch pot using the rich potting mix and move into larger size containers as the root ball becomes compacted.

## Special Problems

Relatively trouble-free. Routine spraying with malathion is in order.

# DIEFFENBACHIA
*Dumbcane*

*Dieffenbachia picta*

Dieffenbachia is the plant that leaves you literally speechless, if you are imprudent enough to chew one of the leaves or stems or even place some of the sap on your tongue. Don't try it—it is painful!

## Origin

This genus, named after the German botanist Dieffenbach, has about twelve notable species and is among the most outstanding foliage plants under cultivation. The lush exotic growth gives a feeling of the tropics which is reasonable since it is a native of the jungles of Central and South America. It is a member of the Arum family (Araceae).

## Description

The plant is classed as a low, shrubby perennial which tends to creep at the base before becoming erect. Old plants tend to drop leaves as a result of age as well as over-watering, which may cause a lot of leaves to become limp and yellow. Depending upon variety, leaves may be 6 to 18 inches long and as much as 8 inches wide. The favorite species is *Dieffenbachia picta* 'Superba, a compact grower with deep green leaves blotched in ivory. For interest look for *Dieffenbachia picta jenmannii, D. bowmannii, D. hoffmannii, D. seguine.*

## Cultivation

Best growing condition is in a fairly even temperature in the 15 to 21°C. range (60 to 70°F.), under filtered sunlight or bright light. Direct sun may cause burning—remember this is a jungle plant growing in nature under high trees. Excessively low humidity should be avoided. Keep the pot on crushed stone above the water level in a humidity saucer or tray.

## Potting

The favorite potting soil mixture for this plant is one part coarsely chopped sphagnum moss, one part chopped fern roots and one part of a mixture of equal parts builders' sand and well rotted manure—in brief, a rich friable potting soil.

## Watering

The plant should be soaked, then allowed to approach dryness and soaked again. The excess water should not be allowed to stand in the saucer.

## Feeding

Most growth occurs between April and September and the plant will respond to supplementary feeding with water soluble general fertilizer during this period.

## Propagation

Old plants that have arrived at a stage of five to six feet of bare trunk with a cluster of leaves at the top, give a fair imitation of a miniature palm tree. It is at this stage that Dieffenbachia owners get somewhat concerned about what to do next—short of making a hole in the roof. Sooner or later the plant has to be stopped and the best method for this is air layering, a technique for re-rooting the top leafy portion and starting a new, short plant. To achieve this, take a sharp knife and make an upward slant cut about 6 inches or so down from the top at a point where a leaf grew previously. The cut will have to remain open, so insert a sliver of wood or small pebble to ensure that the cut does not heal back together. Now take a handful of wet moss and encircle the stem around the cut; if necessary use some thread or soft cotton string to keep the moss in place. To ensure that the moss remains wet, wrap it in clear plastic and fasten above and below with a tie, raffia or string. In three or four weeks when a supply of roots becomes visible, remove the rooted portion from the main trunk by a clean cut just below the moss ball. Remove the plastic and plant the new cutting making sure the pot is large enough to accommodate the new roots. You are on the road to having many more new plants. The old trunk should now be cut back to about 6 inches above the pot where a new bud will form on the stub in a short time. The trunk you have removed may be cut into pieces 2 to 3 inches long. Allow the pieces to dry for a day or two to seal the ends. The pieces are now ready to be rooted in warm, moist sand, perlite or vermiculite. Enclose the pot or rooting box in a closed plastic bag and keep in bright light but out of direct sun. In a few weeks small shoots will begin to appear from the previously dormant

*Dieffenbachia 'Costa Rica'*

leaf nodes. When a good supply of roots has formed, pot up individually. You will probably end up with enough plants for the whole street and your own Dieffenbachia land.

## Special Problems

Above all, remember that the juice of this plant is very toxic and can cause painful swelling of the tongue and mucus glands. Observe strict prophylaxis and watch young children and pets.

# DIZYGOTHECA elegantissima

*False Aralia*

A graceful foliage plant for any room.

## Origin

Genus Dizygotheca, with about fifteen species, is a member of the Ginseng family (Araliaceae) and native to New Caledonia and Polynesia.

## Description

*Dizygotheca elegantissima*, False Aralia, is a graceful small tree growing to 25 feet. Straight stemmed young plants have palmate compound leaves with 6 to 10 narrow petioles that are heavily serrated. The long leaf stems and leaves are mottled with white. The leaves are red and brown in color.

## Cultivation

Grow in a good light without direct sunlight. Average room temperature about 16°C. (60°F.) is satisfactory.

## Potting

Use a mixture of loam, coarse builders' sand, peat moss and rotted or dried manure or compost. Move young plants once a year before new growth starts in spring. Repot older plants only when roots become compacted.

## Watering

Keep evenly moist, with slightly less water during the resting period October to February. Mist spray foliage frequently with clear water to provide extra humidity. Small plants should be grown above a humidity tray.

## Feeding

This is a slow growing plant so feed once a month during the growing season with water soluble general fertilizer.

## Propagation

From seeds that germinate in about 5 days with light. Also from stem cuttings in moist sand or vermiculite and bottom heat.

## Special Problems

Hot dry conditions can produce scale and red spider mites. Control with proper growing conditions and use malathion insecticide spray. Remove individual pests with a cotton swab dipped in rubbing alcohol. Cold wet roots can destroy the plant.

*Dizygotheca elegantissima*

# DRACAENA

Possibly despite your good intentions, you don't give indoor plants all the attention they need and you end up either losing the plant completely or with a less than perfect specimen. Don't despair, nature may have invented the Dracaena just for you. This is a plant that will tolerate a fair amount of neglect and lack of light.

## Origin

The Dracaena belongs to the Agave family (Agavaceae) and is widely distributed in the tropics. It is closely related to the Cordyline and many plants sold as Dracaena are really of this genus.

## Description

Young plants make attractive table decorations, especially when planted in a decorative dish or jardinière. Eventually the plants start to lengthen and form a trunk. Leaves are usually shed as the trunk extends, giving a palm tree effect. Thus you end up with a plant useful for room decoration. *Dracaena fragrans massangeana* has handsome curved foliage, shiny green with a broad yellowy stripe down the center. Some of the leaves are 3 feet long and measure 3 to 4 inches across. This species, along with *Dracaena sanderiana*, is the most suitable for living room conditions *D. sanderiana* is a slender grower with narrow lance-like leaves, grey green, banded in white. *Dracaena indivisa* (Fountain Plant)—a familiar plant often grown in formal beds, tubs and window boxes, is actually *Cordyline indivisa*. However, the appearance and cultural requirements of the two are so similiar that Dracaena is the name most commonly used for both.

## Cultivation

The Dracaena does not have to be grown in a window; it will prosper in a semi-shady to shady location. However, during the dark days of winter it will enjoy being a bit closer to the window. Average room temperature and humidity are suitable for this plant.

## Potting

This plant does not require an overly large pot. In fact a 7 foot specimen can readily be grown in a 6 to 8-inch pot. Like all tropical plants Dracaenas require a light friable rich soil. Use a mixture of equal parts of sharp builders' sand, peat moss and well rotted manure or compost. This will give the proper texture, drainage and moisture retention. Each year remove part of the soil from the top of the pot of older plants. Use a pointed stick for this operation. Replace this lost soil with fresh potting soil.

## Feeding

During spring and summer apply supplementary feeding using a water soluble general fertilizer solution.

## Watering

Keeping the soil just moist at all times produces the best and most luxurious plants. Dusting the leaves with a damp soft cloth keeps them at their best appearance.

## Propagation

When the plant outgrows your ceiling you can air layer the top growth and when roots are in good supply cut it away from the main trunk and plant it in a new pot. The trunk may be cut to a height of your choice and in a few weeks side shoots will start to grow. The portion of trunk that you have pruned away may be used for propagation by cutting it into 1 to 2-inch pieces and burying them in moist sand. Place each piece on its side. Keep the sand evenly moist and warm; covering with clear plastic will help maintain a moist atmosphere. When new growth appears the young plants may be moved into 3-inch pots using the soil mixture discussed under Potting.

## Special Problems

This plant is essentially trouble-free.

*Dracaena fragrans massangeana*

# ECHEVERIA

Beautiful leaf rosettes put these plants high on the list of desirables.

## Origin

Echeveria, named after the Mexican botanical artist, Atanasio Echeverria, is a sub-group of the Stonecrop family (Crassulaceae), which makes it a relative of the Jade Plant (*Crassula argentea*).
There are over 100 species of Echeveria, confined almost entirely to Mexico, but extending from California through Central America into Peru.

## Description

Echeverias are perennials and have fleshy broad leaves, usually in dense rosettes. Many are stemless and some have stems 24 to 30 inches in length. The stemless species are usually considered best for table cultivation and include *Echeveria amonea* with small dense rosettes and numerous off-shoots and *E. setosa* with dense, globular rosettes and flattened 2-inch leaves covered on both sides with long wide hairs.
For window or floor level cultivation look for the stem forming, semi-shrub types with stems up to 30 inches such as: *E. coccinea* with lance spatulate leaves covered with white down, *E. gibbiflora*, with flat wedge-shaped leaves crowded at the end of 24-inch stems and *E. linguaefolia*, with 12-inch branching stems covered with fleshy green leaves which have rose tinges along the edges.
Species native to the Northern Hemisphere normally bloom between winter and spring, while those originating in the Southern Hemisphere bloom between summer and autumn. Flowers are borne on loose spikes from the center of the plant and are generally red tinged, yellow to orange.

*Echeveria amonea*

## Cultivation

Grown as house plants Echeverias look best in low form clay pots, terra cotta or beige in color. Plants need good light both summer and winter. Autumn and winter are the resting periods and the best temperature is 10°C. (50°F.).

## Potting

The drainage hole should be covered with broken shard or pea gravel to a depth of one-third of the height of the pot. The potting mixture should be equal parts coarse builders' sand, rich loam and compost or leafmould.
Young plants may be repotted every year, then at longer intervals as they become larger and older. After potting, plants should be kept dry for a week or so in order that damaged roots may heal. Succulents have a built-in water supply so they will not suffer during the settling-in period.

## Watering

During the resting period water only enough to prevent shriveling of the leaves. During the growing season, spring and summer, more water is in order but always allow the soil to approach dryness before watering.

## Feeding

Supplementary feeding may be given during the growing period which, incidentally, is often confined to only three months.

*Echeveria coccinea*

## Propagation

Propagation is readily achieved by removing side rosettes, by twisting off individual leaves, or by cutting off a leaf with a sliver of the main trunk attached (use a razor blade). Cuttings should be set aside for a few days to allow the broken tissue to dry and to form a callus. Insert the prepared cuttings in coarse moist sand to promote the roots.

## Special Problems

Echeveria is a trouble-free plant. However, too much water can produce root rot and excessive temperature can result in weak spindly growth.

# ECHINOCACTUS and FEROCACTUS

*Barrel Cacti*

Known to distressed desert travellers as a survival plant and a source of water by cutting off the top and mashing the juicy pulp into a viscous drink, barrel cacti are becoming widely used by busy indoor gardeners as tough, non-demanding plants that survive with minimal care. Mexicans find other uses for these plants, particularly the hook spines for fish hooks and bits of the juicy pulp boiled in sugar to make "cactus candy."

## Origin

Two genera *Echinocactus* and *Ferocactus*, qualify as the most popular source for barrel shapes. Both are native to North America from southwest United States through Mexico into Guatemala and are members of the Cactus family (Cactaceae).

## Description

Over the years, in some instances centuries, these plants become immense and somewhat cylindrical in shape. However, during their early years they remain globe-shaped and make durable, manageable, house plants. Of the current recognized nine species of Echinocactus there are three worthy of consideration by the casual gardener:
*E. grusonii* (Golden Barrel) with a light green globe and 21 or more thin high ribs that are covered with golden yellow spines—after many years this plant may reach a diameter of 32 inches with a height of 50 inches. It is a native of Central Mexico. Small yellow flowers appear at irregular intervals for a period of six months.
*E. horizonthalonius* (Eagle Claw Cactus) has curved, pink to red spines, 8 ribs and grows to about 10 inches in height. Small frilled, pale rose to pink flowers appear in summer. It is native to Texas, New Mexico, Arizona and Northern Mexico.
*E. ingens* (Blue Barrel) is somewhat blue to purplish in color with a woolly top. It has 8 ribs and straight brown spines and will grow to 5 feet in height and 4 feet in diameter. A native of Mexico, it has small yellow flowers.
The genus Ferocactus has the greatest number of barrel cacti and of the 30 species the following are the most popular:
*Ferocactus latis pinus*, widely distributed in Mexico into Guatemala, grows to a height and diameter of 16 inches with 15 to 23 ribs. The clusters of 6 to 10 radial spines are white to pale red in color, flowers are bell shaped and about 1 inch in length and rose to purple in color.
*F. rectis pinus* growing 3 to 6 feet high is somewhat cylindrical in shape with clusters of 8 to 12 curved spines and one central, straight spine that reaches 5 inches in length. Flowers are yellow and about 2 inches long. This species is native to lower California.
*F. wislizeni* (Fish Hook Barrel) has black central spines, well hooked and about 2 inches in length. While young, the plant is globular in shape and with great age it becomes cylindrical and about 6 feet tall. The 2-inch flowers may be yellow or red. This plant is found in Texas through New Mexico into Mexico.

*Echinocactus grusonii*

## Cultivation

During summer locate plants in the warmest, sunniest spot. Over winter, during the resting period, September to February, a cool location is best down to 10°C. (50°F.). During the frost-free months plants may be summered on the patio or located in a border with the pot sunk into the ground.

## Potting

Contrary to popular belief, cacti do not grow in pure sand. The basic needs of cacti are perfect drainage, proper aeration of the root system and of course a steady source of nourishment. Commercial packaged soil mixes are available for desert cacti or you may prepare your own by mixing equal parts of coarse builders' sand, garden loam and well rotted leafmould. Add a modicum of bone meal and crushed activated charcoal. Since drainage is vital, the pot should be filled one-third to one-half with broken shard or pea gravel so that drainage is rapid and all surplus escapes. Unlike other plants, succulents in general and more specifically cacti should be potted dry and maintained in a dry condition for at least two weeks to enable broken or damaged roots to heal. Water at this time may bring on a condition of rot and total destruction of the plant. Cacti plants are normally potted with the soil line level with the pot rim to minimize the risk of over-watering.

## Watering

During the growing period, spring and summer, water normally to keep the soil evenly moist. During the winter rest period, keep the plant dry. Plants rested in high temperatures and low humidity may show signs of wrinkled tissue, in which case a small amount of water should be applied to compensate for the excessive moisture loss. Over-watering can induce rot.

## Feeding

Only during periods of active growth with half strength water soluble general fertilizer on a 10 to 14 day schedule.

## Propagation

Readily from seeds that will germinate in five to six days in spring and early summer—much longer at other times. Use the potting mixes discussed previously and allow the seedlings to remain in the seed bed for at least twelve months before potting up to individual pots. Basal offsets that reach handling size may be separated from the parent plant with a sharp knife. Dust cuts with sulphur and powder or powdered charcoal. Allow the cutting to dry in a cool shady spot for at least two weeks, then insert the cutting into barely moist coarse sand. Avoid deep planting. Place in a warm, half shaded spot and keep very moist until new growth indicates that a root system has formed. Plants may be lifted and pot-

*Ferocactus wislizeni*

ted at this time.

## Special Problems

Rot brought on by damaged roots and over-watering. Carelessness and poor growing conditions may result in attacks from aphids, mealy bugs and spider mites, especially on new succulent growth. Pests may be removed with a cotton swab moistened with rubbing alcohol or with an inside house plant spray.

71

# EPIDENDRUM aureum
*Spice Orchid / Cockle-shell Orchid*

These orchids flower in winter and spring.

## Origin
Genus Epidendrum has over 1,000 species all native to tropical and sub-tropical America. It is a member of the Orchid family (Orchidaceae).

## Description
*E. atropurpureum,* the Spice Orchid, is an epiphyte with pear shaped pseudobulbs and leaves to 16 inches. The flower spikes carry up to 13 flowers, 2 to 3 inches across, predominantly chocolate brown, veined magenta with a white lip. It flowers in winter and spring.

*E. cochleatum,* Cockle-shell Orchid, is almost ever-blooming with good light and growing conditions. The spidery, upside down, 3-inch flowers are whitish green with purple and yellow veins.

## Cultivation
Grow in a semi-sunny location in average room temperature. Pseudobulbs are reed-like and old canes should not be pruned since they often bloom a second time.

## Potting
Grow in Osmunda fiber, unshredded sphagnum moss or fir bark. Use clay pots one-third filled with shard, pebbles or pea gravel. Repot when necessary about every two years, in spring or summer.

## Watering
Wet the potting mix and allow to approach dryness before watering again. Relative humidity of 50% or more is required.

## Feeding
Use a diluted 1/10th strength water soluble general fertilizer in place of regular watering.

## Propagation
By division in spring or summer at the time of repotting.

## Special Problems
Avoid stagnant air.

*Epidendrum atropurpureum*

# EPIPHYLLUM oxypetalum (latifrons)

*Queen of the Night, Leaf Cactus, Orchid Cactus, Night Blooming Cereus*

Some of the most spectacular flowers that may be grown by the average gardener are represented in the Epiphyllum, commonly called Leaf Cactus, Orchid Cactus, Night Blooming Cereus or Queen of the Night.

## Origin

Epiphyllum, with about 16 species, is a member of the Cactus family (Cactaceae) and native to Mexico, Central and South America.

## Description

Queen of the Night is a tree dwelling cactus having taken to the high branches of the tropical forest in the same manner as orchids and Bromeliads. It is an "epiphyte" which means it grows upon other plants but is not a parasite. Actually it takes nourishment through aerial roots and from the leaf-mould and mosses caught in the branches and rough bark of the tree it inhabits.

These Cacti have flat leaf-like branches, scalloped along the edges with essentially no spines. Each plant has several cascading branches with strong mid-ribs. Since these plants in nature live in trees, they make nice subjects for hanging baskets with their beautifully scalloped leaves and, in most cases, white scented night blooming flowers. The small flowers are from 2 to 6 inches in diameter while the large are 8 to 10 inches or the size of a dinner plate.

## Cultivation

Unlike their Cacti cousins of the desert, these plants enjoy moisture and humid atmosphere. Growing high up in trees in the accumulated rotting leaves and debris, they enjoy excellent drainage. Living as they do under the leaves in the tree they have bright, filtered light and very little direct exposure to the summer sun. Grown in a 6-inch hanging pot, the plant will be about 3 feet in diameter after eight years.

Each year, in late spring, hang the plant high on an outside wall, placed in such a position that it receives direct skylight and all the rain showers. An eight year old plant will produce up to 35 white tinted blooms 6 inches in diameter on long necks. Flowers open by mid-evening and are finished by mid-morning of the following day. In September the plant should be returned indoors to rest over winter in a light location with a temperature of 7 to 10°C. (45 to 50°F.) with very little water until spring, only enough to prevent it from shriveling.

## Potting

These plants need a soil mixture with plenty of leafmould. Use a mixture made of three parts leafmould, one part well-rotted manure and one part coarse builders' sand and one part good garden loam. This mix will provide a well drained condition and give a mild steady source of food for the plant. Ensure complete drainage with 2 inches or more of pea gravel over the drainage hole.

## Watering

Keep evenly moist and mist stems as often as possible, preferably daily. In winter keep only damp enough to prevent leaf shrinkage.

## Feeding

Very little supplementary feeding is necessary or desirable. Apply bone meal and a commercial fertilizer each spring when the plant begins summer growth and flowering.

## Propagation

Leaf and stem cuttings should be removed with a sharp knife and allowed to dry for a day or so before inserting into moist sand for rooting.

## Special Problems

This plant is essentially trouble-free.

*Epiphyllum oxypetalum (latrifrons)*

# EPIPREMNUM aureum

*Pothos, Devil's Ivy, Ivy Arum*

This climber grows nicely up a moss stick.

## Origin

Genus Epipremnum is a member of the Arum family (Araceae) with about 10 species native to southeast Asia.

## Description

Epipremnum was formerly classified under genus Scindapsus and then Raphidophora.

*E. aureum* is called many names: Pothos, Devil's Ivy, Ivy Arum, etc. and it is the species most commonly grown along with its variegated leaf variety 'Marble Queen,' and 'Golden.' With climbing trailing stems, this plant produces aerial roots at the leaf nodes. Leaves in young plants are heart shaped and up to 6 inches long.

## Cultivation

Grow up a moss stick or fern root pole in bright light out of direct sun. Average room temperature is suitable.

## Potting

Use equal parts loam, builders' sand and peat moss and ensure adequate drainage by placing a layer of pebbles over the drainage hole. Repot only when roots have completely filled the pot.

## Watering

Soak, then let the soil approach dryness before soaking again. This plant tolerates average room humidity. Mist spraying of the foliage with clear water is beneficial especially during the spring to August growing season.

## Feeding

Use water soluble general fertilizer on a 14 day schedule during the growing period.

## Propagation

Readily at any time of the year from stem cuttings with 2 or 3 leaf nodes. Root in moist sand or vemiculite.

## Special Problems

Essentially trouble-free.

*Epipremnum aureum*

# EPISCIA cupreata

*Flame Violet*

A trailing plant with luxurious foliage and bright flowers.

## Origin

Genus Episcia, with ten species, is a member of the Gesneriad family (Gesneriaceae). All are native to the American tropics.

## Description

*E. cupreata*, Flame Violet, is a trailing plant native to the rain forest of Colombia and Venezuela. The 5-inch leaves are oval, soft, hairy, wrinkled and almost entirely metallic copper with clear green and silver variegation. Three to four small 1 ³/₄ inch flowers are borne on flower stems. They are orange-scarlet on the upper side and yellowish with red markings on the lower side. It makes an attractive trailing plant for shelf pots and hanging baskets.

## Cultivation

Grow in semi-shade in average room temperatures that remain above 16°C. (60°F.).

## Potting

Use a rich friable soil mixture of equal parts loam, coarse builders' sand, peat moss and rotted or dried manure or leafmould. Provide full drainage with small pebbles or pea gravel over the drainage hole. Grow in 4 to 6-inch pots or hanging baskets lined with sphagnum moss.

## Watering

Full watering during summer, less from October through February. Higher than normal humidity is required so use a humidity tray.

## Feeding

From March to August use water soluble general fertilizer on a 14 day schedule.

## Propagation

At any time by division of the creeping root or the small plantlets that form on the strawberry-like stolons. Root in moist sand or vermiculite and start off in 3-inch pots.

## Special Problems

Avoid drafts. Treat insect attacks with malathion spray.

*Episcia cupreata*

# ERANTHEMUM pulchellum
*Blue Sage*

Blue Sage is one of the prettiest true-blue winter flowering plants for the windowsill.

## Origin
Native to the tropical regions of India, *Eranthemum pulchellum* is one of thirty species of the genus. It is a member of the Acanthus family (Acanthaceae).

## Description
This plant is a woody shrub growing to 4 feet, bearing ovate leaves that are prominently veined. The flowers are tubular, about 1 inch long, bright blue and borne in early summer.

## Cultivation
Locate in bright light, semi-sun, in average room temperature. Nighttime and winter temperatures must not drop below 16°C. (60°F.).

## Potting
Use shallow azalea type pots and a rich soil mixture of one part loam, one part coarse builders' sand, two parts peat moss and one part dried or rotted manure or leafmould. Repot only in early spring.

## Watering
Keep the soil evenly moist at all times and place the plant in a humidity tray to maintain a higher than normal humidity. Mist spray occasionally with clear tepid water.

## Feeding
Use water soluble general fertilizer on a two week schedule between April and September.

## Propagation
From cuttings rooted in moist sand in a temperature of 24 to 27°C. (75 to 80°F.). Enclose the rooting bed in a plastic bag and keep out of direct sunlight.

## Special Problems
Attacks of scale, red spider mites or aphids should be controlled with an insecticide such as malathion. Individual pests may be removed with a cotton swab dipped in rubbing alcohol.

*Eranthemum pulchellum*

# EUCOMIS
*Pineapple Lily*

This plant grows from a bulb and produces greenish flower trusses resembling a pineapple.

## Origin

Native to South Africa, Eucomis is a member of the Lily family (Liliaceae).

## Description

The plant sends out a basal rosette of leaves that are 2 inches wide and up to 24 inches long. The flowers are greenish white and grow about one inch above the base around the stout, main flower stock which reaches 18 inches. The top of the flower stock is crowned with a second rosette of smaller leaves that bears a strong resemblance to the top of a pineapple. There are about twelve species of Eucomis, mostly native to South Africa and the commonly grown are: *E. punctata* (Pineapple Lily) from a 2 to 3-inch diameter bulb bears half inch green flowers in a 12-inch cluster. *E undulata* from a 2 to 3-inch diameter bulb similar to *E. punctata* with a shorter flower spike.

## Cultivation

Grow in bright light in an east or south window preferably in a temperature range of 10 to 15°C. (50 to 60°F.). Bulbs planted in autumn bloom in late spring. Spring planted bulbs bloom by mid-summer. Plants may be summered outside, in or out of pots.

## Potting

Use a soil mix of equal parts rich loam, coarse builders' sand, peat moss and rotted or dried manure. Plant bulbs about one inch below the surface in a 4 or 5-inch pot, using a generous amount of drainage material over the drainage holes. Plants can remain in the same pots for several years with a program of supplementary feeding.

## Watering

Give little water until growth is active.

## Feeding

Use water soluble general fertilizer on a 14 day schedule during periods of active growth and flowering.

## Propagation

Usually from offsets taken from the mother bulbs. These produce flowering size plants much faster than from seeds.

## Special Problems

This plant is essentially trouble-free and a healthy bulb will last for many years.

*Eucomis punctata*

# EUPHORBIA lactae

*Candelabra Plant*

The Candelabra Plant looks so much like a Cactus that it takes a real expert to say it is not one of the Cacti species.

With one exception, (*Cactus genus Mammillaria*), the presence of white latex sap distinguishes Euphorbia from Cactus and usually provides the first test in the absence of flowers. The flowers normally provide the final test.

## Origin

While Cacti have their origins in the Americas, Euphorbia have come from the old world with most members originating in the tropical, semi-tropical regions.

Botanists consider this a classic example of how two groups of plants, widely separated, have arrived at the same solutions to overcome dry, desert, and generally inhospitable conditions. The Candelabra Plant is native to India, Ceylon and the East Indies.

*Euphorbia lactae* is a member of the Spurge family (Euphorbiaceae) of which there are over 1,000 species worldwide with many distinguished plants such as Poinsettia, Crown of Thorns, etc. Not all are succulents, although genus Euphorbia contains most of the succulents of the family.

## Description

The Candelabra Plant is a tree-like plant, often reaching 8 to 12 feet in height. However, during its extended youth it makes a controllable addition to the succulent collection. The candelabra-like branches are three angled, deeply scalloped and bear black spines in pairs. The branches are dark green with a greenish white marbled band down the center.

## Cultivation

During summer, locate plants in the warmest, sunniest spot. Over winter, during the resting period, September to February, a cool location is best, down to 10°C. (50°F.). During the frost-free months, plants may be summered on the patio or located in a border with the pot sunk into the ground.

## Potting

Contrary to popular belief, succulents do not grow in pure sand. The basic needs of succulents are perfect drainage, proper aeration of the root system and, of course, a steady source of nourishment.

Commercial packaged soil mixes are available for succulents or you may prepare your own by mixing equal parts of coarse builders' sand, garden loam and well-rotted leafmould. Add a modicum of bone meal and crushed activated charcoal.

Since drainage is vital, the pot should be filled one-third to one-half with broken shard or pea gravel so that drainage is rapid and all surplus water escapes.

Unlike other plants, succulents in general shoud be potted dry and maintained in a dry condition for at least two weeks to enable broken or damaged roots to heal. Water at this time may bring on a condition of rot and total destruction of the plant.

Succulents are normally planted with the soil line level with the rim of the pot to minimize the risk of overwatering.

## Watering

During the growing period, spring and summer, water normally to keep the soil evenly moist. During the winter rest period, keep the plant dry. Plants rested in high temperatures and low humidity may show signs of wrinkled tissue, in which case a small amount of water should be applied to compensate for excessive moisture loss. Overwatering can induce rot.

## Feeding

Only during periods of active growth with half-strength water soluble general fertilizer on a 10 to 14 day schedule.

## Propagation

Propagation by stem cuttings, best taken during summer. Wash away the milky latex sap from the cut end and set aside to dry for a few days in a shady, dry location. Plant in a mixture of coarse sand and powdered charcoal and keep barely moist. Avoid deep planting. Formation of new growth indicates that a root system has formed. Plants may now be lifted and potted as described previously.

## Special Problems

Rot brought on by damaged roots and over-watering. Carelessness and poor growing conditions may result in attacks from aphids, mealy bugs and spider mites, especially on new succulent growth. Visible pests can be removed with a cotton swab moistened with rubbing alcohol or with an inside house plant spray bomb. **CAUTION:** The milky sap or latex is very bitter, it burns and is sometimes poisonous. Keep away from eyes, mouth and open cuts.

*Euphorbia lactae*

# EUPHORBIA milii

*Crown of Thorns*

This is a much loved house plant.

## Origin

Genus Euphorbia with over 1,600 species is a member of the Spurge family (Euphorbiaceae).

## Description

*Euphorbia milii*, Crown of Thorns, is native to Madagascar. It is a woody, spiny shrub climbing to 4 feet. The stems are covered with thick spines and bright green leaves are carried on young growth. The small flowers of variety 'Splendens' are surrounded by bright red bracts. Plants may be summered on the patio when given shelter and support.

## Cultivation

Grow this plant in a sunny to semi-sunny location in average room temperature. As with all succulents, a cooler temperature is desirable over winter during the resting period.

## Potting

Use a rich, open, friable soil mixture of equal parts loam, coarse builders' sand, peat moss and rotted or dried manure, or compost. Provide for thorough drainage with a generous layer of pebbles and pea gravel over the drainage holes. Repot young plants when roots become compacted, older plants only when absolutely necessary.

This plant is heavily armored— protection with leather gloves is in order when handling. After repotting withhold water for at least a week until roots have had a chance to heal.

## Watering

As with other succulents, water heavily, then allow the soil to become quite dry before soaking again. Less water is required during the winter resting period. Normal room humidity is suitable.

## Feeding

Use water soluble general fertilizer on a two week schedule from spring to autumn.

## Propagation

Stem cuttings taken in spring will root in moist sand. Such cuttings should be allowed to stand in the open air for a few days to allow drying of the cut end and formation of a callus before inserting in the rooting bed.

*Euphorbia milii*

## Special Problems

Leaf drop may result from over-watering as well as a cold location. Weak forced growth can bring on an attack of aphids and white fly. Control with malathion insecticide. Avoid skin contact with the white, milky sap, which is generally considered to be a bit poisonous and irritating. Accidental contact should be washed away with lots of water and soap.

# EUPHORBIA pulcherrima

*Poinsettia*

The Poinsettia has been a highly prized plant for centuries. The legend is that on a Christmas Eve long ago, Pepita, a little Mexican girl, was very sad. She wanted more than anything to give a fine present to the Christ Child at the church service that evening. But she was very poor and had no gift. As she walked sorrowfully to church with her cousin, Pedro, he tried to console her. "Pepita," he said, "I am certain that even the most humble gift, given in love, will be acceptable in His eyes." So Pepita gathered a bouquet of common leaves from the roadside and entered the church. As she approached the altar she forgot the humbleness of her gift as she placed it tenderly at the feet of the Christ Child. Then there was a miracle!

Pepita's insignificant weeds burst into bloom. They were called "Flores de Noche Buena," Flowers of the Holy Night—we call them Poinsettias.

## Origin

The Poinsettia flourished in a wild state near present day Taxco and Cuernavaca. It was highly prized as a symbol of purity by the kings of the Aztecs right through to the untimely demise of Montazuma II in 1521. A crimson dye was made from the color bracts and a fever medicine from the milky latex sap. During the 1600's a Franciscan priest settled near Taxco and began using Poinsettia in the Christmas Nativity procession—Fiesta de Santa Pesebre—the natural blooming period for Poinsettia

being at that time of year. The botanical designation of *Euphorbia pulcherrima* was made known in 1833 by Johann Friedrich Klotzsch (1805-1860), curator of the Royal Herbarium at Berlin, as having been previously assigned by German botanist Karl Ludwig Willdenow (1765-1812).

Joel Robert Poinsett, the first U.S. Ambassador to Mexico, observed the plant growing in Taxco and in 1852 sent plants to his home in Greneville, S.C. and to John Bartrum of Philadelphia. Bartrum, in turn, supplied Robert Buist, a commercial grower, who sold the plant as Euphorbia Poinsettia. Today the name Poinsettia is the accepted name in English-speaking countries.

Albert Ecke (Ex Switzerland 1902) started raising field

flowers in 1906 with the help of sons Hans and Paul in the vicinity of Hollywood. Poinsettia, which flourishes in the Southern California climate, was raised and sold as a fresh cut flower. Eventually root stock was sold and shipped to growers in the cold climates to produce blooming plants in their greenhouses. Upon the death of his father in 1919, Paul disposed of all the family farming business except for two large fields of Poinsettias which his father had on leased ground on Sunset Blvd. near LaCieniga, Los Angeles. The business was expanded and although fresh cut Poinsettias were still sold from roadside stands at Christmas, concentrated effort was given to providing root stock to the eastern United States. Paul made per-

## Cultivation

Proper care will ensure maximum enjoyment and long life for this holiday plant. The important considerations are light, water and temperature.

It is important that the plant receives as much light as possible. Full daylight is best—near a window is ideal. Dim light or darkness will shorten its life. During the day it must have light. In the evening place it wherever you can enjoy it the most.

Ideal temperatures should never exceed 21°C. (70°F.) during the day or 18°C. (65°F.) at night. They really do best at 16°C. (60°F.) with high humidity. Temperatures above 24°C. (75°F.) with low humidity are detrimental to any Poinsettia plants. Avoid hot dry air, drafts or sudden changes. The top of a television set is a disaster area because of the heat generated by the set.

### Re-growing a Poinsettia

Generally, it is a challenge to re-grow a Poinsettia plant at home that will compare with one commercially grown in the greenhouse under controlled conditions. However, it is worth the experience and the important thing is to remember that the plant must be given tender care during spring, summer and autumn with the proper light and temperature treatment starting in October. A Poinsettia is past its prime when it has lost its green foliage and the colored bracts begin to wither. At this point, reduce watering and when nothing but bare stems remain, remove the plant to a dark, cool, 10 to 12°C. (50 to 54°F.) location and keep barely moist until April. Pruning the stems back to 4 to 6 inches above the soil may be undertaken before storage or delayed until later. Check the plant regularly during

storage to ensure that everything is in order.

Early in May take the plant out of storage and prune back to 4 to 6 inches above the soil level. The pruning will cause the buds located at the leaf axils or nodes to develop and grow.

Remove the root ball from the old container by turning it upside down and tapping the rim to loosen. Shake off loose soil slightly exposing the root tips. This helps stimulate new root growth.

Select a new pot, one to two sizes larger, place 1 to 2 inches of drainage material such as pea gravel over the drainage hole. Add a small amount of potting mix of equal parts commercial potting soil, peat moss and builders' sand. Center and place the root ball on top and add more potting mix. Gently firm the mix with fingers or a blunt stick then tap the pot sharply on a bench or table to ensure proper settling in. Make certain that the soil level is half an inch below the rim for ease of watering. Immerse the plant in a pan of tepid water to thoroughly wet the soil and thus bring the roots in close contact with the soil particles. Don't water again until the soil approaches dryness and then only lightly until new growth develops. Soft prune by pinching off all but three shoots. As soon as the weather settles (by the end of May or after danger of frost), bury the pot to the rim in an outdoor location that has some light shade.

Poinsettias are naturally tall growers; in fact, they are shrubs by nature and around the middle of August it should look quite lush with all the new growth. To control the height and shape of your plant, prune back all growth by at least one-third well

before the end of August. These prunings may be treated as cuttings. Before frost arrives, the plant must be moved indoors where an 18 to 21°C. (65 to 70°F.) daytime temperature and a 15°C. (60°F.) minimum at night prevails.

The Poinsettia is a "photo period sensitive" plant which means it is sensitive to light and only begins to form flower buds as autumn and winter nights become longer. The key point now is to ensure that the plant is kept in total darkness for 14 continuous hours per day, starting in October and no later than October 10th if it is to perform for the holiday season. Once the color of the bracts is developed, this treatment can terminate. Darkness may be accomplished by placing the plant in a dark closet at six o'clock each evening and leaving it there until 8 o'clock the next morning or you can put a cardboard box over the plant for 14 hours using the schedule mentioned. During the day keep the plant in sunny window. Ordinary light in the home in the evening will prohibit the development of the flowering buds. The optimum temperature during the dark period is 15 to 18°C. (60 to 65°F.). If the temperature is too high, the setting of buds may be delayed or halted.

Your Poinsettia should be fed regularly throughout the growing season and then feeding should be reduced to half strength during the flowering period.

## Potting

See Cultivation, section entitled Re-growing, for details.

## Watering

Check the plant daily. Some plants need watering every day while others sonal visits throughout the U.S. introducing the plant and instructing growers how to make the plant bloom for Christmas. Eventually his efforts carried him into Europe. In the 1920's Sunset Blvd. began to build up and land became expensive. To cope with the ever-increasing demand for Poinsettias, a ranch was acquired in Encinitas on the coastal belt of San Diego County and this remains the Poinsettia capital of the world today.

## Description

In cultivation, the Poinsettia grows from 2 to 10 feet high bearing large, deep green leaves and greatly enlarged brilliantly colored floral bracts surrounding numerous inconspicuous flowers.

Poinsettia breeders have had tremendous success during recent years in developing hardy varieties. They are now grown in a wide selection of sizes and shapes in shades of red, pink, white and marble.

The modern era of Poinsettia culture really began in 1923 with the introduction of the seedling variety 'Oak Leaf' which, according to reports, was grown in Jersey City by a Mrs. Enteman. From 1923 to the early 1960's, all of the principal varieties of commercial importance were from this 'Oak Leaf' seedling.

A new era started in 1963 with the introduction of the 'Paul Mikkelson' variety developed by Jim Mikkelson of Astabula, Ohio. This variety had stiff stems and foliage retention qualities and was the first so-

called "longer lasting" variety of commercial importance. The first 'Annette Hegg' variety, an extremely hardy type, was grown in 1964 in Oslo, Norway, by Thermod Hegg.

Long lasting qualities from hybrid varieties revolutionized the Poinsettia industry in 1970. Paul Ecke added a new dimension in 1975 with the 'Ekespoint' variety with bracts up to 12 inches in diameter in shades of red, white, pink and hot pink. There is also a 'Pixie of Hegg' variety which grows under 12 inches for use in small containers.

not so often. Water thoroughly when the soil is dry to the touch. Discard water that collects in the receptacle—Poinsettias do not like wet feet.

## Feeding

Feed regularly throughout the growing season and then reduce to half strength during the flowering time. Fertilizers and plant foods come in many forms and potencies. They all have one thing in common: the rating numbers which indicate the percentages of nitrogen, phosphorus and potassium, in that order. The proper balance for Poinsettias is when the amount of nitrogen approximately equals the sum of the percentages of phosphorus and potassium together, i.e., 10-6-4. Follow the manufacturer's instructions and measure carefully using your own experience with other house plants. Your plant is properly fed when it maintains a continuous rich green growth.

## Propagation

From cuttings of new growth. Root in moist builders' sand and peat moss, or in vermiculite. When roots have formed, pot the young plants in a mixture of equal parts loam, builders' sand and peat moss.

## Special Problems

Excessive dryness may result in attacks from white fly, mealy bug, scale and even red spiders. Mist spray the leaves with clear water. Spray regularly with malathion.

*Euphorbia pulcherrima*

# xFATSHEDERA lizei

*Botanical Wonder, Tree Ivy*

This plant is ideal for offices.

## Origin

Fatshedera sometimes called Botanical Wonder is a hybrid plant which originated in France by crossing *Fatsia* *japonica* variety 'Moseri' with *Hedera helix* variety 'Hibernica.'

## Description

*Fatshedera lizei* produces weak stems up to 8 feet in height. Glossy dark green, ivy shaped leaves with 3 to 5 lobes grow up to 12 inches long and 8 inches wide with 3 to 5-inch leaf stalks. A variegated form also exists with creamy white markings along the leaf edges.

## Cultivation

Grow in a sunny to semi-sunny location. Average room temperature is tolerable with a cooler location over winter. Prune yearly to encourage bushiness.

## Potting

Use a rich soil mix of equal parts loam, builders' sand, peat moss and rotted or dried manure or compost. Provide drainage with small pebbles or pea gravel over the drainage hole. Repot in March or April when roots become crowded.

## Watering

Keep evenly moist and mist spray the leaves to provide extra humidity.

## Feeding

Use water soluble general fertilizer on a 10 day schedule from spring to autumn.

## Propagation

By root division or stem cuttings at any time.

## Special Problems

Excessive dryness will damage the leaves and encourage red spider mites. Control with malathion spray.

*XFatshedera lizei*

# FATSIA japonica
*Castor Bean Plant, Japanese Aralia, Castor Oil Plant.*

A durable indoor plant sometimes called Castor Bean Plant because of similarly lobed leaves.

## Origin

Fatsia, with only one species, is a member of the Ginseng family (Araliaceae) and is a native of Japan.

## Description

*Fatsia japonica* is a compact evergreen shrub growing 15 to 20 feet. The leathery, glossy, dark green leaves are 7 to 11 lobed, with tooth edges and up to 16 inches across. The leaf stems may be as long as 16 inches. This is a highly decorative plant much used in commercial as well as home settings.

## Cultivation

Locate the plant in a cool location in good light even at a north window. Outside on the patio in summer, provide shade. Room temperature in the 16°C. (60°F.) range is ideal.

## Potting

Use a soil mixture of equal parts loam, coarse builders' sand, peat moss and rotted or dried manure or compost. Repot in early spring when roots become compacted.

## Watering

Water freely during the spring through summer growing period. Use less water during the resting time. Judgment is required in view of the extra large foliage. Mist spray foliage frequently to enhance humidity.

## Feeding

Use water soluble general fertilizer on a 10 day schedule during the growing period.

## Propagation

From seeds that germinate in warmth in about 15 days—also from cuttings rooted in moist sand with bottom heat.

## Special Problems

Excessive dryness will damage the leaves and encourage red spider mites. Control with malathion spray.

*Fatsia japonica*

# FICUS
*Rubber Plant/Fiddle Leaf Fig/Weeping Chinese Banyan, Weeping Fig*

Ficus the Fig is a vast natural genus that has more than 600 species widely distributed in tropical and warm temperature zones. Among the principal species is the famous Banyan tree (*Ficus benghalensis*), growing to 100 feet and notable for its spreading horizontal branches that send down aerial roots which take hold in the ground and develop into secondary supporting trunks. With this type of growth, one tree can expand to occupy a large area. One story reports that the Banyan tree under which Alexander camped with 7,000 men measured 2,000 feet in circumference and had 3,000 trunks and could shelter 20,000 people.

No less important are *Ficus carica* (Common Fig), grown for its edible fruit, *Ficus elastica* (Rubber Plant), *Ficus lyrata* (*pandurata*) (the Fiddle Leaf Fig) and *Ficus benjamina* (Weeping Fig), the last three being popular house plants. All are members of the Fig family (Moraceae).

## Ficus elastica
### Origin
*Ficus elastica* is a native of India and Malaya and at one time was cultivated for its white latex sap (the original source of India rubber). It grows to a height of 100 feet or more. Growing wild in its native tropics the tree is a strangular fig that can envelope and destroy other trees.

### Description
The Rubber Plant achieved great popularity as a house plant around the turn of the century and it is not unusual today to find a large pot or tub of this plant in the family room as well as the living room providing a decorative touch with its brown stems and large, handsome elliptic leaves. The modern variety of this plant is *Ficus elastica decora* with leaves 12 inches long and 6 inches wide, dark green and glossy above with a lighter green on the under side. The veining is moderate and adds to the overall attractiveness and shape of the leaves.

## Ficus lyrata
### Origin
Originating from tropical West Africa, *Ficus lyrata* was formerly identified as *Ficus pandurata*. It is commonly called the Fiddle Leaf Fig and was introduced around 1903 and became popular because of its interesting, decorative foliage.

### Description
The leaves are about 18 inches in length, deeply veined, light green and shaped like a fiddle.

## Ficus benjamina
### Origin
This is one of the most beautiful of the evergreen figs growing up to 50 feet high in the humid parts of India, Burma and the Philippines. It is commonly known as Weeping Chinese Banyan or Weeping Fig.

### Description
In recent years it has become almost as common as the Rubber Plant and makes an outstanding specimen for banks and shopping plazas as well as the home. It makes a graceful poplar-like tree with slight pendulous branches. The thin elliptical leaves are quite glossy and dark green. They are only 2 to 4$^{1}/_{2}$ inches in length, which sets them apart from *elastica* and the Fiddle Leaf Fig with their large jungle-like foliage. Grown indoors Benjamina may be kept in a dwarf state for many years. You will find four to five foot specimens readily available at most tropical plant stores.

## Cultivation
### Ficus elastica
Although the plant can stand a lot of abuse, it really thrives on tender, loving care, becoming well branched and eventually growing itself out of a home for it often reaches 15 feet or so in the course of a few years. Ficus does best in an east or west window and will tolerate a fair amount of shade. Average room temperature and humidity above 30% make for ideal growing conditions. This species has a slower tendency towards leaf drop and the ultimate appearance of an inverted feather duster. However, when this condition and appearance ultimately arises, surgery is in order and it is best to cut back to a height of 12 inches to force new shoots that will appear in a few weeks. To develop a compact plant, it is necessary to pinch prune the new shoots before they reach a 6-inch size. Remember the sap is a latex so protect furniture and rugs from the drips.

### Ficus lyrata
This is a distinctive and valuable looking plant but somewhat more temperamental than *Ficus elastica*. If you allow the soil to become too dry between soaking it will drop leaves. It will tolerate lots of heat but needs good direct light to prosper.

### Ficus benjamina
Grow in semi-sun in average room temperature with 30% or more humidity.

## Potting
Use a soil mixture of equal parts coarse builders' sand, peat moss and rotted or dried manure. Thorough drainage is a must and a generous amount of crushed stone, pea gravel or broken crockery should be used over the drainage holes to a depth of at least 2 or 3 inches. While the plant is young keep it in vigorous growth by moving it up a pot size as soon as the root ball becomes crowded. Once the finishing size, which is usually a tub 12 to 14 inches, is achieved, remove the top soil annually with a pointed stick and replace with potting soil mixture discussed previously.

## Watering
Keep the soil evenly moist during the growing season but reduce water during winter dormancy.

## Feeding
Established plants should be fed once a month with water soluble fertilizer and every two weeks during periods of active growth.

## Propagation
An alternative to pruning back immediately is to first develop a second plant by using a propagation technique known as air layering. To achieve this, select a spot on the stem just below the remaining leaves and make a long upward cut about half way through the stem. Depending upon the diameter of the stem, try for a slope cut 1 or 2 inches in length. Keep the cut open with a small wedge (a wooden match stick, a small pebble or a small piece of charcoal) to prevent the cut from healing and growing together again. Place a large handful of clean, wet, sphagnum moss around the stem to cover the cut and hold in place with raffia or soft cord. Finally, cover the wet moss with a piece of plastic film and twist-tie top and bottom so that the moss will not dry out. Roots form best during the spring and summer growing season.

After the roots become visible and plentiful in the moss, allow another two weeks before cutting off the new plant just below the moss ball. Carefully pot up the new plant in a porous soil mixture and protect from direct sun as well as drying out until it becomes firmly established. At the time of separation you may prune back the main stem on the mother plant to 12 inches and proceed with shaping the new growth as described previously.

## Special Problems
Given proper care, this plant is essentially problem-free.

*Ficus elastica*

# FITTONIA

A good plant for dish gardens and planters.

## Origin

Genus Fittonia has only two species and is a member of the Acanthus family (Acanthaceae), all native to South America. The name was given in honor of the sisters Elizabeth and Sahara Mary Fitton who published *Conversations of Botany of 1817*.

## Description

This is a low creeping plant of the tropical rain forest. The elliptic leaves are 4 inches in length with white or colored veins. The principal species, *F. verschaffeltii* has three varieties:
 Argyroneura' with light green leaves, white mid-ribbed and veined; 'Pearcei,' olive green leaves with veins, and mid-ribbed bright carmen; 'Verschaffeltii,' dark green leaves veined pink to red.

## Cultivation

Grow in semi-shade with enough light to develop full color. Average room temperature is suitable, below 13° C. (55° F.) is fatal.

## Potting

Use a soil mix of equal parts loam, coarse builders' sand, peat moss and rotted or dried manure or leafmould. Provide drainage by putting pebbles or pea gravel over the drainage hole. Use low azalea or bulb pots for best appearance. Repot in early spring only when roots have outgrown the container.

## Watering

Keep evenly moist at all times. Grow plants over a humidity tray.

## Feeding

Use half strength water soluble fertilizer on a two week schedule between spring and late summer.

## Propagation

Insert tip cuttings in moist sand with bottom heat. Enclose rooting bed in a clear bag to maintain high humidity.

## Special Problems

Drafts and cold below 13° C. (55° F.) will destroy the plant. Control pests with malathion spray.

*Fittonia verschaffeltii*

# FUCHSIA
*Fuchsia, Lady's Eardrops*

Commonly called Lady's Eardrops because of the handsome, pendulous flowers, Fuchsia remains one of the most popular house plants.

## Origin

Native to South America, the Caribbean and New Zealand, Fuchsia is the most notable genus of the Evening Primrose family (Onagraceae). It was first described by Father Charles Plumier (1646-1706) in his book, *Nova Plantarium Americanarum Genera*, and was given the name Fuchsia in recognition of the celebrated botanist Leonard Fuchs (1501-1565).

## Description

In their native habitat, Fuchsias are shrubs or trees with considerable variations among the species. *F. exorticata* of New Zealand reaches a height of 30 to 40 feet. *F. triphylla* from the West Indies reaches 18 inches and has red flowers. *F. procumbens* from New Zealand is a trailing Fuchsia that is widely used as a hanging plant.

Over the years, growers have developed innumerable strains and species and it is possible to find flowers in both single and double forms in color tones ranging from pure white through pale pink to rose, crimson, purple, magenta and blue in some hybrids. Few plants offer so much satisfaction with so little care. They are beautiful in hanging baskets and pots, absolutely arresting when grown as standards and outstanding as a bedding plant, particularly in a raised bed.

## Cultivation

Fuchsias prefer a cool temperature, 15 to 18°C. (60 to 65°F.) when growing and 7 to 10°C. (45 to 50°F.) while resting. They grow best in good light with protection from sun in summer— east or west window light is ideal.

Plants summered outside should be returned indoors before heavy frosts. When plants have finished flowering, usually in October, they should be rested by placing them in a cool dry spot and withholding water except for the small amount needed to keep the stems and wood from drying out. By mid-January bring the plant out of storage, prune back and repot. In 30 days or so there will be enough new shoots that some may be used for softwood cuttings to start new plants. The remainder, once they have reached the 6 to 8 leaf stage, should be pinch pruned to develop bushy plants. It takes about 6 weeks for flower buds to form after final pinch pruning.

## Potting

Proper drainage is essential for a healthy plant and a generous amount of pea gravel or broken shard must be used to cover the drainage holes. A rich soil mixture is a must. Use equal parts rich loam, peat moss, coarse builders' sand, and rotted or dried manure. Moisten the mixture to full capacity and allow to ripen for a few days. Young plants should be moved into larger pots as soon as the root ball fills the existing pot, continuing until the pre-determined finishing size has been reached.

Plants brought out of storage in January should be allowed to sprout, then trimmed to shape. Repotting should be undertaken at this time by turning the plant out of its pot, removing all loose soil and dead roots and returning it to the pot with fresh potting soil. Treated in this manner Fuchsias will last for many years and will attain specimen size.

## Watering

Keep the soil evenly moist at all times during the growing period. Overhead mist spraying is very beneficial since the plants enjoy a humidity of 50% or more. Out of doors, try to locate plants in a spot protected from prevailing winds to minimize drying and wilting.

## Feeding

Established plants require supplementary feeding to maintain rapid growth and profuse flowering. This may take the form of watering one day with ordinary water, then the following day with a diluted solution of water soluble general fertilizer at one-quarter the usual label strength. The alternating treatment should be carried on from spring to autumn. The program is sup-plemented by a regular leaching of the soil with floods of water every two weeks to prevent build-up of excessive fertilizer or toxic salts in the soil. The main objective is for the plants to have usable food and water available at all times.

Fuchsias perform best in a slightly acid condition and an occasional watering with a mixture of one teaspoon of ammonium sulphate to one gallon of water helps maintain the desirable, slightly acidic condition over and above the peat moss present in the soil mix.

## Propagation

Propagation may be accomplished from seed which takes about 25 days to germinate. Light is required for proper germination. The most favored method is from 3-inch cuttings of new growth from February into early summer. Treat cut ends with rooting hormone and place in moist coarse builders' sand or vermiculite. Pot individual rooted cuttings in 2-inch pots and move into larger pots as roots fill the containers.

## Special Problems

Hot dry atmosphere will damage flowers and cause leaf drop. Control aphids, green and white flies with malathion spray.

# GARDENIA

Gardenia, well known as the button-hole flower, is much admired for its spicy fragrance. Plants in bud and flower are readily available at most nurseries and more often than not at supermarkets.

## Origin

Gardenia is a genus of the Madder family (Rubiaceae), which also includes coffee, quinine and other medicinal plants. There are approximately 250 species in the genus native to the tropical and sub-tropical areas of Africa and Eastern Asia. The plants are mostly evergreen shrubs, sometimes small trees.

This genus of plants was named Gardenia by Carl Linnaeus (1707-1778), in honor of Alexander Garden, a Scottish science graduate from Aberdeen, born in Charleston, S.C. around 1730. He set up a medical practice there in 1755 and had a botanical association with John Bartram (1699-1777) who is considered to be the first American botanist.

## Description

Gardenia is a tender, evergreen shrub with dark, glossy, leathery leaves that are essentially stemless, oval in shape and up to 4 inches in length. The white to yellowish double velvety flowers are usually borne singly and are notable for their delicious fragrance. The mature height is around 6 feet and the double white flowers measure about 3 inches in diameter. Flowering occurs mostly from October to June, but will vary with the time that the plants were propagated and the temperature conditions for the setting of the flower buds.

Native to China, *Gardenia jasminoides* (Cape Jasmine) and hybrid *'Veitchii'* have once again become the choice for house plants.

## Cultivation

Gardenia requires semi-sunny conditions over winter with only bright light, during the summer. This plant is considered to be a two temperature range plant: daytime 21°C. (70°F.) and above—at night 16 to 18°C. (62 to 65°F.). A constant temperature of 21°C. (70°F.) and above usually results in a failure to set flowering buds.

Plants summered outside must be returned indoors well before the first frost.

## Potting

Use a soil mixture of equal parts rich loam, coarse builders' sand, peat moss and rotted or dried manure. Avoid the use of lime since this is an acid-soil plant (pH 5.0 to 5.5). Repot every two to three years just as new growth begins.

When repotting, plant at the same level and handle gently to avoid damage to the fine rootlets. Provide for drainage with a generous layer of shard or pea gravel at the bottom of the pot over the drainage holes.

## Watering

Water only with tepid water and keep the soil moist at all times—never dry or soggy. Humidity is very important and pots should be positioned on pebbles in a humidity tray, above the water line. Frequent mist spraying with clear water is very beneficial. Under extreme conditions enclose the plant in a clear plastic bag to make a temporary terrarium.

## Feeding

Use water soluble general fertilizer in solution on a 14 day schedule between January and September. Alternate with

*Gardenia jaminoides*

a solution of ammonium sulphate (one-half ounce to one gallon water) to maintain an acid soil condition.

## Propagation

Use half-ripened shoot tips placed in moist sand with bottom heat around 24°C. (75°F.). Place in a plastic bag to maintain humidity. After planting, pinch prune early growth once to produce bushy plants.

## Special Problems

Gardenias are almost as well known for bud drop as they are for beauty and fragrance. Bud drop can result from sudden changes in growing conditions, lack of moisture, insufficient light as well as an alkaline soil condition.

Attacks of spider mites and mealy bugs can be controlled with malathion spray. A cotton swab dipped in rubbing alcohol is also helpful for isolated colonies.

# GASTERIA

*Oxtongue, Cape Hart's Tongue*

The unusual form and growth of this plant makes it a desirable addition to the indoor garden.

## Origin

From South Africa, genus Gasteria, with over 50 species, is a member of the Lily family (Liliaceae), along with the Aloes.

## Description

The thick tongue-shaped fleshy leaves are 6 to 7 inches long and about half an inch thick at the base. They grow opposite each other rather than in rosettes. The leaves are deep green with white blotches. During spring and summer the plant sends up a graceful curvy spike topped with loosely hanging bell-shaped flowers that are light red, tinted with green.

## Cultivation

Gasterias make remarkably tough house plants. They are able to tolerate cramped quarters, poor light, lack of water and often downright negligence. Given reasonable care they make outstanding and attractive plants for the apartment and home collection. If possible, maintain the temperature at 15°C. (60°F.) with bright light winter and summer. If you summer the plant out of doors protect it from hot sun to avoid leaf scald.

## Potting

While all succulents like well drained quarters, they will not grow in pure washed sand. They require a rich soil as with cacti and other plants. A mixture of equal parts of coarse builders' sand, peat moss, leafmould and rotted or dried manure is ideal with just a modicum of bone meal—up to a tablespoon per pot. Repotting should be undertaken when the plant outgrows the existing container. Use a plastic or clay pot with drainage holes to allow the escape of excess moisture. The half height Azalea-type pots give the best appearance for this type of plant. Cover the drainage holes with 2 inches or so of pea gravel or other drainage material.

## Watering

During the spring and summer growing season keep the plant moderately moist. From October to February allow the plant to rest by substantially reducing the water.

## Feeding

During the growing season, spring and summer, apply water soluble fertilizer at half strength every 10 to 14 days.

*Gasteria hybrida lapaxii*

## Propagation

Propagation is usually from offsets around the base of the plant or leaf cuttings that are removed with a sharp knife and allowed to heal for a week or so, then rooted in coarse moist sand. Plants grown from seed rarely come true to type.

## Special Problems

Gasteria is essentially a pest-free plant and will stand an unusual amount of neglect. The only enemy appears to be the gardener who over waters and over fertilizes and brings on rot and final destruction.

# GREVILLEA robusta
*Silk Oak*

So readily raised from seed, no one need be without a beautiful foliage pot plant.

## Origin
Genus Grevillea of the Proteaceae family has about 250 species mostly native to Australia. It was named to honor Charles F. Graville (1794-1865) as patron of botany.

## Description
*Grevillea robusta*, the Silk Oak, has fern-like foliage and grows to 150 feet in its native habitat, Queensland, Australia. As a tree it produces outstanding clusters of yellow-orange flowers, as a pot plant there are no flowers. Over the years it has become a popular fern leaf pot plant and makes an outstanding specimen 2 to 5 feet tall.

## Cultivation
Grow in full sun, south window over winter and half shady during summer —east or west window. While it may be grown in average room temperature it thrives best at around 16°C. (60°F.).

## Potting
Use a mixture of loam, coarse builders' sand, peat moss and rotted or dried manure or compost. Use pebbles or pea gravel over the drainage hole. Transplant seedlings into 3-inch pots. Repot when roots fill the container. Young plants should reach a 6-inch pot size in 12 months.

## Watering
Keep evenly moist and mist spray foliage with clear water especially in spring when new growth begins.

## Feeding
During summer, feed with water soluble general fertilizer on a 14 day schedule.

## Propagation
Readily from seed sown in late winter or early spring. Normally seed is sown annually to keep a supply of fresh young plants.

## Special Problems
High winter temperature encourages white and green fly. Control with insecticide malathion spray.

*Grevillea robusta*

# GYNURA aurantiaca
*Velvet Plant*

This is a popular ornamental with large velvety leaves.

## Origin
Genus Gynura has about 100 species and is a member of the Composite family (Compositae). It is native to the tropics of Africa and Asia.

## Description
Velvet Plant, *Gynura aurantiaca*, is a native of Java. It has velvety fleshy leaves and is covered throughout with purple hairs. The elliptic, toothed leaves grow up to 8 inches. The orange-yellow flowers produced in late summer are attractive but a secondary feature.

## Cultivation
Grow in best possible light to maintain coloring, shape and flowering. Average room temperature is suitable. Keep young plants erect by pinch pruning.

## Potting
Use a soil mixture of equal parts loam, coarse builders' sand, peat moss and rotted or dried manure or compost. Provide for drainage with pebbles or pea gravel over the drainage hole. Repot when roots become compacted.

## Watering
Keep evenly moist. Average room humidity is adequate.

## Feeding
Use water soluble general fertilizer on a 14 day schedule during summer.

## Propagation
From cuttings taken at any time of year. Root in moist sand or vermiculite.

## Special Problems
Poor light will produce sprawling plants with poor color. Control green fly with insecticide malathion spray.

*Gynura aurantiaca*

# HEDERA helix

*English Ivy*

A widely grown, much admired climbing shrub for indoor gardens.

## Origin

Genus Hedera is one of over 80 members of the Ginseng Family (Araliaceae). In turn, *helix* with over 80 varieties is one of five species of Hedera. Species *helix* is a native of Europe, North Africa and Asia.

## Description

This evergreen, climbing, self-clinging shrub has over 80 varieties. There is a wide selection covering plants with small leaves, large leaves, three and five lobed, ruffled, curled and edged in white and yellow.

## Cultivation

Grow in a sunny to semi-sunny location in winter and shade to semi-shade during summer. While average room temperature, 21°C. (70°F.) and below is acceptable, coolness is a key to success as long as the area is frost-free.

## Potting

A rich soil mixture is required. Use equal parts loam, coarse builders' sand, peat moss, rotted or dried manure and leafmould. Incorporate a modicum of bone meal or ground lime stone into the mix. Use pebbles or pea gravel over the drainage hole.

## Watering

Keep constantly moist, never allow the plant to become dry. Less water is needed during winter in cool locations. Above average humidity is desirable—use a humidity tray and spray mist frequently with clear water, especially in warm quarters.

## Feeding

From spring to August apply water soluble general fertilizer every two weeks.

## Propagation

Any time of year, root 3 to 4-inch terminal growth cuttings in moist sand or vermiculite. Ivy is noted for a self-mutation characteristic, thus cuttings are best taken from older wood to assure duplication of the parent plant.

## Special Problems

Excessive warmth and dry air will encourage attacks of red spider and scale, followed by sudden leaf drop. Use insecticide malathion spray regularly especially from autumn until spring. For small plants, showering and washing the stems and leaves with water is very beneficial.

*Hedera helix*

92

# HELXINE soleirolii

*Baby's Tears, Irish Moss,
Paddy's Wig, Corsican Curse,
Mind-your-own Business,
Peace-in-the-Home.*

This is a tiny creeping plant with many names, but Baby's Tears, is the most commonly used.

## Origin

*Helxine soleirolii* is a member of the Nettle family (Urticaceae) and is native to the islands of Corsica and Sardinia.

## Description

The thread-like stems of the plant are freely branched and intertwined to form a dense mat of bright green. Individual leaves are almost circular and no more than one-quarter inch in diameter.

It is widely used as a ground cover in terrariums where the high humidity causes rapid spread even up the inside walls of the container. Specimen plants may also be grown with sufficient moisture.

## Cultivation

Locate in a semi to full shade location in average room temperature. A relative humidity of 50% or more is desirable, which is somewhat difficult outside of a terrarium. However, use of a humidity tray and frequent mist spraying with clear tepid water will be helpful. Enclosing specimen plants in clear plastic bags will also be useful during difficult periods of low humidity.

## Potting

Use an open rich mixture such as equal parts loam, sand, peat moss, rotted or dried manure or leafmould and provide for prompt drainage with crock or pea gravel over the drainage holes. Use clay pots to provide a moist surface for the trailing stems.

## Watering

Keep evenly moist at all times and mist spray frequently.

## Feeding

Apply water soluble general fertilizer solution on a 14 day schedule.

## Propagation

Divide clumps or root stem cuttings in moist sand.

## Special Problems

This plant is essentially problem-free.

*Helxine soleirolii*

# HIBISCUS rosa-sinensis

*Rose-of-China, Chinese Hibiscus, Blacking Plant*

The bright hollyhock-like flowers of *Hibiscus rosa-sinensis* (Chinese Hibiscus) remain open for only one day and remain fresh for only one day in or out of water as well as on the plant.

## Origin

Now seen everywhere in the tropics, the Chinese Hibiscus is a native of China even though Hawaii has adopted it as a national flower. The genus Hibiscus is a member of the Mallow family (Malvaceae) and is made up of 150 to 200 species that may be catalogued in four groups: annuals, herbaceous perennials, hardy shrubs and tropical shrubs. Chinese Hibiscus is a tropical shrub.

## Description

The foliage is bold in texture, bright green and coarsely toothed making an attractive plant even when there is no bloom. Each flower lasts only one day with a replacement appearing each morning at the leaf axils on new growth. The flowers are somewhat shaped like the hollyhock with stamens projecting well beyond the petals. They range up to 5 inches in diameter, both single and double, and come in many colors including pale yellow to amber, shell pink to rose, bright vermilion (a classic) and white. Most flowers are produced in spring and summer. In Northern climates this plant must be treated as a tender evergreen pot or tub plant. It may be grown as a small bush or allowed to grow somewhat taller if it fits in available sunny locations.

## Cultivation

Located in a bright sunny window over winter, plants will usually produce at least one colorful blossom each day, after reaching the 12-inch pot size. Plants may be used outside after danger from frost.

Pinch prune new growth to control size and shape. However, it should be noted that flowers come from fresh new growth rather than the old wood. Hibiscus may be trained into a standard form by removing all side growth and allowing the main stem to grow to a desired height of 3 to 4 feet before pinch pruning the top to start branching.

## Potting

Drainage is very important to the health of this plant and a rich friable potting soil should be used. A suitable mixture can be made from equal parts rich loam, coarse builders' sand, peat moss and rotted or dried manure or compost. Since plants begin blooming when only a few inches high, it is possible to keep a plant well within the space available. Repotting should be undertaken in early spring.

## Watering

This leafy plant is very thirsty and the soil should be kept evenly moist. Drying out will cause leaf drop.

## Feeding

Feed on a 10 to 14 day schedule with water soluble general fertilizer during the growing period. Since the plant requires a slightly acid growing condition it should be watered once a month with a solution of one teaspoon of ammonium sulphate to one quart of water.

## Propagation

From 4-inch soft tipped cuttings in late spring dipped in rooting hormone powder and placed in coarse moist sand or vermiculite. Bottom heat of 24 to 27°C. (75 to 80°F.) should be maintained along with high humidity which may be arranged by enclosing the rooting setup in a clear plastic bag.

## Special Problems

Red spider mites and mealy bugs may be controlled by regular spraying with malathion solution. Mist spraying of the foliage with clear water will help maintain humidity and prevent flower bud drop.

*Hibiscus rosa-sinensis*

# HIPPEASTRUM
*Amaryllis*

Few plants for pot culture are so truly sensational or more easily grown than Hippeastrum, commonly called Amaryllis. The choice bulbs are those from Holland which are large and very expensive. However, this is not a one-time, one-bloom investment, since the Amaryllis can bloom year after year when given the proper care and rooting.

## Origin

Hippeastrum from Peru and South Africa is the plant from which most of today's popular forms of Amaryllis originated. It is a member of the Amaryllis family (Amaryllidaceae).

## Description

Bulbs produce flowers 7 to 10 inches across, usually with three or four flowers on a spike and often two to three spikes per bulb. The huge trumpet-shaped flowers are breathtaking in scarlet, crimson, pink and white as well as in combinations of these colors.

*Hippeastrum*

## Cultivation

Dormant Holland bulbs are usually available in November and December while those from South Africa may be in stock as early as September, in which case it is possible to have bloom by Christmas. To keep the first bloom up to standard, try to buy bulbs as soon as they arrive at the garden shop and plant them immediately to preserve any and all live roots on the bulb. A single bulb can be grown in a 5 or 6-inch pot and thorough drainage is essential. The potting soil must be porous and moisture-retentive. A mixture of equal parts coarse builders' sand, peat moss and rotted or dried manure or compost is ideal. Most bulbs will be around 3 inches in diameter and a 6-inch pot is a good size to use. Since water-logged soil is death to Amaryllis roots, it is necessary to take special care to insure good drainage by placing a generous amount of broken crockery and pieces of activated charcoal over the drainage hole.

The bulb should be planted with the top one-third above the soil level and the final soil level should be at least one half inch below the rim of the pot to facilitate watering. While planting, handle any live roots on the bulb with care by holding the bulb in place and gently working and compacting the soil into place.

When active growth is occurring, avoid damage to the tall flower stems by supporting them with a small cane and tie. Begin this early to keep the stems growing straight up. Development at this time is usually rapid and blooming occurs 6 to 8 weeks after planting. As the flower stalk lengthens, turn the pot daily at least a quarter turn to keep the growth equalized. Don't be surprised if the leaves do not appear until after the flower buds open. The Amaryllis will enjoy a sunny window in winter and will prosper in any skylight enclosure.

## Rebuilding the Bulb

The large sized bulbs of the Dutch hybrids usually produce two and sometimes three stocks of blooms at intervals over a few weeks during the blooming season. As soon as the flowers fade, cut the flower stalk off at the base and direct your attention to rebuilding the bulb for next year's performance. Since flower production has used up plant food from the bulb, it is somewhat smaller than when it was planted. You can build it back by encouraging growth of luxuriant foliage. Each leaf blade broadens out at its base to become a scale of the bulb. The more leaves, the more scales, and the larger the bulb. Foliage growth is strongest during spring and summer so the plants must be maintained in a suitable place, well fed and well watered. After flowering they should remain in the window until late May, when it is warm enough to move them. The best procedure is to sink the pot in the ground within an inch of the top. Choose a location sheltered from the wind and with the morning and evening sunlight, much the same as with tuberous begonia.

## Resting Period

Most hybrid Amaryllis are deciduous and by August the leaves will start to turn yellow and die. When this occurs, cease feeding and reduce water. Before frost, the pots must be lifted and stored in a cool part of the basement. They must not be allowed to freeze. The best resting temperature is 15 to 20°C. (60 to 70°F.). Use only enough water to prevent shriveling of the roots.

## New Growth

By early December, after a two to three months' rest, bring the Amaryllis back to warmth and light. Some of the bulbs will already be showing buds at this stage.

## Potting

Use a mixture of equal parts coarse builders' sand, peat moss and rotted cow manure or compost. Ensure good drainage by placing a generous amount of broken crockery and pieces of activated charcoal over the drainage hole. A single bulb should be planted in a 5 or 6-inch pot with the top one-third of the bulb above the soil level. The final soil level should be at least half an inch below the rim of the pot. Handle any live roots with care.

Complete repotting is necessary only every three or four years as the bulbs resent root disturbance and will flower best when pot bound. However, each year before starting the bulbs in growth, the surface soil should be scraped away with a pointed stick so that a top dressing may be applied using fresh potting mix. Obviously, when the bulb gets too large for the pot, it will have to be moved up to a larger size.

## Watering

After planting, water thoroughly and place in a warm location, 24 to 26°C. (75 to 80°F.). Water should be given sparingly until growth is active. The soil must not be allowed to dry out once growth has started. The emergence of a large fat bud from the neck of the bulb signals the reawakening and start of growth. At this point the bulb should be placed in a bright location at 18 to 21°C. (65 to 70°F.) and watering gradually increased. Only lukewarm water should be used.

## Feeding

After flowering, a routine feeding with water soluble general fertilizer should be given every two weeks.

## Propagation

From offsets that develop around the base of the bulb.

## Special Problems

This plant rarely suffers from diseases or pests.

# HOFFMANNIA refulgens
*Taffeta Plant*

This splendid foliage plant is excellent for use as a bright accent.

## Origin
Genus Hoffmannia, with around 100 species, is a member of the Madder family (Rubiaceae). All are native to Mexico into South America.

## Description
*Hoffmannia refulgens,* Taffeta Plant, grows 6 to 12 inches with narrow ovate leaves which may have many close set parallel veins running from the mid rib to the leaf edge. The upper surface is dull green blotched in irridescent shades of purple and brown. The under surface is pale red to wine color. Small red flowers are produced.

## Cultivation
Grow in semi-shade in average room temperature.

## Potting
Use a soil mixture of equal parts loam, builders' sand, peat moss and rotted or dried manure or leafmould. Repot when the roots become compacted.

## Watering
Keep evenly moist and grow plants over a humidity tray with frequent mist spraying to maintain the high humidity required by this plant.

## Feeding
During the summer growing season, use water soluble general fertilizer on a 14 day schedule.

## Propagation
Use cuttings dipped in hormone powder and place in coarse builders' sand or vermiculite with humidity and warmth.

## Special Problems
Control pests with malathion spray.

*Hoffmannia refulgens*

96

# HOWEA

*Kentia Palm, Curly Palm, Thatch Leaf Palm*

Early in the century potted palms were widely used to decorate the living room as well as the ice cream parlor. The recent environment and green survival themes have re-awakened interest in palms and they are readily available in many sizes in stores specializing in green foliage plants.

## Origin

While grasses are number one in an economic importance, palms rank a close second and have more applications to human needs than any other group of plants. Food, clothing, shelter, oils, fats, sweet drinks, wine, beetle nuts, etc. all are available from one or more of 1,500 species that form the Palm family (Palmacea). Fossils indicate the presence of palms at the time of the dinosaurs as well as their existence in nearly all parts of the world in past ages. Today, palms are confined to the tropical and sub-tropical areas and are widely grown in Florida, the Gulf states and California. In the north, palms are confined to pots and tubs. Probably the most decorative and beautiful of the palms for home culture is the genus Howea, a native only to the Lord Howe Island, a tiny speck of land in the South Pacific. Kentia is the capital of this island and the palm has in times past been called Kentia Palm.

## Description

The two species, *Howea belmoreana* (30 feet) and *Howea forsteriana* (50 feet), in their juvenile state, show very little difference in appearance and continue for many years as pot plants and eventually tub plants. Most species of these feather leaf palms have graceful, arching, spineless leaves that can be over 7 feet long when mature specimens.

## Cultivation

This palm requires very little light, which makes it ideal for the darker corners of the living room. In nature this plant starts off as undergrowth beneath the jungle forest and is conditioned to survive in the deepest shade. It may be kept indoors throughout the year or summered out of doors in a shady spot. Indoor winter temperatures should be 18 to 21°C. (65 to 70°F.) during the day and 15°C. (60°F.) at night. Protect the plant from sudden cold drafts, from open doors or windows as this will cause the leaves to turn brown.

## Potting

Repotting should be undertaken only when absolutely necessary and preferably only from spring into early summer. Palms grow best when their roots are confined so it is best not to over-pot. Move to a pot only one size larger.

Cover the drainage hole with an inch or so of shard, crushed stone or pea gravel so that stagnant water will not collect at the bottom of the pot. Use a potting soil of equal parts rich loam, builders' sand and leafmould or rotted or dried manure. Mix in a small amount of bone meal. Two or three plants are normally grown in each container.

## Watering

Watering should be maintained year round. Avoid daily sprinkling of the soil. The best technique is to water thoroughly by soaking the pot in a pail or pan of tepid water for ten minutes or so, or until air bubbles cease to rise. Drain thoroughly and discard water that collects in the saucer. This treatment once a week should suffice but will be dependent upon the room humidity and temperature.

*Howea belmoreana*

## Feeding

Supplementary feeding with water soluble fertilizer on a 10 day schedule may be given from March through July. Make certain that the potting soil is moist before application of the fertilizer, otherwise the roots may be damaged.

## Propagation

Howea is propagated from seeds sown in March or September in a seed bed with bottom heat about 26°C. (78°F.). Freshness of the seed is very critical. Even in the best of circumstances, germination may take from 60 days up to nine months. For the novice it is best to begin with young plants for growing on.

## Special Problems

Mealy bugs and scale can be kept under control by spraying regularly with malathion. Red spider mites will be discouraged by mist spraying the leaves with clear water as well as by regular dusting of the foliage with a soft damp cloth.

# HOYA

*Wax Vine, Wax Plant*

This long lived plant was named in honor of Thomas Hoy, a gardener to the Duke of Northumberland and was introduced into England around 1850.

## Origin

Genus Hoya is a member of the Milkweed family (Asclepiadaceae) with about 200 species. It is native to South China, India, through the islands into Australia.

## Description

Commonly called the Wax Vine because of the firm wax-like flowers, this genus consists of evergreen, tropical, root climbing vines and trailing shrubs. The evergreen, glossy, leathery, oval pointed leaves growing up to 3 inches are found in pairs on the opposite sides of the stem. The showy umbrella-like flower heads are borne from short stems or spurs originating from the leaf axils on old wood. Flowers are borne from the same spurs for several years and unfamiliar growers often destroy potential flowering by cutting away these spurs after the flowering period. Faded flowers should be removed gently by hand rather than by cutting. The principal species grown include:

*H. bella* from India, a dwarf (1 to 2 feet) branched shrub with clusters of flowers, (8 to 10), white with a crimson center. It is often grown in a hanging basket.

*H. carnosa*, commonly called Wax Plant, is found from South China to Australia and grows 5 to 8 feet in height. The fragrant flowers, white with a pink center, grow in clusters of 12 or more. There is also a species, *H. carnosa variegata*, with white edged leaves. It is less floriferous.

*H. imperialis (sussuela)*, from Borneo, is a natural tall grower that begins flowering when only 3 to 4 feet tall. The individual flowers of the flower head are 2 to 3 inches across. They are a deep, dull purple with a white crown. This plant was introduced into England by Sir Hugh Low (1824-1905), before 1850.

## Cultivation

This summer flowering plant (May to August), requires a location in bright light (sunny to semi-sunny), and may be grown in average home temperature and humidity. The resting period for Hoya is autumn and early spring and more vigorous plants are produced if a temperature in the range of 10 to 16°C. (50 to 60°F.) can be maintained during this period.

## Potting

Hoya requires a rich, friable soil that drains freely. An ideal mixture is equal parts loam, coarse builders' sand, peat moss and rotted or dried manure or leafmould. A generous layer of small stones or pea gravel should be used over the drainage hole to ensure prompt drainage. Young plants should be repotted as soon as the root ball fills the container, older plants only when absolutely necessary, to a slightly larger pot or with root pruning and returned to the same size container.

## Watering

Water freely during the growing period, spring to autumn. Keep barely moist during the resting period.

## Feeding

During the growing and flowering period, use supplementary feeding on a two week schedule with a water soluble fertilizer.

## Propagation

Cuttings of terminal growth taken during June may be rooted in coarse builders' sand, with heat and humidity. Use a rooting hormone powder and enclose the rooting bed in a clear plastic bag located out of direct sun. Air-layering may also be used by pinning a stem onto a pot of soil mixture.

*Hoya imperialis*

Select a semi-mature stem, cut a small slit with a sharp knife, below a leaf node, pin to the soil, cover with soil and keep moist.

## Special Problems

Soft, forced growth may be attacked by green fly and mealy bugs. Control with an insecticide such as malathion or a cotton swab dipped in rubbing alcohol to remove the individual pests. Pruning of flowering spurs will reduce future flowering. Avoid altering light conditions in any way during the bud forming and flowering period to reduce premature drop.

# HYACINTHUS orientalis
*Hyacinths*

Of all the hardy bulbs, Hyacinths are probably the easiest and most rewarding for indoor forcing. The perfection and beauty of the Hyacinth flower depends on bulb size and the strength of the roots.

## Origin

Most of our present day Hyacinths are decended from *Hyacinthus orientalis*, a native of Asia Minor that was introduced into Europe in the early 1500's.

## Description

Hyacinths are available in colors ranging from white to blue and purple, with a few yellows. Generally, two or more flower spikes are produced from a bulb.

*Hyacinthus orientalis*

## Cultivation

### Culture in Soil

Hyacinths are the easiest of the hardy bulbs to force into bloom indoors, months earlier than in the spring garden. Anyone, child or adult, can force Hyacinths by following a few simple steps.

Bulbs for forcing should be plump, solid and free from blemishes. The largest size is the best; the size and strength of the plant is already determined by the size of the bulb. It is far better to buy fewer good bulbs than a larger quantity of average quality. You will find that most dealers offer prepared or pre-treated, pre-cooled bulbs, which means they can be readily forced to produce blooms for Christmas.
A loose crumbly soil is best for potting.

*(see over)*

# HYACINTHUS (continued)

Builders' sand, peat moss or vermiculite may be added to loosen the soil. Garden loam or commercial potting soil will probably require further conditioning. Avoid using soil in which Hyacinths have been grown before and never use fresh manure. If you use a mixture of one part soil, one part peat moss and one part builders' sand, you will have a potting mix that gives best possible root development and the all-important drainage.

Almost anything that will hold potting mixture can be used for a container as long as it is at least twice as high as the bulb and has a bottom drainage hole. Clay pots should be soaked in water for at least 12 hours before using.

Top size bulbs can be planted one to a 5-inch pot. Smaller sizes can be planted three to five depending on the container. Place a layer of broken shard or pea gravel over the drainage hole, partially fill the container with the soil mixture, gauging or predetermining the amount so that when the bulb is placed on top, the tip will just be level with the edge of the container. Water thoroughly by setting the container in water about half way up and allow it to soak until the soil surface looks wet and feels moist. Label or mark the pot showing date of planting, variety and color since it will be out of sight and mind most of the 12-week rooting period.

All spring bulbs require 10 to 12 weeks of cold to develop a suitable root system. The easiest method is by rooting bulbs in a cold, dark location under cover such as a cellar, garage or shed close to the house. A cold frame is ideal and a basement window well is useful. The temperature in the rooting location should be between 5 to 10°C. (40 to 50°F.). Lower than 5°C. (40°F.) lengthens the rooting period, while temperatures above 10°C. (50°F.) prevent rooting. If you have an old refrigerator in the garage or basement you can fill it with potted bulbs and turn the temperature down to 5°C. (40°F.). Keep the door closed as much as possible but check at least once a week to make sure there is no excessive drying. Keep the soil moist at all times. At the end of the rooting period, sometimes as early as nine weeks with precooled bulbs, the pot will contain a mass of roots that are visible through the drainage hole. Sprouts will be about 2 inches high. If the roots are not visible, invert and tap the rim of the pot to check the extent of root growth. Check at two week intervals until you are satisfied that the root structure is extensive and well developed.

When the rooting is completed, place the plant in a semi-dark spot for 7 to 14 days in a temperature no higher than 15°C. (60°F.). Then the plant can be placed in a room temperature of 21°C. (72°F.) with more light. Keep the plant out of direct sunlight and away from heating ducts and radiators.

## Culture in Water

You can amaze your friends and neighbors and fascinate the children in your family by growing Hyacinths in a glass. They will stand in all their splendor with roots, bulbs, stems, leaves and flowers, fully visible. They will also provide a delicate exquisite perfume.

Next to Paperwhite Narcissus, Hyacinths adapt readily to water culture either individually in Hyacinth glasses or in bowls and jars with the bulbs held in place with small pebbles.

For water cultivation, use only the extra select top size bulbs. You will find that varieties such as 'King of the Blues' (deep steel blue), 'Myosotis' (Forget-Me-Not blue), 'L'Innocence' (pure white), 'La Victoire' (brilliant red) and 'Pink Pearl' (rich deep pink) will give more than satisfactory results in water culture. Most garden outlets now offer a few pre-cooled or conditioned bulbs, which means they have been stored for nine weeks at 4°C. (40°F.) and thus may be forced into bloom before January. Otherwise, results would be disappointing if forcing were undertaken without sufficient cool conditions. It is during this cool period that subtle chemical changes take place within the cells of the bulb that normally occur over winter in outdoor cultivation. Thus, the bulb, after sufficient cooling (usually 8 to 12 weeks), is deceived into spring awakening and coaxed into bloom.

Select plump top size bulbs and clean their bases by clipping away any dead dry roots as these will not grow and will only end up clouding the water.

Hyacinth glasses are available in clear as well as blue and amber. The classic clear smooth glass that gives a full undistorted view of the developed roots is by far the first choice.

Place a few small bits of wood charcoal in the glass to help keep the water pure and sweet. Locate the clean bulb in the bulb receptacle and fill the glass with water to a level that just touches the base of the bulb. This level must be maintained throughout the life of the project, with evaporation replaced regularly. The planting is now ready for the dark, cool, storage period, preferably 4°C. (40°F.).

In about 8 to 10 weeks, the developing roots will fill the glass and the flower shoot should be about 3 inches in length. Continue to keep the plant in the dark until the shoot reaches about 5 inches. Growth at this point will be pale and sickly looking, but don't be alarmed.

Gradually move the plant into light. In a few days it will be a rich green and in a few more days flowers will start to unfold. For this phase, 15°C. (60°F.) is the best temperature.

To keep growth straight, the plant should be given a quarter turn clockwise each day so that leaning towards the light will be minimized.

Plantings in dishes are accomplished in much the same manner as with Paperwhite Narcissus. The container must be at least 4 inches deep to allow for sufficient space for water and root development. Spread a layer of 2 to 3 inches of small pebbles in the container. Then position the clean bulbs close together without touching and add more pebbles to hold the bulbs in position. Now add water just to the base of the bulbs. Storage and rooting conditions are the same as for Hyacinth glass planting. In the apartment you might be able to take over a small corner of the refrigerator for the cool rooting period.

## Potting

For bulbs grown in soil, use a mixture of one part commercial potting soil, one part peat moss and one part builders' sand. Cover drainage hole with a layer of shard or pea gravel.

See Cultivation for detailed instructions on how to pot.

## Watering

For bulbs grown in soil, water moderately.

For bulbs grown in water maintain water at a level that just touches the base of the bulbs.

## Feeding

No feeding is necessary.

## Propagation

See Cultivation for growing Hyacinths from bulbs.

Bulbs cannot be forced a second time. However, if allowed to mature, they may be stored cool and dry and planted in the lawn or garden the following September. Results, of course, will not be the same as from new bulbs.

## Special Problems

Grown properly, Hyacinths are problem-free.

# HYDRANGEA macrophylla
*Hydrangea*

This plant is a favorite for Easter and Mother's Day. The showy clusters of white, pink or blue flowers are quite spectacular.

## Origin

This plant is a member of the Saxifrage family (Saxifragaceae) and is native to Japan. Carl Peter Thunberg, a Swedish physician and botanist, employed by the Dutch Trading Company in Japan, is credited as being the first European to describe this Asian shrub around 1775. Reportedly, this shrub had been cultivated for many years in Eastern Asia prior to his discovery.

## Description

This plant is a perennial, deciduous shrub growing to 12 feet in its native habitat. As a pot plant it is usually grown as a single stem, usually three to a 6-inch pot. The large, handsome foliage is ovate, up to 6 inches long on short leaf stems, pale green with serrated edges. The flowers grow in large clusters almost spherical, 8 to 10 inches, in well grown plants. The sterile flowers last for a long time and may be white, pink to carmine and blue.

## Cultivation

With care, Hydrangea may be kept in bloom for a month or longer even though as a gift plant it was in full bloom when received.

This plant needs bright light during the day with a temperature no higher than 21°C. (70°F.). If possible, place it in a cool location 15 to 18°C. (60 to 65°F.) at night.

To carry the plant over for another year, cut the stems back about half way after the flowers have faded and repot. Carefully work the old soil away from the roots and replant in a fresh potting mix of equal parts rich loam, coarse builders' sand and peat moss. Keep the plant well watered. After the last spring frost, place the pot outdoors in a half shade location. Keep it well watered and feed alternately with water soluble general fertilizer and a solution of iron sulphate (1 ounce to two gallons of water), every two weeks. This will give the proper soil acidity required for *Hydrangea macrophylla*.

If the plant is growing too tall or if you want to make a bushier plant, pinch out the young growing tips but only up until the first week of July. This will allow ample time for development of new shoots and flower buds. Before danger of hard frost which can destroy the flower buds, bring the plant indoors. Stop supplementary feeding, place the plant in a cool dark storage 8 to 10°C. (45 to 50°F.) and keep barely moist. While in storage the leaves will wither and drop. They should be collected and destroyed to prevent mildew.

After Christmas and before late January, begin forcing the plant into growth at a temperature of 15°C.(60°F.)in a semi-sunny location. To have the plant in flower for Easter plan on about thirteen weeks from the time the plant is taken out of storage. Once the new growth is underway the feeding program should be started again.

If you are opting for early summer blooms in the garden, keep your plant in storage until late March.

Hydrangea can be left outside over winter but flower buds are damaged at temperatures below -8°C. (18°F.).Some gardeners in cold regions report occasional success by enclosing the plant in a wire cage and packing it full of leaves after the first frost. If the flower buds are damaged there will be no flowers since they come from year-old ripened wood.

## Color Development of Flowers

The coloring of the pink and blue varieties is determined by the degree of soil acidity and the fertilizing program. A plant that is pink one year may be turned into blue for another. The white flowering Hydrangea has no coloring pigment, it cannot be changed to pink or blue.Pink flowers are produced with a general fertilizing program and iron sulphate. Blue flowers require a feeding program which makes use of a fertilizer with no phosphorous present since this element makes aluminum unavailable to the plant. Aluminum is essential for the formation of blue flowers and is provided in three or four applications of aluminum sulphate in solution (3 ounces to one gallon of water). Some authorities recommend puncturing the root ball with a stiff wire or pointed pencil to damage the roots just prior to the aluminum application.

## Potting

Use a potting mix of equal parts rich loam, coarse builders' sand and peat moss.

## Watering

Careful attention is required since this is a very thirsty plant. The best technique is to submerge it in a pan of water until air bubbles cease to rise from the pot. Mist spray the leaves with clear water to maintain humidity and top-notch appearance.

## Feeding

During the active growing period, spring to fall, feed alternately with water soluble general fertilizer and a solution of iron sulphate, (one ounce to two gallons of water), every two weeks.

## Propagation

The flowers of Hydrangea are sterile and propagation is accomplished from leaf bud cuttings. This is achieved in late spring by cutting the stem just above a pair of leaves then splitting through the middle of the cut away portions so that each segment has a leaf and a 2-inch piece of stem. Coarse builders' sand, perlite or a mixture of perlite and peat moss may be used as a rooting medium. The cutting must be kept moist at all times and enclosing in a clear plastic bag will help maintain this condition. It will take about three weeks at 15° C. (60° F.) for the cutting to produce roots. Transplant into individual pots in soil mixture discussed previously and treat in the same manner as for a plant being carried out for a second season.

## Special Problems

Red spider mites and plant aphids can be controlled by regular spraying with malathion solution.

# IMPATIENS

*Patience Plant, Touch-Me-Not,*
*Snap Weed, Busy Lizzie*

For a faithful flowering windowsill plant, don't overlook Impatiens with their simple leaves and showy flowers.

## Origin

Genus Impatiens is one of two members of the Balsam family (Balsaminaceae). It has over 500 species widely distributed around the world, mainly in mountainous regions in warm temperate and tropical zones. A common characteristic is the manner in which ripe seed pods curl at a touch to expel the seeds. This has led to the common names Snap Weed and Touch-Me-Not.

## Description

This is a tender plant having thick succulent watery stems with simple, pointed elliptical leaves. Depending upon the species, height can range from 6 to 24 inches. Two species are of interest to the indoor gardener: *Impatiens sultanii*, so named in honor of the Sultan of Zanzibar. It is probably the most widely known and cultivated. This species reaches 12 inches in height with bright green foliage. This plant first reached England in the latter part of the 19th century, having been collected by Dr. John Kirk while he was Counsel General at Zanzibar. In its original form, *I. sultanii* produced rich scarlet flowers; now from the attention received over the years from plant breeders, constant flowering varieties are available ranging from white, through orange, rose, scarlet to orchid and purple varieties. Dwarf varieties (5 to 6 inches) of recent introduction have further enhanced use as pot plants and bedding plants.

*I. holstii*, grows to 3 feet in height and was introduced from tropical East Africa around 1906. It grows in the mountainous regions up to 3,000-foot elevations. The branches of this species are marked red and burgundy. Many hybrids have been developed, many of which bear strong resemblance to *I. sultanii*.

## Cultivation

Impatiens require good light for best performance. During winter provide full sun, during summer give light shade. Normal room temperature 21 to 22°C. (70°F.) is suitable for this heat loving plant. Temperatures below 15°C. (60°F.) may cause the plant to sulk and drop leaves. Humidity above 30% is desirable and locating the plants in a humidity tray filled with gravel and water will assist in maintaining this condition. Mist spray the foliage with clear water, but avoid wetting the flowers.

Plants will do well out of doors after danger of frost in a semi-shade location. Plants may be set directly in the border or kept in their pots.

## Potting

A rich humusy soil is required such as equal parts rich loam, coarse builder's sand, peat moss and rotted or dried manure or compost. Plants may be maintained in 4 to 6—inch size pots. Delay repotting.

Plants that have been set out in the border for the summer may be rescued before frost. Prune back plants you wish to save, lift and pot in the rich potting soil described above. Use a pot of sufficient size to accommodate the roots. Ensure prompt drainage by covering the drainage hole with about 2 inches of pea gravel. Place in a sunny window and you will have a continuous display of colorful blooms for the winter months.

## Watering

Impatiens need a bit more water than most house plants, so take care that the soil always stays moist and never dries out. Mist spray the foliage with water but don't wet the flowers.

## Feeding

During periods of active growth and flowering, use water soluble general fertilizer on a 10 to 14 day schedule.

## Propagation

Impatiens is easily grown from seeds which are available from most mail order house in mixtures as well as individual colors.

Sow the seed in sand or vermiculite and cover sparsely because light is required for germination. If a pot is used as a seed bed, place it in a large, clear plastic bag to maintain a moist atmosphere in a fairly large air space. Place the seed bed in bright light out of direct sun. Best germination occurs in a 21 to 26°C. (70 to 80°F.) temperature range and should take place within 15 days. The seed is rated very sensitive to low temperature, lack of moisture and darkness. Seed may be sown at any time of the year and those which are sown around February 1st will provide 3-inch pot size plants by the end of May.

When germination becomes evident keep the seedlings shaded from direct sun and water from below to minimize damping off. When the seedlings are large enough to handle (3 to 4 leaf stage), remove from the seed bed and plant individually in small pots.

Impatiens is one of the easiest plants to root from cuttings and they may be taken at any time of the year. They will root in a glass of water; however, stronger roots develop from those rooted in sand, perlite or vermiculite. Select a small healthy branch 3 or 4 inches long and make a clean cut at a leaf node. Dipping the end in a hormone powder does much to hasten the rooting. When roots have formed, pot up individually as described for seedlings. Cuttings taken during January and early February will provide healthy blooming size plants by May.

## Special Problems

Red spider mites arrive when conditions become hot and dry. Plant lice and white fly are also fond of this plant. Regular spraying with malathion solution will control these pests.

*Impatiens sultanii*

# IXORA
*Flame-of-the-Woods*

An outstanding shrub for a warm location.

## Origin

Genus Ixora, with over 400 species, is member of the Madder family (Rubiaceae) and native to the tropical areas of the world.

## Description

*Ixora coccinea*, Flame-of-the-Woods, a native of India, is an outstanding, 4-foot shrub, with a good bushy habit that makes it suitable as either a large or small flowered pot plant. The glossy, evergreen, leathery leaves are 4 inches in length. Flowering commences in April and continues over a long period. Flowers appear in dense, wide spreading clusters of scarlet tubular flowers.

Individual tubes are over 1½ inches in length. Some other favorites include:
*I. chinensis* from Malaya has orange red flowers.
*I. duffii* from Caroline Island has deep red flowers and long leaves.
*I. paviflora* from India has fragrant white flowers in 6-inch clusters.

## Cultivation

Grow in a sunny location with protection during the March to August period (semi-sunny). Average room temperature 18 to 21°C. (65 to 70°F.) is suitable. Temperatures below 16°C. (60°F.) will cause leaf drop and loss of flower buds. Pruning should be undertaken immediately after flowering.

## Potting

A rich new textured soil is required. Use equal parts loam, coarse builders' sand, peat moss and rotted or dried manure or compost. Cover the drainage hole with pebbles or pea gravel to ensure adequate drainage. Young plants should be moved to larger pots before they become root bound to develop plants of the desired flowering size. Mature plants can remain in the same pots for up to four years before repotting if the supplementary feeding program is followed.

## Watering

Keep evenly moist throughout the year. Grow plants over a humidity tray and mist spray the foliage for additional humidity, especially during the spring and summer period.

## Feeding

Apply water soluble general fertilizer on a 10 day schedule during the growing and flowering period.

## Propagation

During spring, use cuttings of half ripened wood with 3 to 4 pairs of leaves or leaf nodes. Dip cut ends in rooting hormone powder and place in moist sand or vermiculite. Maintain humidity and a bottom heat of at least 21°C. (70°F.).

## Special Problems

Low temperature may cause leaf drop. Dryness can bring on attacks of scale and mealy bugs. For control use malathion insecticide spray.

*Ixora rosea*

# JACARANDA

Grown in a flower pot, Jacaranda is a far cry from the 60 feet it achieves in its native environment where it is a tall slender tree with a smooth three-foot diameter trunk.

## Origin

Jacaranda is a member of the Bignoniaceae family and native to the Guyanas, Venezuela and Colombia. Specimen plantings are found in southern California and Florida as well as the warm Mediterranean. It is one of the most widely grown ornamental trees in Brazil.

## Description

While the feathery fern-like foliage is enough to make it a desirable plant, the unbelievable clusters of azure blue flowers give it an un-paralleled distinction that is much appreciated by northerners who manage to escape to the warm climates in mid-winter and early spring. The flowers are bell shaped, about 2 inches long and are produced in great branch clusters. The flowers wilt and soon drop off after full bloom, covering the ground with a blanket of blue.

## Cultivation

This tropical plant requires a bright sunny location with some shade and above average humidity. Frequent mist spraying of the foliage with clear water is desirable and the winter temperature should be kept above 15°C. (60°F.).

## Potting

Use a rich mixture of equal parts coarse builders' sand, peat moss, loam and rotted or dried manure. Lime must be avoided. Repotting should take place as soon as roots outgrow the container. Once the plant has reached the 12-inch tub size it can be held by regular root pruning and partial repotting every second year. A generous layer of shard or pea gravel must be used over the drainage hole to ensure prompt drainage and aeration of the root ball. Pinch pruning will maintain the plant to shape and size.

## Watering

Do not over water this plant—the soil should be kept evenly moist.

## Feeding

Supplementary feeding with water soluble fertilizer should be confined to spring until early autumn.

## Propagation

Jacaranda propagates readily from seed at a germination temperature of around 24°C. (75°F.). Seed is offered by many of the specialty seed houses.

## Special Problems

There are no special problems.

*Jacaranda acutifolia*

# JASMINUM
*Jasmine*

A popular perfumed plant.

## Origin

Genus Jasminum, with about 200 species, is a member of the Olive family (Oleaceae) and is native to southeast Asia and the Pacific regions into Australia.

## Description

Jasminum varies in habit and form—some are erect shrubs, others climbers, some are deciduous. Most have small, glossy dark green leaves either simple or compound. Tubular flowers, white or yellow, appear in clusters and are perfumed. Some of the principal species are:

*J. grandiflorum*, the Royal or White Spanish Jasmine from India, is evergreen and nearly erect growing with drooping branches. It is one of the best whites flowering in summer and autumn. It is widely grown for the essential perfume oil of the flowers.

*J. mesnyi*, (primulinum), from China, is a non-climbing evergreen growing to 10 feet. Flowers are yellow with a darker throat.

*J. nudiflorum*, a native to China, is a nearly erect form, growing to 12 feet with yellow flowers. It drops its leaves in autumn. It was introduced into England by Robert Fortune (1812-1880) around 1846.

*J. officinale* is a slender grower up to 30 feet with clusters of droopy white flowers that are rich in essential oil. Native to Kashmir and China.

*J. sambac* is an evergreen climber from India with clusters of white flowers that take on a purplish cast as they fade. It is a source of Jasmine flowers for jasmine tea.

## Cultivation

With the exception of *sambac* which accommodates average room temperature, the others require a 16°C. (60°F.) environment. Grow in full winter sun and provide partial shade during spring to autumn.

## Potting

Use a rich friable soil mixture of equal parts loam, coarse builders' sand, peat moss and rotted or dried manure or compost. Move young plants up to 6-inch pots as soom as roots fill available space. Mature plants can remain in the same condition for a few years if fed regularly. This plant resents soggy conditions. Use a generous layer of pebbles and pea gravel over the drainage hole.

## Watering

Keep evenly moist and mist spray with clear water to provide above average humidity. Grow small plants over a humidity tray.

## Feeding

Apply water soluble general fertilizer on a two week schedule during summer to encourage growth and flowering.

## Propagation

Use 3-inch cuttings of terminal, half ripened wood during spring. Dip cut ends in rooting hormone powder and place in sand, vermiculite or a mixture of sand and peat moss. Maintain temperature in range of 21 to 24°C. (70 to 75°F.).

## Special Problems

High temperatures with dryness can bring on attacks of scale, aphids, mealy bug and red spider. Control by regular spraying with malathion insecticide. Remove individual pests with a cotton swab dipped in rubbing alcohol.

*Jasminum*

# JUSTICIA brandegeana
*Shrimp Plant*

This very attractive house plant, with a shrimp-like appearance, need not be protected from the midday sun.

## Origin

Genus Justicia is a member of the Acanthus family (Acanthaceae). This genus has around 300 species of plants and shrubs, mostly native to the tropical areas.

## Description

Shrimp Plant, *Justicia brandegeana* (formerly *Beloperone guttata)*, is a small evergreen shrub growing to 3 feet. Pot culture, of course, reduces the size relative to the pot used. The bright green, hairy leaves are ovate shaped and about 3 inches long. The terminal flower spikes are composed of overlapping bracts, much like shingles, and red-brown, violet to yellow-green in color. The total effect is a shrimp-like appearance.

## Cultivation

Grow in a sunny to semi-sunny location indoors. Average room temperature is acceptable; however, the best plants are produced in a temperature of 16°C. (60°F.). Pinch prune plants to maintain shape and bushiness. Heavier pruning should be carried out in early March. Outdoors, in summer, grow in a semi-shady location.

## Potting

Use a soil mixture of equal parts loam, coarse builders' sand, peat moss and rotted or dried manure or compost. Provide for drainage by using a generous layer of pebbles or pea gravel over the drainage hole.

## Watering

From early spring through August, water by soaking thoroughly then allow the root ball to approach dryness before soaking again. Maintain higher than normal room humidity by growing young plants over a humidity tray and mist spray the leaves with clear water occasionally.

## Feeding

Use water soluble general fertilizer on a 14 day schedule from spring to September.

## Propagation

Use stem cuttings at any time of the year. Dip cut ends in rooting hormone powder before inserting in moist sand or vermiculite. Bottom heat will accelerate the rooting time.

## Special Problems

Control white flies, mealy bugs and red spider mites with malathion spray.

*Justicia brandegeana*

# KALANCHOE

*Velvet Elephant Ear, Velvet Leaf* and *Panda Plant*

Commonly known as Velvet Elephant Ear, this plant, along with Cacti, is a member of the group of plants known as "succulents." Such plants have adapted to semi-arid locations by collecting and storing a large volume of water in their fleshy stems, branches and leaves. Not all are found in the semi-arid regions, many exist on high mountains as well as on tall trees. However, all these sites share one thing in common—the scarcity of water.

## Origin

Kalanchoe is a genus of the Stonecrop family (Crassulaceae) and they originate mostly from Madagascar. Genus Kalanchoe has over 200 species.

## Description

These perennial evergreen plants make undemanding house plants. They can range in size from 4 inches to 12 feet. The most familiar and widely grown species includes *K. beharensis*, commonly known as Velvet Leaf or Velvet Elephant Ear. It is a woody succulent shrub growing to 10 feet high with large thick leaves often 12 inches across and 18 inches long. They are broadly arrow-shaped, lobed, rich green in color but densely covered with rusty hairs above and silver hairs below. Each leaf has its own leaf stalk from the main trunk. This is an outstanding bold plant, the largest species of Kalanchoe genus.

*K. blossfeldiana*, also native to Madagascar is an 8 to 10-inch branching plant with small, ovate, glossy green leaves. Clusters of bright red flowers are normally borne in January, but by giving short day treatment as with Chrysanthemums it may be forced into bloom in time for the Christmas season. To achieve this, the plant must be kept in total darkness from 7:00 p.m. to 7:00 a.m. each day, starting around October 10th. *K. tomentosa*, the Panda Plant growing to about 30 inches is native to South Africa. This is a beautiful succulent with erect branching and soft, spoon-shaped leaves entirely covered with white silvery hairs except at the edges which are covered in reddish brown hairs.

## Cultivation

Locate in a sunny to semi-sunny spot with normal or lower than normal room temperature, lower especially during resting period. Average house humidity is suitable. The plants may be summered outside.

## Potting

The potting soil should be one part coarse builders' sand, one part rich garden loam and one part well rotted leafmould, or rotted or dried manure, or compost, with a light sprinkling of bone meal, bearing in mind the basic needs are perfect drainage with good aeration and nourishment when needed.

Since succulents are very susceptible to rot from excessive moisture in the soil, especially when the roots have been disturbed or pruned, it is considered prudent to plant not only in a dry pot but in dry soil as well and to leave the plant dry for several days.

Place a generous amount of broken crockery or pea gravel over the drainage hole then a layer of dry soil. Center the plant over this material and add more soil around the roots until the container is half full. Tamp or bump the pot to compact the soil, continue filling the container, tamp and compact leaving reasonable space at the top for watering. Bury the roots and stems to the same depth as before. If the roots are sparse it may be necessary to support the plant with a small stake until the roots have developed sufficiently to anchor into the soil. After several days, water sparsely for 30 days or so and allow the roots to return to healthy vigor. Don't use a saucer under the container unless it is first filled with crushed stone.

## Watering

Plants making fresh growth in the spring or summer may be watered as often as the soil dries out. In autumn and winter water only enough to keep the plants from shriveling since during the resting period the plant will use water mainly from its own tissue. When water is indicated, it is preferable to water heavily to remove the stale air from around the roots, then allow the plant to approach dryness before watering again.

## Feeding

Feed occasionally during the growing season with water soluble general fertilizer.

## Propagation

Roots readily from stems and individual leaves, even parts that fall on the soil. Make cuts with a sharp knife and allow the moist ends to dry before inserting in moist sand or vermiculite. The fastest rooting occurs during springtime.

## Special Problems

Essentially trouble-free except for root rot that can result from poor drainage and over-watering.

*Kalanchoe beharensis*

# LABURNUM
*Golden Chain Tree*

Some deciduous flowering trees make worthwhile additions to the indoor garden when grown as tub plants. Golden Chain Tree (*Laburnum watereri vossi*) may be forced into bloom from March onward to provide an exciting prelude to spring.

## Origin

Laburnum is a member of the Pea family (Leguminosae) which is composed of ornamentals as well as food and forage plants: peas, beans, clover, alfalfa, lupines and wisteria. Golden Chain is a native of Southern Europe and Central Asia and is widely grown in the U.K. where it is much admired for its colorful spring display. All parts of Golden Chain are poisonous, especially the pods and seeds.

## Description

Golden Chain is a deciduous tree with attractive green bark and light green foliage. It is a small tree that grows to 20 feet in the garden and has small three-part leaves, somewhat like overgrown clover. It normally blooms in late spring or early summer with long, 12 to 15-inch hanging clusters of bright, golden yellow pea-shaped blossoms, much like Wisteria. This plant cannot take temperatures below –5°C. (23°F.). It can be grown in a tub over summer, moving the plant indoors to a light cool area 5 to 10°C. (41 to 50°F.) from November to May. The plant may be grown as a standard with a four foot stem or trunk and kept trained to a mock head shape. This keeps the tree relatively small as well as attractive.

## Cultivation

During summer place in full light on the patio or balcony. From autumn to May grow in bright light at a temperature of 5 to 10°C. (41 to 50°F.) With increased daylight and a rise in daytime temperature to 16°C. (60°F.) from February on, Golden Chain may be flowered from mid-March into April well before the outdoor blossom time. Any pruning required to keep the plant in shape should be undertaken immediately after floweing.

## Potting

It is best to start off with dormant plants in early spring, either bare root or container, from the local or mail order nursery. Using a 14-inch container, like western red cedar, place a generous layer of pea gravel 1 to 2 inches deep at the bottom over the drainage holes. Root prune the plant to fit the container and add a soil mixture composed of equal parts coarse builders' sand, peat moss, rotted or dried manure and garden loam. Firm the soil in and around the roots, maintaining the trunk at the same level as previously grown. Flood with water to compact the soil in and around the roots. Adjust the level with additional soil to about one inch below the rim of the container. Every two to three years, remove the tree from the tub and cut away a slice of soil and roots from one side and return the plant to the tub. The free space is then filled with fresh soil mixture as described previously, firmed in place and watered.

## Watering

Keep evenly moist at all times. Less water will be required during the resting period.

*Laburnum watereri vossi*

## Feeding

Fertilize with water soluble general fertilizer on a 10 to 14 day schedule during periods of active growth.

## Propagation

Propagation may be achieved from seeds planted in spring about half an inch deep. Choice varieties are usually raised from cuttings or by grafting or budding onto seedlings of less desirable varieties.

## Special Problems

Aphids can be controlled with malathion spray solution.

### Caution

Reportedly all parts of Golden Chain are poisonous, especially the pods and seeds which contain a poisonous substance called "cytisine."

# LANTANA
*Shrub Verbena*

With enough light, this plant can bloom continuously.

## Origin

Genus Lantana, with over 100 species, is a member of the Verbena family (Verbenaceae). They originate mostly in tropical and sub-tropical America.

## Description

*L. camara* is a small hairy shrub, sometimes with short hooked spines, that grows to 4 feet. The oblong toothed leaves grow 4 to 5 inches. Verbena-like flowers are borne in 2-inch flat top heads. Flowers start off yellow or creamy yellow and change to orange-red or red with age. With enough light, flowering goes on continuously. This plant may be trained to a standard form with a 3 to 4 foot trunk.

*L. montevidensis* is a trailing or weeping shrub with 3-foot stems and rosy lavender flowers. It is an excellent plant for hanging baskets.

## Cultivation

Grow in full sun for continuous blooms. Average room temperature is suitable.

## Potting

Use a rich friable soil mixture of equal parts loam, builders' sand, peat moss and rotted or dried manure. Cover the drainage hole with pebbles or pea gravel. Repot in early spring.

## Watering

Keep evenly moist at all times. Plants pruned back during mid-winter will obviously need less water. Mist spray the foliage to provide above normal humidity.

## Feeding

Use water soluble general fertilizer during the growing and flowering season.

## Propagation

Readily from seed that may take 30 days or more to germinate or from stem cuttings taken in spring and summer.

## Special Problems

Lack of sun reduces flowering. This plant is dearly loved by white fly. Spray regularly with malathion insecticide before they gain a foothold.

*Lantana montevidensis*

# LILIUM longiflorum

*Easter Lily, White Trumpet Lily*

Accepted as symbolic of Easter and purity, the White Trumpet Lily is widely used as an Easter gift plant.

## Origin

Lilies have a long association with ancient cultures and reportedly some species have been used as food. Genus Lilium, with nearly 100 species and native to the North Temperate Zones, is a member of the Lily family (Liliaceae).

## Description

*Lilium longiflorum* 'Croft' is the variety in general use for forcing. The plant grows from a scaly bulb that is graded by its circumference. Large size bulbs of 11 inches in circumference produce the most flowers. Growth of the single stem reaches about 24 inches with glossy-green, lance-like leaves that are about 7 inches long at the base, becoming progressively shorter towards the top, thus producing a pyramid-like shape. The stem is topped with white, funnel-shaped flowers with long stamens and a greenish-yellow throat. Species *longiflorum* is native to Japan. Variety 'Croft' was developed in the Pacific Northwest U.S.A. It is not reliably hardy when grown in the outside border in the cold regions.

## Cultivation

Gift plants need full sun during the day and may be moved for best viewing during the evening. While average room temperature is suitable, flowers last longer at 16 to 18°C. (60 to 65°F.). Place the plant in a cool location over night to achieve the longest enjoyment. Remove faded flowers and keep the plant growing for recycling.

## Potting

Lilies require a coarse, porous potting soil that drains promptly. Use a mixture of rich loam, coarse builders' sand and rotted or dried manure. Incorporate about one-quater cup of agricultural lime for each 6-inch pot. Drainage is critical so use at least two inches of small pebbles or pea gravel over the drainage hole.

Bulbs normally become available in early autumn into October and November. Select top size and plant once to a 6-inch pot covering the tip with about half an inch of soil. Professional growers usually receive stock in November after a six-week pre-cooling period at a temperature just above freezing 1°C. (33°F.). Potted bulbs are started in a temperature of 16°C. (60°F.) about 115 to 120 days before Easter. Root growth is rapid and green growth appears in about seven days. Locate the plant in full sunshine to avoid production of a weak elongated stem.

The first bloom should appear about 40 days after the appearance of the flower buds. Growth is readily manipulated by increasing or lowering the growing temperature.

After flowering keep the plant in growth and move outside after the last frost. Remove from the pot with the root ball intact and plant 6 to 8 inches deep. When the plant yellows and goes dormant in late summer, harvest the bulb and repot as described previously.

*Lilium longiflorum*

Without pre-cooling, plants require about 180 days to flowering.

## Watering

Keep the soil evenly moist and thoroughly drained. Examine decorative wrappings on gift plants to ensure that the drainage hole is uncovered. Average room humidity is suitable. Mist spraying of the leaves with clear water is beneficial but avoid wetting the flowers.

## Feeding

Use only low phosphorous fertilizers. Use water soluble general fertilizer (such as 4:1:4) on a 14 day schedule at regular strength or substitute a very weak solution for regular watering.

## Propagation

Individual scales from the bulb may be rooted in moist sand, however it will take several years to produce forcing-size bulbs. With time, patience and care, plants can also be grown from seed that takes 30 days or more for germination.

## Special Problems

Root diseases and poor root growth are a result of wet soggy soil mixtures. Weak elongated stems result from lack of light and high forcing temperatures. Control aphids with malathion spray.

# MALPIGHIA coccigera
*Miniature Holly*

Miniature Holly has pale pink flowers in spring and summer that stay pretty for months.

## Origin
Genus Malpighia with 30 to 40 species is a member of the Malpighia family (Malpighiaceae) and native to tropical America.

## Description
*Malpighia coccigera,* Miniature Holly, native to the West Indies, is a smooth leaved, evergreen shrub growing to 3 feet. The leaves are glossy, spiny, margined and about one inch in length. Small, half inch pink flowers appear in summer and are followed by round red fruit.

## Cultivation
Grow in a sunny to semi-sunny location in normal room temperature.

## Potting
Use a potting soil of equal parts loam, coarse builders' sand, peat moss and rotted or dried manure or compost. Cover the drainage hole with shard, pebbles or pea gravel.

## Watering
Keep evenly moist and maintain a slightly higher than normal room humidity by growing young plants over a humidity tray and mist spraying the foliage with clear water.

## Feeding
During the period April to August, use water soluble general fertilizer on a 14 day schedule.

## Propagation
By seeds or stem cuttings in spring. Use rooting hormone powder on the cut ends before placing in moist sand or vermiculite. Maintain humidity and warmth.

## Special Problems
Essentially a trouble-free plant.

*Malpighia coccigera*

# MANDEVILLA splendens

Sometimes identified as *Dipladenia splendens*, this plant from the moist jungles of Brazil is achieving new popularity.

## Origin

Genus Mandevilla, with over 100 species, is a member of the Dogbane family (Apocynaceae) and native to tropical America. The name is in honor of Henry J. Mandeville (1773-1861) who introduced two species into Britain around 1837.

## Description

*Mandevilla splendens* is a smooth stemmed woody climber (8 to 10 feet) with glossy, leathery leaves, elliptic in shape and up to 8 inches long. Leaves appear in pairs along the twisting stems. Funnel shaped flowers appear from summer into autumn in groups of three to five on long flower stems. They are 3 inches across with a rose-pink tube and throat.

## Cultivation

Grow in a light semi-sunny location in average room temperature. During the winter resting period, January through February, keep the plants slightly cooler at 13 to 16°C. (55 to 60°F.).

## Potting

Use a soil mixture of equal parts loam, coarse builders' sand and peat moss. Prompt drainage of excess moisture is essential. Use a generous layer of pebbles or pea gravel at the bottom of the tub. Plants succeed best when grown in tubs or 12-inch pots and over. Repot only in early spring when new growth begins.

## Watering

Keep evenly moist except during the winter rest period when water should be used sparingly. High humidity is required especially from March on when flower buds are being formed.

## Feeding

Use water soluble general fertilizer on a two week schedule except during the winter months.

## Propagation

From seeds and cuttings in coarse builders' sand with bottom heat. Mist often or enclose rooting bed in a clear plastic bag.

## Special Problems

Dry air and hot direct sun will damage the foliage. Control insects with malathion spray.

*Mandevilla splendens*

# MARANTA leuconeura

*Prayer Plant, Rabbit's Foot*

An interesting foliage plant and a symbolic gift for a sick friend.

## Origin

Genus Maranta, with over 20 species, is a member of the Arrowroot family (Marantaceae) and native to tropical America. It was named in honor of Bartolomme Maranti, a botanist at Naples, circa 1550.

## Description

Prayer Plant, *Maranta leuconeura massangeana*, has spreading stems. Its oval 6-inch leaves are up to 4 inches wide and carried on 6-inch stems. The olive green leaves have dark brown markings along the central vein. All veins carry a silver grey pattern. The other side of the leaves is reddish purple. At night the leaves fold upward, resembling hands in prayer. *M. l. kerchoveana* is slightly less spreading; its leaves are more pointed, dark green and have red blotches between the veins.

## Cultivation

Grow in good light out of direct sun. Average room temperature is suitable as long as it is maintained above 16°C. (60°F.).

## Potting

Use a soil mixture of loam, coarse builders' sand, peat moss, rotted or dried manure or leafmould. Drainage is critical so use a generous layer of pebbles or pea gravel over the drainage hole. Repot during spring when roots become compacted.

## Watering

Keep evenly moist; slightly drier over winter. Above average humidity is desirable. Grow young plants over a humidity tray and mist spray foliage with clear water.

## Feeding

During the period April to August, use half strength water soluble general fertilizer on a 14 day schedule.

## Propagation

Only by division at repotting time.

## Special Problems

Essentially trouble-free.

*Maranta leuconeura massangeana*

# MESEMBRYANTHEMUM

*Ice Plant/Sea Fig/Hottentot Fig*

This delightful plant, when allowed to cascade from a hanging basket, will reach a length of one to two feet in one season.

## Origin

Around the turn of the century, explorations in South Africa disclosed that Mesembryanthemum, a genus of the Fig-Marigold family (Aizoaceae), was one of the largest groups of succulents ever discovered. Almost overnight the family grew from 300 species to over 2,000. Botanists then divided the species into 150 genera according to special characteristics of the flowers and fruit. Despite all this botanical reorganization, the average gardener and seed catalogues still use the name Mesembryanthemum (Ice Plant) even though Ice Plant is now officially *Cryophytum crystallinum*. The plants are mostly native to the hot and dry, barren areas of South Africa.

## Description

In the north, plants are tender and are treated as house plants or as annuals in the garden. However, in the Mediterranean area and in Southern California several species have become naturalized in sandy places along the coast. Among the group of trailing Mesembryanthemum the favorites used for ground cover and trailers for hanging baskets and pots are: *M. cryophytum crystallinum* (Ice Plant), a plant with fleshy creeping stems often reaching 3 to 5 feet. The flat fleshy leaves and stems are covered with watery sparkling bubbles resembling ice crystals. While the one-inch white to slightly pink flowers are not particularly striking, the unusual glistening foliage makes it an interesting drapery for hanging basket, a wall or a bank. *M. carpobrotus chilensis* (Sea Fig) is a large trailing, fast growing plant with three sided leaves, bright green, tinged red. The large rosy purple flowers are 4 to 5 inches in diameter. *M. carpobrotus edulis* (Hottentot Fig) is very similar to the Sea Fig but with 4-inch flowers mostly yellow. The fast growing characteristics of the Sea Fig and Hottentot make them valuable for holding drifting sands as well as stabilizing dirt fills and hillside cuts along highways. *M. roseum* which has 2 feet upright stems, greyish leaves and dark pink flowers is the most often seen shrubby kind.

## Cultivation

The culture requirements of Mesembryanthemums vary to some degree since they have a wide spread origin in South Africa. The plants require maximum sunlight, good air circulation and protection from frost.

## Potting

While the trailing types are not difficult to grow in essentially any soil, they will respond to a basic soil mixture of two parts coarse builders' sand, one part well decayed leafmould and one part good garden loam. To achieve even sharper drainage add another part of crushed stone or small gravel. Ensure that the drainage hole in the pot is well covered with broken shard or pea gravel.

## Watering

Don't over water as the danger of rotting is always present. The plant should be kept on the dry side especially during the winter rest period.

## Feeding

During period of growth, fertilize with water soluble fertilizer on a 10 to 14 day schedule.

## Propagation

All types of Mesembryanthemums may be grown from lightly covered seed, which germinates in about two weeks. Cuttings should have a bit of

*Mesembryanthemum*

stem attached. Make cuts with a sharp knife and allow wet ends to dry before inserting in moist sand or vermiculite. Early spring is the best time of year to undertake propagation.

## Special Problems

These species are essentially trouble-free.

# MIMOSA pudica
*Sensitive Plant, Humble Plant, Touch-me-Not*

Mimosa is usually treated as a curiosity of the plant world because its leaves fold when touched or shaken. The leaves also fold during darkness. History reports that it was introduced into China in 1753 by Pierre Nicholas le Chéron d'Incarville, a missionary who achieved imperial favor from the emperor when he presented a plant grown from seed originating in America.

## Origin
Genus Mimosa is a member of the Pea Family (Leguminosae) with nearly 500 species native to the tropical and sub-tropical regions.

## Description
*Mimosa pudica*, from tropical America, is a shrubby, small plant growing from 12 to 30 inches, with woody spiny stems. The feathery compound leaves fold at the slightest touch and with repeated stimulation, the leaf stem also bends down for which it is sometimes called the Humble Plant. Small mauve-pink flower heads, much like small powder puffs, are produced during summer and autumn.

## Cultivation
Grow in semi-sun to semi-shade in average room temperature, preferably at a constant minimum temperature of 20°C. (70°F.). Fresh young plants should be grown annually since older plants become scraggly.

## Potting
Use a mixture of equal parts loam, coarse builders' sand, peat moss and rotted or dried manure. Cover the drainage hole with pebbles or pea gravel. Repot young plants as soon as the root system fills the pot.

## Watering
Keep evenly moist at all times and grow plants over a humidity tray. Mist spray the foliage frequently with clear water to provide extra humidity.

## Feeding
Feed with water soluble general fertilizer on a 14 day schedule.

## Propagation
By seeds sown annually from February to March. The seed germinates in about 8 days. Young plants should receive no pruning.

## Special Problems
Avoid chilling the plant and protect against aphids and red spider mites by spraying with malathion.

*Mimosa pudica*

117

# MONSTERA deliciosa

*Swiss Cheese Plant, Ceriman,*
*Mexican Bread Fruit, Hur-*
*ricane Plant, Fruit Salad Plant*

Probably no plant has been subjected to so much name calling as the *Monstera deliciosa*. It is often referred to as the Swiss Cheese Plant, Ceriman, Mexican Bread Fruit, Hurricane Plant and Fruit Salad Plant. It is even mistakenly called split leaf Philodendron and *Philodendron pertusum* to which it is related.

## Origin

Monstera is a genus of the Arum family (Araceae) and species *deliciosa* is native to Mexico and Guatemala.

## Description

This plant is a tall tropical climber rising far above the jungle floor by attaching its aerial roots to convenient tree trunks. The leathery, cut and ventilated leaves are well designed to withstand the tropical winds. The oblong leaves of Monstera plants can be very wide, often as much as 3 feet across. For this reason only young plants are grown indoors, and even these need lots of space as well as large slabs of bark covered wood or tree fern root for climbing and support. The long aerial roots are cord-like and while many never reach the ground level, most do so, and their tips should be buried in the potting soil. The club-like flower spike rises from a creamy white enveloping leaf about 12 inches long and eventually develops into a cone-like edible fruit which is green in color until it ripens. At that time there is a tinge of yellow, and the outer rind comes off in bits and pieces at a touch. The edible ripened fruit has a flavor between pineapple and banana. Warmth and humidity are required for flowering and fruit production. Since this is a vigorous growing plant, it soon reaches a large pot or tub size. The Monstera's glossy leaves are a bright dark green, almost too good to be true and many say almost too beautiful to be real. New growth is always much lighter in color and makes an effective contrast with the older foliage. All in all, this is a bold impressive plant that is suitable for the home as well as the office.

## Cultivation

Monstera is very tolerant of poor light but responds best to bright light as in an east window. However, it will tolerate a northern exposure and even an interior location. This strong survival characteristic, along with average room temperature and humidity, makes it a natural for the beginning home gardener.

## Potting

The potting mixture should be rich and porous to enable prompt drainage. Use a mixture of equal parts loam, coarse builders' sand, peat moss and rotted or dried manure over a generous layer of pea gravel at the bottom of the pot.

## Watering

Keep the soil evenly moist during periods of growth. During late autumn and early winter months lessen the water supply until about the end of January when the plant will begin to show a renewed growth cycle.

## Feeding

During the summer months, growth is rapid and plenty of water will be required along with a regular ten day supplementary feeding with water soluble general fertilizer.

## Propagation

Propagation is by air layering or stem cuttings in warm moist sand. Young plants are readily available in garden supply stores as well as supermarkets.

## Special Problems

The plant is essentially pest-free, and since the tough leathery foliage will allow frequent wiping and washing, most would-be invaders are readily dislodged.

*Monstera deliciosa*

# MUSA

*Banana*

When plants of outstanding tropical effect are needed especially around indoor swimming pools, nothing can match Musa. This plant is commonly known as Banana and is best described as a tree-like herb since it grows from 5 to over 25 feet tall.

## Origin

Musa is a genus of the Banana family (Musaceae). It was named after Antonio Musa, physician to Octavius Augustus. It is a native to tropical Asia, Africa and Australia and is more or less a food staple in the tropics.

## Description

While Musa looks very much like a tree, there is no woody trunk. The long leaf stocks are wrapped tightly together and as each new leaf appears at the top of the stock, it looks very much like a tightly rolled green cigar. As each leaf emerges it adds further height to the stock and plant. The leaves can be truly gigantic—often 1 to 2 feet wide and 6 to 10 feet long. The banana is one of the oldest known fruits. A medium size banana has about 100 calories and contains vitamins A, B and C. Chemical analysis of the fruit is approximately 75% water, 22% carbohydrate and 1.5% protein.

Of the decorative bred bananas, *Musa enseta* (Abyssinian Banana) is the most widely grown. In the south it may reach 30 to 40 feet in height. *Musa arnoldiana* is a more modest grower reaching only 12 to 15 feet while *Musa cavendishii* may be considered a dwarf at 4 to 6 feet.

## Cultivation

In the north, Musa must be treated as a tender perennial because it can tolerate only the slightest frost. Give the plant full sun year round in a south or west window. Plants may be summered outside during the frost-free months but wind protection should be provided to prevent tearing of the leaves. Tub culture results in considerable dwarfing of the plant and with supplementary feeding it is possible to accelerate or slow down leaf development. A winter temperature of 15°C. (60°F.) is satisfactory.

## Potting

Use an extra rich friable potting mixture such as one part rich loam, one part coarse builders' sand, one part peat moss and two parts compost or rotted or dried manure. Plants should be repotted as soon as roots become compacted. A fairly large plant can be held in a 14-inch tub.

## Watering

Keep the soil evenly moist. Mist spray the leaves with clear water to maintain humidity. During the winter less water is required while the plant is being rested or stored.

## Feeding

During the growing period over summer, supplementary feeding with water soluble general fertilizer may be given as often as twice a week.

## Propagation

Usually from suckers around the base of older plants. They should be separated from the old plant with a piece of root attached. Use a sharp knife. The cuttings should be potted in a 4 or 5-inch pot using the rich potting mixture previously described. Enclose the cuttings in clear plastic bags to maintain a humid atmosphere to encourage rapid growth of new roots. Cuttings are best started in early March.

A few species such as *Musa enseta* may be started from seed. The seed is very hard and the outer casing should have holes filed in it and then soaked in warm water for 48 hours. The seed bed should have a lot of heat to ensure germination which may take up to 50 days. Pot the young plants in a rich potting mixture and keep the night temperature around 21°C. (70°F.).

## Special Problems

This plant is essentially problem-free.

*Musa enseta*

# NARCISSUS
*Daffodils*

It is possible to enjoy Daffodils from mid-winter on, long before the normal time, by forcing indoors in pots.

## Origin

Narcissus are native to Central Europe in the Mediterranean region, eastward through Asia. They are members of the Amaryllis family

(Amaryllidaceae).

## Description

Daffodils are bulbous plants that send up a set of narrow, flat, erect, strap-like leaves, usually 6 to 8. These surround the angular flower stem which, in the case of variety 'King Alfred,' is a bright yellow trumpet-shaped flower or cup surrounded by a set of petals of the same color. There are 11 divisions and 18 sub-divisions of Narcissus as recognized by the International Registry. 'King Alfred' belongs to Division 1, which is the trumpet type. 'King Alfred' was introduced around 1900 and has remained the most popular daffodil of all time. Always select bulbs with care especially for forcing. Select clean healthy bulbs with several growing tips. There are no real bargains in bulbs, so go for the top size since the complete plant and flower is already formed and dormant in the bulb.

## Cultivation

Successful indoor forcing requires well developed roots before light and warmth is provided to start the bulb into growth.

Pot the bulbs in a mixture of equal parts garden loam, coarse builders' sand and peat moss, to achieve a coarse friable mixture that will hold moisture, yet drain thoroughly. No additional fertilizer is required.

Select containers with bottom drainage and cover the drainage hole with pea gravel, broken crockery or charcoal lumps. Fill the container to within 3 inches of the top, place the bulbs in position and cover with more of the soil mixture so that the tips are just showing about half an inch below the rim of the container. Set the container in a pail of water until the soil is thoroughly moist, remove and set aside to drain.

The next step covers a period of two months or so, wherein the bulbs must be kept at a temperature of 2 to 5°C. (36 to 41°F.), moist and in darkness. This may be achieved in a cold frame or basement window well, which is somewhat easier than burying them in the ground for the period. The latter can give some problems if the spot is not well insulated against freezing and early snow. You might try a pot or two in the main part of the kitchen refrigerator, if you can innovate for darkness and moisture requirements. Modern, no-defrost models keep the air Sahara dry, so try a plastic bag cover for protection.

At the end of two months check the pots for root formation. If they are not growing out of the drainage holes by this time, return for another week or so. Once the rooting has occurred, the pots may be removed and placed in a cool dark room with the temperature around 10°C. (50°F.). In about two weeks the buds will be visible and the pots may be brought into a lighted room and gradually into a sunny window.

The Daffodil is a spring plant, so best results are achieved in a room or window temperature around 15°C. (60°F.). Blossoming should occur in about four weeks after removal from darkness. The time interval between removal from darkness to blooms becomes shorter the longer the bulbs are left at the rooting stage and the closer the time to their natural blooming. Bulbs cannot be forced a second time.

## Potting

Use a mixture of equal parts garden loam, coarse builders' sand and peat moss. Cover drainage hole with pea gravel, broken crockery or charcoal lumps. See Cultivation for further potting instructions.

## Watering

The soil must be kept evenly moist at all times from early rooting to faded blossoms.

## Feeding

No additional fertilizer is needed.

## Propagation

Bulbs cannot be forced a second time. Purchase new bulbs from your garden center.

## Special Problems

Daffodils are essentially trouble-free.

# NEPETA hederacea

*Ground Ivy*

This plant makes a nice basket plant and is also useful as ground cover for plants in large pots.

## Origin

Genus Nepeta has over 200 species and is a member of the Mint family (Labiatae).

It is found in the Northern Hemisphere as well as tropical Africa.

## Description

*Nepeta hederacea variegata* is the species most commonly grown. Ground Ivy is a perennial plant with creeping stems that take root at the leaf nodes. It forms a dense mat of roundish deeply notched leaves. The green leaf form is the bane of lawn gardeners. Blue or white flowers are produced in whorls on a short flower stem during spring and summer.

## Cultivation

Grow in full sun and a cool location.

## Potting

Use a soil mixture of equal parts loam, coarse builders' sand, peat moss and rotted or dried manure or compost. Place pebbles or pea gravel over the drainage hole.

## Watering

Keep evenly moist at all times. Will tolerate average room humidity.

## Feeding

During the summer growing season, use water soluble general fertilizer on a 14 day schedule.

## Propagation

Roots readily from stem cuttings in moist sand or vermiculite.

## Special Problems

A tough, problem-free plant.

*Nepeta hederacea*

# NEPHROLEPIS
*Boston Fern*

Ferns are flowerless plants and don't rely on any special season for their appeal but rather on the great beauty of their leaves in their various forms as well as the many subtle shades of green.

## Origin

Nephrolepis is a member of the Fern family (Polypodiaceae). Ferns appear almost everywhere in the world. Some varieties grow north of the Arctic Circle and some at altitudes over 15,000 feet. Ferns flourished on earth thousands of years ago notably during the carboniferous period and supplied a considerable amount of the vegetative matter which later formed the great coal deposits.

## Description

There are literally thousands of varieties of ferns. Boston Fern *(Nephrolepis exaltata bostoniensis)* was first discovered in 1896 as a bud sport of the native Nephrolepis of sub-tropical regions and because of its more attractive leaf formation it immediately took over as the preferred fern for cultivation and decoration. Shortly after this time other sports of *N. exaltata* were discovered and named 'Sotti,' 'Rooseveltii'and 'Whitmannii.' These became much favored house plants at the turn of the century since they prospered in the cool moist conditions of the homes of that period.

## Cultivation

With our central heating and dry air, Boston Fern requires a bit more attention for luxurious growth. Boston Fern must be kept out of the sun. However, it does need a good bright light since it will not prosper in a dark corner of the room. Best growing temperature is 12 to 15°C. (55 to 60°F.) so try to locate the plant in a cool spot. Never place it over a radiator because it objects to heat. Fortunately Boston Fern is reasonably tough and will prosper better than most other types that can only be successfully grown in a terrarium with its controlled atmosphere.

## Potting

While Boston Fern will grow in almost any soil as long it is well drained, the recommended mix is one containing equal parts of fibrous loam, peat moss, leafmould, coarse builders' sand and activated charcoal. Pots should be cleaned inside and out and the drainage holes covered with 1 inch or so of crushed stone to ensure complete drainage. When the fern has completely filled its pot with roots move it to the next size using the soil mix discussed above.

## Watering

Although ferns must be kept constantly moist, their roots will not tolerate soggy wet feet and sour soil finishes them off in no time at all. Water daily with this in mind. The soil should never dry out.

Ferns do require more humidity than most other house plants and it is pretty much a necessity to place them in a tray filled with pebbles and water making certain that the bottom of the pot does not extend below the water line. Regular misting of the fronds with warm water from a mister or salvaged window spray bottle is very beneficial. Mist as often as you wish, the more the better.

*Nephrolepis exaltata bostoniensis*

## Feeding

Boston Fern should receive regular feeding at 10 to 14 day intervals with a water soluble general fertilizer. However, fern roots are easily injured and burned with fertilizer so be sure to water the plant first before applying the solution.

## Propagation

Boston Fern is propagated from runners that develop in all directions from stock plants. The runners are allowed to take root in the soil of a prepared bed and later detached and planted in individual pots. It takes 10 to 14 months to produce a 6-inch pot size plant. Propagation can also take place from spores (primitive seeds) which take somewhat longer. Propagation of ferns in the home is best confined to division of larger plants.

## Special Problems

Brown scraggly foliage will result from a number of conditions; soggy soil, bottom heat, sun scald and location in a traffic area where the foliage is being constantly brushed by passers-by. An infestation of white fly can also bring about this condition. Spray regularly with malathion to prevent such an invasion. When the undersides of fronds show brownish spots in symmetrical rows, don't be alarmed as these are the spore cases and a natural part of a fern's reproductive process.

# NERIUM oleander

*Oleander, Rose Bay*

This old-fashioned evergreen shrub has been cultivated in Western Europe over 300 years. In countries with mild climates, it forms the background of borders and hedges. In this country, it must be grown in pots and tubs for summer flowering both indoors or outside.

## Origin

Genus Nerium is a member of the Dogbane family

(Apocynaceae) and species *oleander* is native to the complete Mediterranean region and especially the moist areas of the Holy Land.

## Description

The evergreen shrub reaches a height of 6 to 12 feet, sometimes to 20 feet in native outdoor plantings. The plant is attractive at all times with its narrow, dark green, leathery leaves that are willow-like in shape and often 8 inches in length. The flowers are borne in terminal clusters during the summer months. The color range is white to dark red with double as well as single flowers 1½ to 3 inches in diameter. In California, the plant is widely grown with irrigation and the long median strip planting of Oleander on the Los Angeles to Riverside Highway is a joy to behold. The profusion of bloom and the delicate scent is enough to convert the world to at least one pot of Oleander. The plant may be trained into a standard form by allowing only one stem to grow to 3 feet or so and removing all side growth below. Once desired height is reached, the center growth is pinch pruned to induce branching in the standard tree form.

## Cultivation

During the growth and flowering period, locate the plant in the sun and average room temperature. Cooler temperatures down to 7 to 10° C. (45 to 50° F.) in bright light are desirable during the resting period between September and March.

The plant is easy to grow if attention is given to resting and pruning of shoots immediately after flowering. Good, well-ripened shoots are necessary for flowering and, for this reason, the plant must receive plenty of light and air. When a plant forms buds which open poorly or not at all, the condition is usually due to imperfect ripening of the wood.

Remove young shoots as they appear underneath the flower buds, otherwise blooms will be hidden by foliage.

## Potting

Use a mixture of equal parts loam, sand and peat moss ensuring adequate drainage by placing shard or pea gravel over drainage hole.

## Watering

During active spring growth and all during the flowering period, plants should receive lots of water. After blooming, the plant should receive less water.

## Feeding

Provide supplementary feeding using water soluble general fertilizer during spring growth and flowering period.

## Propagation

Propagation is usually performed after the flowering period. Good size cuttings are used. They will take root readily in moist sand or vermiculite, or

*Nerium oleander*

even in a bottle of water. After the roots have formed in about three to four weeks, cuttings are potted individually in 4-inch pots. Use a soil mixture of equal parts loam, sand and moss and keep moist. During February or March, active growth will start and young plants should receive lots of water and regular supplementary feeding with water soluble general fertilizer. In late spring move the plant up to a 6-inch pot and, if possible, grow outdoors for the summer. In September, move the plant indoors for a second winter. You can expect the plant to start blooming the following summer.

## Special Problems

The chief problems with Oleander are scale and mealy bugs. The scale may be sponged off with a bit of cotton and soapy water. Spray with malathion to control mealy bugs.

### Caution

A word of caution is in order to point out that all parts of this plant are poisonous—leaves, flowers and stems. Some people have actually been poisoned by using Oleander twigs to hold marshmallows for toasting.

# NIDULARIUM

Nidularium is excellent for planters and north windows.

## Origin

Genus Nidularium, with over 20 species, is a member of the Pineapple family (Bromeliaceae) and native to the rain forests of Brazil.

## Description

This is an epiphytic plant with tightly formed rosettes of prickly margined leaves. Stemless flowers grow from ivy colored bracts in the center of the rosette. Two species provide a good introduction to this genus:

*N. fulgens* with pale green leaves spotted dark green, 12 inches long and 2 inches wide. It produces low, bright colored bracts with white flowers. *N. innocentii* has purple to purplish-black leaves, red-brown flower bracts and white flowers.

## Cultivation

Grow in shade to semi-shade, even in a north window. Average room temperature is satisfactory. A 16°C. (60°F.) nighttime temperature is beneficial during the winter rest period.

## Potting

Plants may be grown on driftwood or old branches by wrapping the base with sphagnum moss and wiring into position. For pot culture, use osmunda fiber, ground bark or very coarse loose leafmould.

## Watering

Keep the rosette filled with water during spring and summer. Use less water during the winter rest. Average room humidity is suitable with occasional mist spraying during spring and summer.

## Feeding

Feed very little, possibly only once during summer with one-quarter strength water soluble general fertilizer.

## Propagation

From basal offsets of the parent plant. Remove with a sharp knife when large enough to handle. After flowering, the parent plant will wither and die, thus it is best to leave at least one offset for replacement.

## Special Problems

A trouble-free plant when grown properly.

*Nidularium innocentii lineata*

# OSMANTHUS fragrans

*Fragrant Olive, Sweet Olive*

A fragrant plant for the indoor gardener.

## Origin

Genus Osmanthus has over 30 species mostly from east Asia. It is a member of the Olive family (Oleaceae).

## Description

Fragrant Olive, *Osmanthus fragrans,* is the most valuable species for pot culture. It grows to 30 feet with elliptic toothed leaves up to 4 inches in length. Small white, half inch, fragrant flowers are borne in clusters almost year round.

## Cultivation

Grow in full sun over winter, semi-shade during summer. Average room temperature is suitable. Rest the plant in late winter around 16°C. (60°F.) to ripen the wood for autumn and winter flowering.

## Potting

Use a soil mix of equal parts loam, builders' sand, peat moss and rotted or dried manure or compost. Place small pebbles or pea gravel over the drainage hole. Don't over-pot this plant and repot only when the root ball is compacted and drainage impaired.

## Watering

Keep evenly moist with less water during the rest period. Above average humidity is desirable. Use a humidity tray for small plants and mist spray the foliage with clear water.

## Feeding

Use water soluble general fertilizer on a 14 day schedule during the growing and flowering period.

## Propagation

Usually from cuttings of half ripened wood taken during summer. Use rooting hormone powder on the cut ends before inserting in moist sand or vermiculite. Maintain humidity and warmth. Seeds take over 12 months to germinate.

## Special Problems

Control mealy bugs with malathion insecticide spray.

*Osmanthus fragrans*

# OXALIS
*Good Luck Plant, Lucky Clover*

Sometimes called the Good Luck Plant because of the clover-like leaves which, along with the flowers, close up at night as well as on dull days, these plants are ideal for hanging baskets or pots.

## Origin

Genus Oxalis is a member of the Wood-Sorrel family (Oxalidaceae). There are over 800 species originating from all continents with the greatest representation coming from South Africa and South America. Francis Masson (1741-1806) is credited with introducing 48 South African species in Kew Gardens around 1772.

## Description

This group of plants grows from bulbs, tubers and sometimes a perennial creeping root stock. The small rounded plants are rarely over 12 inches in height with clover-like leaves borne on long stems as well as small trumpet-like flowers. This plant is commonly grown on the windowsill as well as in hanging baskets and is available in shades of white, pink, red, violet and yellow. Some of the species grown include:
*O. bowiei (bowieana)*, originating from South Africa, is a summer to autumn blooming species with 3 leaves and pink to rose-purple flowers up to 2 inches across.
*O. cernua (pes-caprae)* also from South Africa is spring blooming with 1½ inch showy bright yellow flowers. The three lobed, mottled leaves are borne on 5 inch stems. It is sometimes called Bermuda Buttercup.
*O. crassipes* from South America bears clusters of white or rose-pink flowers on stems up to 18 inches in length. The three part leaves are borne on short stems. It is nearly ever-blooming.
*O. deppei* from Mexico is sometimes called the Good Luck Plant because of the four part leaves. The flowers are red with a yellow throat.
*O. hirta* from South Africa is winter flowering with white, violet or purple flowers. It grows to 12 inches with three lobed leaves.
*O. lasiandra* from Mexico grows to 12 inches and has reddish three lobed leaves and crimson flowers.
*O. rubra* from Brazil grows to 12 inches from a woody root crown. Flowers are dark veined, pink or rose. The leaves are three lobed.

## Cultivation

Oxalis should have full sun to produce abundant flowers. Average room temperature is suitable but the best plants are produced around 16°C. (60°F.). In general, summer flowering species are dormant over winter and vice versa.

## Potting

Use a rich friable soil mixture such as equal parts loam, coarse builders' sand, peat moss and rotted or dried manure or leafmould. Cover the drainage hole with a generous layer of pebbles or pea gravel. Plant 3 or 4 tubers to a 5-inch pot and replant in fresh soil each season. Ever-blooming species need to be repotted each year in late summer or autumn. Trim back to encourage new growth.

## Watering

Keep the soil evenly moist during the growing period. Place the plant in a humidity tray and mist spray the foliage with clear water to maintain humidity.

## Feeding

Apply water soluble general fertilizer on a two week schedule. Alternate with a solution of ammonium sulphate—1 teaspoon to 1 gallon of water to provide a slightly acid condition.

## Propagation

Propagate by division of the tubers or from offsets that increase rapidly. Ever-blooming varieties should be divided in January or February. Seeds planted in February and March germinate and grow rapidly.

## Special Problems

Excessive heat causes the foliage to wilt. Control green fly with an insecticide spray such as malathion.

*Oxalis bowiei*

# PANDANUS veitchii
*Screw-Pine*

A durable and decorative foliage plant.

## Origin
Genus Pandanus has over 500 species and is a member of the Screw-Pine family (Pandanaceae). It is native to Africa and Asia tropics.

## Description
*Pandanus veitchii*, Screw-Pine, is the principal species for pot culture. The long linear leaves, up to 3 feet in length, have marginal spines and are a light green with longitudinal white stripes. Young plants somewhat resemble a Dracaena. This plant was introduced into England from Samoa by John Gould Veitch around 1865.

## Cultivation
Grow in full sunlight during autumn, winter and spring. Diffused sunlight should be provided in summer. Average room temperature is suitable.

## Potting
Use a mixture of equal parts loam, coarse builders' sand, peat moss, rotted or dried manure and leafmould. Cover drainage hole with broken shard, pebbles or pea gravel. Repot when roots become compacted at the beginning of new growth.

## Watering
Keep evenly moist during the growing period mid-winter to summer, less at other times. This plant requires high humidity especially during the growing period. Mist spray frequently with clear water and grow young plants over a humidity tray.

## Feeding
Use water soluble general fertilizer on a 14 day schedule during the growing period.

## Propagation
Suckers that arise from around the base can be removed at repotting time. Cover the cut ends with rooting hormone powder and insert in coarse builders' sand or vermiculite. Use humidity and bottom heat to accelerate the rooting.

## Special Problems
This plant is essentially trouble-free.

*Pandanus veitchii*

128

# PASSIFLORA

*Passion Flower, Passion Vine*

When first discovered by early Spanish explorers in the South American forest, the odd flowers were a source of great wonderment.

## Origin

Passiflora, with its 400 species and with the exception of a few Malayan, Chinese and Australian species, is a native of tropical and sub-tropical America. It is a member of the Passion-Flower family (Passifloraceae).

Legend and superstition has it that the early explorers believed the parts of the plant were emblematic of the crucifixion of Christ and since it was growing in such profusion and climbing on high, it was surely a token that the Indians were to be converted to Christianity. Thus evolved the names Passion Flower and Passion Fruit with nothing to do with libido.

## Description

While the family includes some shrubs and trees, it is chiefly composed of woody evergreen vines, many of which are cultivated, some as curiosities, others for the beauty of the flowers and the dark green three-lobed leaves, and a few for the plum-shaped fruits. The leathery, thin shell of Passion Fruit contains numerous flat edible seeds in a juicy yellowish pulp and is an outstanding source of Vitamins A and C.

A five year old plant in a 10-inch pot can readily cover a 100 square foot area and produce dozens of blooms and a few small fruits. The individual flowers are short lived, lasting only one day before fading. Cut flowers make attractive table arrangements when floated in a decorative dish of water along with a few leaves.

## Cultivation

In Northern climates Passion Flower must be grown as a pot plant. With planning, the plant may be moved outside for the summer months. It may remain in its pot or tub or be planted directly in the ground in prepared soil. Even though Passion Flower becomes more hardy after the first year's growth and will survive temperatures down to -4°C. (25°F.), it really should be rescued in autumn before hard frost. If planted directly in the ground, it should be lifted and returned to a 10 or 12inch pot. Prune back the top growth sufficiently to compensate for any loss of roots and water thoroughly.

You can have the plant in bloom all year but the best practice is to cut back during January and repot in a fresh soil mix to encourage young vigorous growth. A few of the new shoots may be rubbed off as they form to prevent over-crowding. Excessive pinch pruning of the new growth to keep the plant in bounds can be detrimental to flower production.

The vine needs support and this is easily supplied with string to hold the tendrils. The best growing location is a sunny south window but the plant will soon make a total block-out if unrestrained.

## Potting

The plant prospers in a well drained, and rich friable soil. Use a mixture of equal parts loam, coarse builders' sand, peat moss and rotted or dried manure. Provide for prompt drainage with 2 inches or so of pea gravel at the bottom of the pot over the drainage holes.

## Watering

Keep the soil evenly moist during the growing period. With so much foliage, this is a thirsty plant. Frequent mist spraying with clear water is most beneficial.

*Passiflora*

## Feeding

On a regular 10 to 14 day schedule with water soluble general fertilizer during active growth.

## Propagation

Passion Flower is readily grown from seed or from cuttings of young shoots 4 to 6 inches in length taken during the spring months.

## Special Problems

Frequent mist spraying with water from a window spray bottle will discourage red spider mites and provide humidity for this moisture-loving plant.

# PELARGONIUM

*Geranium*

The Geranium (Pelargonium) is one of the most widely cultivated plants in the world. It is grown inside as well as outside with relative ease.

## Origin

Pelargonium, a member of the Geranium family (Geraniaceae), originally came from South Africa and was cultivated in England and Holland as early as 1690. The two original parents of today's bedding geraniums were introduced into England in 1710 and 1714.

## Description

The Geranium has received much development and attention over the past 200 years. The species are numerous and most of them are unknown to the average gardener. However, there are four large familiar groups.
(1) Garden Geranium *(Pelargonium hortorum)* is the most common bedding species with scalloped leaves mostly with zonal markings (horseshoe shaped markings of brownish green). The round clusters of flowers are carried above the leaves and are red, pink and white. They come in various forms—carnation flowered, cactus flowered, etc. There are also tri-colored foliage types such as 'Skies of Italy.'
(2) Ivy Geranium *(Pelargonium peltatum)* a trailing plant currently very popular in hanging planters. The foliage is glossy green sometimes variegated. The stems are more or less zigzag, angled with flowers as colorful and attractive as the bedding types.
(3) Fragrant Leaf Geranium *(Pelargonium crispum, P. graveolens, P. odoratissimum, P. tomentosum)*. The foliage is ornamental and may smell like lemon, apple, rose (often used to flavor jellies), mint, etc. This group is grown chiefly for the foliage fragrance.
(4) Martha Washington *(Pelargonium domesticum)* is another large species and is often referred to as the show or fancy geranium. They grow well in cool night temperatures. They usually bloom in the spring. A temperature below 13°C. (55°F.) is required for flower bud formation.

*Pelargonium hortorum*

## Cultivation

During the winter months Geraniums need full sun to continue blooming, so place them in the sunniest, coolest window preferably 15 to 18°C. (60 to 65°F.). In summer, plants will do well in sunny or semi-sunny locations and may be used outside during the frost-free months. Plants will tolerate the average house humidity of 30%.
To have plants in flower during the latter part of May, established plants or cuttings should be given a hard pinch early in February or a soft pinch during the first part of March.

## Standards

Select two straight cuttings that have just been rooted and start training them into a single stem by pinching out all side shoots. Do not pinch out the terminal or top growth—keep it growing straight up. When the plant is 10 to 12 inches high support it with a 30 to 36-inch bamboo stake, using plant ties of soft cord or cloth. When the plant stem grows to 28 to 30 inches pinch out the top to start branching in the formation of a flowering head. Continue pinch pruning until you get the size and shape required. The plant should be shifted to larger pots as growth progresses until large enough for a final 8 or 10-inch pot. A tree Geranium is as dramatic as a Fuchsia Tree and since it is portable it can become a focal point for any occasion.

## Potting

Plant rooted cuttings in 2¼-inch pots in a coarse friable soil mixture that will give good drainage. A mixture of equal parts loam, builders' sand, and peat moss with a modicum of super phosphate and lime is ideal. When the plants have grown sufficiently to fill the 2¼-inch pot with roots, and just before they become hard root bound, they should be moved into 4-inch pots using the same coarse friable soil mixture. Make certain the drainage hole remains unobstructed so as to provide complete drainage—use pea gravel or shard.

## Watering

Soak, then allow the soil to approach dryness before soaking again. Discard excess water that collects in saucers.

## Feeding

Fertilize regularly with water soluble general fertilizer. After the first blooms appear cut back on nitrogen by using one which is mainly phosphate and potash to assist the plant in producing flowers rather than excessive foliage.

## Propagation

Geraniums may be grown from seed and a 4-inch size plant may be grown in about the same time as from a cutting. Seed of a carefree group of geraniums F-1 hybrids is readily available. Propagation from cuttings is relatively easy and remains the most popular method. During autumn, select at least one plant as a stock plant for next summer's Geranium crop. This can be achieved by feeding the plant regularly with water soluble general fertilizer and encouraging it to grow as tall and leafy as possible. Late in November pinch out the terminal tips of the plant to promote growth of side shoots. Around mid-January stem tip cuttings 3 to 5 inches long may be taken, followed by a second crop of stem cuttings in early February as well as the leaf bud cuttings that are available. These bud cuttings are made by cuttings the stem into sections 1 to 2 inches long. Each section should have one leaf with some growth showing at the juncture of the leaf with the stem. A large pot or box of coarse builders' sand, perlite or a mixture of perlite and peat moss may be used for rooting the cuttings.
After the cuttings are placed they should be well watered and from then on, only sparingly to prevent drying out. Keep out of direct sunlight in a 15°C. (60°F.) temperature and rooting will occur in three to four weeks. If the location is excessively dry, lightly cover the pots or rooting box with clear plastic bags or film to keep high humidity without excessive wetness of the rooting medium. Plant rooted cuttings as described under Potting.

## Special Problems

Pelargoniums are sensitive to gas, even the slightest leakage, which may mean no Geraniums in the kitchen window. Excessive nitrogen or insufficient light may cause weak spindly growth. Browning and dropping of leaves can result from excessive watering as well as insufficient watering, root damage and low humidity. Control aphids with a malathion spray solution.

# PELARGONIUM peltatum

*Ivy Geranium*

Ivy Geraniums are exceedingly showy and floriferous plants and because of their trailing nature they are ideal for hanging containers. The 5 to 8 flower clusters are carried on long stems extending beyond the foliage which gives the plant an elegant, airy feeling—almost like butterflies in flight.

## Origin

The Ivy Geranium, a member of the Geranium family (Geraniaceae), originated in South Africa and came into England at the beginning of the 18th century. Since that time many hybrid forms have been developed.

## Description

The long, trailing, angled stems often reach 4 to 6 feet in just one season. The leaves are thick, smooth, glossy and bright green and rarely more than 2 to 3 inches across. They are five-lobed like English Ivy *(Hedera helix)* and hence the common name Ivy Geranium. The flowers are carried on long stems extending beyond the foliage. The flower head has usually 5 to 8 flowers. The five petals of each flower are nearly equal in length with the two upper petals somewhat broader and usually veined. The color range includes pink, cerise, lavender and white.

## Cultivation

While Ivy Geraniums have been popular for many generations, chiefly because of their endurance in a wide range of growing conditions, responsible attention to the basic needs of the plant will bring forth vigorous growth and lots of flowers. Geraniums are not shade plants; they require full sunlight for at least part of the day and, if possible, for the whole day. Some afternoon shade will help pastel colored flowers to retain their full color. The plant is tolerant of a wide range in temperature but a night temperature of 13 to 18°C. (55 to 65°F.) coupled with a 21°C. (70°F.) daytime temperature is considered the best for maximum development. Plants grown in a window indoors should be turned regularly to keep them evenly balanced. During the dull winter months Ivy Geranium will usually stop flower production but by the end of February they are back and usually better off for the period of rest.

*Pelargonium peltatum*

## Potting

The best soil mixture for this plant is a fairly heavy garden loam that is friable plus enough humus and coarse builders' sand to achieve a soil porous enough to give free drainage of excess moisture.

## Watering

Plants grown indoors may need water every day during the hot summer weather. During dull, cold weather, the plant uses less water and care should be taken not to over-water during such periods.

## Feeding

While the plants are young, care must be taken that the soil is not overly rich, since too much nitrogen and too wet a soil will result in a vegetative plant with excessive leaf growth and few, if any, flowers. Once the plant reaches a 6-inch pot size, a program of supplementary feeding may begin either in dry or liquid form. Select a fertilizer which is low in nitrogen to achieve the most blossoms.

## Propagation

The fastest way to increase stock of Geraniums is by cuttings or slips from old, healthy plants. The cuttings may be taken from the stem or a branch, preferably from a recent mature growth. Old, woody growth does not give good root formation and young, soft growth has a tendency to rot. Cuttings should be made with a sharp clean knife, just below a node or joint. Root the cuttings in a mixture of sand and peat moss, keep in a well lit spot but avoid hot sunshine. Frequent misting with water is beneficial. Roots will form in 2 to 3 weeks and once they are half an inch in length they may be transferred to 2½-inch pots and moved on to larger pots as soon as they become root bound. Plants should bloom in about 11 to 12 weeks from the time the cuttings are started.

## Special Problems

With proper care, Ivy Geranium is essentially trouble-free.

# PELLAEA rotundifolia

*Button Fern, Cliff-brake*

A cliff-brake that grows in limestone rocks, the plant is low growing and spreading.

## Origin

Genus Pellaea, with about 80 species, is a member of the Fern family (Polypodiaceae) with a wide distribution.

## Description

Button Fern, *Pellaea rotundifolia*, from New Zealand, is a small plant growing to about 12 inches. The narrow fronds carry small circular leaves. Of all the species, it is the one most amenable to indoor cultivation.

## Cultivation

Grow in semi-sun to semi-shade in normal room temperatures except over winter when a range of 10 to 16°C. (50 to 60°F.) is desirable.

## Potting

Use a soil mix of equal parts loam, coarse builders' sand and leafmould. Add a modicum of ground limestone. Repot in spring when the plant outgrows the pot. Cover the drainage hole with a generous layer of pebbles and pea gravel as fast drainage is essential.

## Watering

Keep evenly moist in summer with less water over winter; however, the root ball must never become dry. Average room humidity is suitable. Avoid high humidity and do not mist spray the foliage. Never allow the pot to sit in water.

## Feeding

During the period spring to August, use water soluble general fertilizer on a 14 day schedule.

## Propagation

Leaf spores caught in sphagnum moss and germinated around 16 to 18°C. (60 to 65°F.).

## Special Problems

Excessive dryness or excessive humidity can be equally damaging.

*Pellaea rotundifolia*

# PELLIONIA

*Watermelon Begonia, Watermelon Pellionia*
*Satin Pellionia*

Trailing foliage plant for baskets and planters.

## Origin

Genus Pellionia, with around 50 species, is a member of the Nettle family (Urticaceae). The name originates from J. Alphonse Pellion, a French officer in the Freycinet's Expedition to South America and the South Pacific circa 1817.

## Description

Two species are usually grown: *P. daveauana*, Watermelon Begonia or Pellionia, from the rain forest of Burma and Vietnam is a creeping plant with pink stems up to 24 inches in length. The close-set leaves are oblong, up to 2 inches in length, and dark olive green with brownish purple margins and pale green central striping. The undersides have a pinkish cast.
*P. pulchra*, commonly called Satin Pellionia, has green leaves with a blackish brown mid rib and veins. Undersides have a purplish cast.

## Cultivation

Grow in good light, semi-shade, never direct sunlight. Average room temperature is suitable.

## Potting

Use a mixture of equal parts loam, coarse builders' sand, peat moss and rotted or dried manure or compost. Use pebbles or pea gravel over the drainage hole.

## Watering

Water freely in summer, less over winter. Above average humidity is desired. Grow young plants over a humidity tray and mist spray foliage with clear water.

## Feeding

During the period April to August, use water soluble general fertilizer on a 10 day schedule.

## Propagation

Easily propagated at any time from stem cuttings rooted in moist sand or vermiculite.

## Special Problems

Avoid chilling the plant. Control green fly and red spider mites with malathion insecticide spray.

*Pellionia pulchra*

# PEPEROMIA

*Watermelon Begonia/Emerald Ripple/Radiator Plant/Pepper Face, Baby Rubber Plant*

This is an outstanding foliage plant for table, window, planter or terrarium.

## Origin

Genus Peperomia, with literally hundreds of species, is a member of the Pepper family (Piperaceae) with wide distribution in tropical and semi-tropical areas.

## Description

Species that are readily available include: *P. argyreia*, commonly called Watermelon Begonia, is from Brazil. The dark green, ovate leaves have bands of silver between the radiating veins. It grows 6 to 12 inches.

*P. caperata*, commonly called Emerald Ripple, is from Brazil. The leaves are corrugated and glossy dark green. It grows to 6 inches.

*P. maculosa*, commonly called Radiator Plant, from the West Indies has dark green leaves, veined in light green to white and spotted in red. It grows to 12 inches.

*P. obtusifolia*, Pepper Face or Baby Rubber Plant, grows 6 to 12 inches with waxy green 2 to 3-inch ovate, concave leaves. There are several varieties with markings of cream and creamy yellow and bright red. This makes a good plant for dish gardens.

*P. dahestedii (fosteri)* has short, thick, dark green leaves in whorls of three, along slendered red vining stems. It roots readily at the leaf nodes and is sometimes grown as an epiphyte.

## Cultivation

Grow in good light but with no direct sun for any length of time—north or east window year around, west is suitable in winter. Average room temperature is suitable.

## Potting

Use a soil mixture of equal parts loam, coarse builders' sand, peat moss, rotted or dried manure and leafmould. Drainage is critical so use a generous layer of pebbles and pea gravel over the drainage hole.

## Watering

Water with care and allow surface to become dry between watering. Water sparingly during winter. Average room humidity is suitable.

## Feeding

During the period April to August, use water soluble general fertilizer on a 14 day schedule.

## Propagation

Use stem or leaf cuttings placed in moist sand.

## Special Problems

Plants tend to rot in cool, wet conditions.

*Peperomia obtusifolia*

# PERSEA americana

*Avocado*

Avocado, the palm tree of the apartment dweller, can be grown by just about everyone. It tolerates the heat and dry atmosphere of the apartment to an amazing extent. Some plants last for ten years though most are finished in three or four. They are easy to grow and you can always have new plants coming along at regular intervals at no cost since you buy the fruit for guacamole or salad and get the seed free.

## Origin

Avocado *persea americana* is a sub-tropical evergreen native to the West Indies, Mexico, Central America and South America. It has been cultivated for centuries. In fact, the name is a corruption from the Aztec "Ahuacatl."

## Description

Three species of avocado are cultivated. Those originating from the West Indies with large, tender fuits that ripen in summer and autumn; the Guatemalan variety with large fruit that ripens in winter and spring, while the somewhat smaller Mexican type ripens from late spring to early autumn. Thus you will get some variation from one species to the other and the time of year will roughly determine which is destined to become your apartment palm.

Out of doors in southern climates, Avocado makes a tall beautiful shade tree often reaching 50 to 100 feet tall. From a dietary point of view Avocado contains nine vitamins, is low in carbohydrates and over 90% of its oil is unsaturated, digestable fatty acid. The oil content may vary as much as 5 to 20% depending upon the species.

So if you buy an Avocado to start a plant, don't overlook the nutritious value of the fruit and of course, the rich buttery nut-like flavor. Use lemon or lime juice on the prepared fruit to prevent darkening.

*Persea americana*

---

## Cultivation

Grow plant in a warm sunny location. See Propagation for starting plant.

## Potting

Use a 6 to 10-inch pot with a generous covering of crushed stone or shard over the drainage hole. A mixture of equal parts builders' sand, rich loam, peat moss and rotted cow manure or compost is ideal.

See Propagation for potting method.

## Watering

Water regularly to maintain the soil in a just moist condition.

## Feeding

Regular feeding with water soluble fertilizer will keep the plant in full foliage. Use a general water soluble fertilizer for this purpose.

## Propagation

There are two basic methods for starting a plant. Both call for removal of the seed from the surrounding oily flesh and stripping off the paper brown covering. Prior to this the fruit should stay at room temperature for a few days until it is soft and ripe, especially if it is hard at the time of purchase. Cut the fruit in half with care so as not to damage the seed. Remove the seed from the oily meat and wash with tepid water. You will note the paper brown covering which will have to be removed either at the time of washing when it will often slide right off or by soaking overnight or sometimes by allowing it to sit for a day so that the brown skin becomes dry enough to peel off. Don't use a knife or peeler in this operation, it might damage the seed. Once the covering is removed wash the pit again to remove any traces of covering and the oily flesh that might encourage early decay.

### Toothpick Method

Place three or four wooden toothpicks into the seed about one-third to one-half the distance down from the pointed end. This you can gauge from the size and shape of the seed. Position the peeled seed over a wide mouth glass so that the flat end is pointing downward. Add a piece of activated charcoal to the glass and fill with warm water so that the bottom one-third of the seed is submerged in water. Set the planting aside in a convenient dark spot, since you will need to change the water at least once a week. A kitchen cupboard or under the sink are both likely spots providing the glass won't be tipped over. Roots may begin to show as early as one week. However, it may take as long as two months so be patient. If the pit starts to show signs of rotting throw it out and start over. Soon a small sprout will start to show at the pointed end and it will grow very rapidly. When it reaches 6 to 8 inches in height cut it back one-half with a sharp knife. Return to the dark for a further two or three weeks during which period the roots will become stronger and will be more plentiful and a new shoot will start out either from the cut back sprout or an entirely new one will appear directly from the seed. This early cutting back or pruning ensures a much bushier plant rather than one that will look like a bean pole. The young plant is now ready to be placed in soil.

Use a 10-inch pot with a generous covering of crushed stone or shard over the drainage hole. Fill the pot about one-half with a rich friable soil mixture. A mixture of equal parts builders' sand, rich loam, peat moss and rotted cow manure or compost is ideal. Now remove the rooted seed from the glass and remove the toothpicks if they come out readily, otherwise leave them in place. Remember the roots are extremely brittle, don't force the roots into the soil, hold them around the soil level in the pot and gently add soil by hand under and around. Don't pack—the roots will be squashed. Keep adding soil until the top third of the seed remains above soil level. Now water thoroughly with tepid water to compact the soil around the roots. You will need to add more soil to keep the seed two-thirds covered.

### Pot Method

This procedure calls for planting the seed directly into a 6-inch pot using the rich friable soil mix as described previously. Don't forget the layer of crushed stone over the drainage hole. The seed is positioned and firmed into the soil so that the pointed end is just above soil level. Place the pot with your other house plants in good light and keep moist. As long as the seed stays pink and firm keep on watering. If it starts to shrivel and turn black you have lost the plant so start over again with a fresh seed. Avocado plants thrive best in full sunshine, with regular watering to maintain the soil in a just moist condition.

## Special Problems

This plant is essentially free of insects and diseases.

135

# PHALAENOPSIS
*Moth Orchids*

Moth Orchids make breathtaking house plants.

## Origin
Genus Phalaenopsis, with over 35 species, is native to tropical Asia and Australia. It is a member of the Orchid family (Orchidaceae).

## Description
This epiphytic plant, *Phalaenopsis lueddemanniana,* has no pseudobulbs and is classed as monopodial. The leaves are about 12 inches in length. The flower spike is often branched and carries yellowish white flowers with cinnamon and amethyst markings. It is native to the Philippines. Flowering occurs in spring and summer and with care it may be kept in flower for 10 months.
*Phalaenopsis equestris* (formerly *Phalaenopsis rosea*) has 8·inch oblong leaves and produces up to 14 flowers on a 12·inch flower stalk (scape). The flower petals are white with a blush and tinge of rose-pink.

## Cultivation
Grow in a semi-sunny location in average room temperature.

## Potting
Use Osmunda fiber or shredded bark in clay pots one-third filled with pebbles or pea gravel. Repot every two years.

## Watering
The potting material must be kept evenly moist at all times since there are no pseudobulbs. Relative humidity of 70% is required.

## Feeding
Replace watering with a 1/10th strength water soluble general fertilizer.

## Propagation
By division at the time of repotting.

## Special Problems
Stagnant air can induce attacks of fungi. Pruning of flower spikes can reduce flowers. Remove faded flowers with very little stem. Allow main flowering spike to remain until it withers and dies.

*Phalaenopsis equestris*

# PHILODENDRON selloum
*Philodendron, Lacy Tree*

Growing where there is more shade than sunshine is what the Philodendron does best and this could be its major attribute for interior decoration if it were not for its leathery, attractive foliage.

## Origin

Philodendron has over 250 species all of which are native to the jungles of Central and South America. It is a member of the Arum family (Araceae). Species *P. selloum* is native to Brazil.

## Description

*Philodendron selloum* belongs to the non-climbing self-heading group of Philodendrons. Rather than growing up, it grows out, and in the process eventually requires a lot of room to accommodate the handsome 3-foot, dark green, deeply notched leaves that are held on 3 to 4-foot stems. Strong aerial roots are produced on older plants.

## Cultivation

This plant is very tolerant of dim light, average room temperature and humidity. Frequent misting and wiping of the leaves with clear water will encourage luxurious growth. Direct aerial roots into the potting soil.

## Potting

Use a rich friable soil mixture of equal parts loam, coarse builders' sand, peat moss and rotted or dried manure or compost. Use a generous layer of pea gravel or broken shard at the bottom of the pot. Repot to a larger size when roots become cramped. When a 12 or 14-inch size pot is reached, root prune every second or third year by removing a slice of root from one side only and returning to the same container. Fill space with potting mix.

## Watering

Soak, then allow plant to approach dryness. More water is required during summer.

## Feeding

Feed every 10 to 14 days during the summer growth period. Use water soluble general fertilizer.

## Propagation

*P. selloum* is propagated from off-shoots of the main plant. Root in coarse moist sand or vermiculite at 21 to 27°C. (70 to 80°F.).

## Special Problems

This is a durable trouble-free plant. Extended dryness may cause browning of leaf edges.

*Philodendron selloum*

# PHOENIX
*Date Palm*

Phoenix is one of the showiest and most graceful palms to grow indoors.

## Origin

Genus Phoenix, with 15 or more species, is a member of the Palm family (Palmaceae), all native to the tropics and sub-tropics of Africa and Asia.

## Description

Date Palm, *P. dactylifera*, from North Africa is grown commercially for fruit. It is a single stemmed plant that grows to 100 feet with a slender trunk. Multi-leaved, arching fronds reach up to 20 feet in length. Many gardeners have started their own plants from fresh un-pasteurized date stones rescued from the kitchen scraps.

*P. roebelenii* is a miniature plant growing to 6 feet with a slender roughened trunk. The multi-leaved fronds grow up to 4 feet in length.

## Cultivation

Grow *P. dactylifera* in full sun. *P. roebelenii* requires less sun. Average room temperature is suitable. Best winter temperature for *P. dactylifera* is around 10°C. (50°F.) and *P. roebelenii* not below 16°C. (60°F.).

## Potting

Use a mixture of equal parts loam, builders' sand, peat moss and rotted or dried manure. Use a generous layer of shard, pebbles or pea gravel over the drainage hole. Repot with care because of the delicate root system and only when the roots have become compacted. This becomes evident when water applied at the top takes a long time to soak in and drain away.

## Watering

Water is best supplied by soaking the root ball and allowing it to approach dryness before soaking again. Average room humidity is suitable. Occasionally wipe the foliage with a soft wet cloth.

## Feeding

Use one-half strength water soluble general fertilizer on a 10 day schedule from spring to August.

## Propagation

From seeds that take 50 to 60 days to germinate. Bottom heat of 24 to 27°C. (75 to 80°F.) should be used. Also from basal offshoots that may be separated and planted when large enough to handle.

## Special Problems

Red spider mites and scale can be controlled with malathion insecticide. Use a cotton swab moistened in rubbing alcohol to control individual pests.

*Phoenix roebelenii*

# PHYLLITIS scolopendrium

*Hart's Tongue Fern*

This plant, set in a decorative container to show off its beautiful shiny bright green fronds, makes an exquisite centerpiece.

## Origin

Genus Phyllitis, with 8 species, and a member of the Fern family (Polypodiaceae), is found in tropical and temperate regions.

## Description

*Phyllitis scolopendrium*, Hart's Tongue Fern, is a rare small fern found in America as far North as Owen Sound, Canada. It is evergreen and winter hardy with straight, sometimes wavy, shiny leaves 10 to 15 inches long and up to 3 inches wide. A well grown tuft may have 50 or more leaves.

## Cultivation

Grow in shade in a cool room. In winter grow in the range of 7 to 10°C. (45 to 50°F.).

## Potting

Use a mixture of loam, builders' sand, and peat moss. Incorporate chopped activated charcoal and a modicum of bonemeal. Repotting should be undertaken in spring.

## Watering

Keep evenly moist. Wet soggy conditions can induce root rot. Never allow the pot to stand in water. Frequent mist spraying of the leaves will help provide the extra humidity required by this fern.

## Feeding

Use only a weak solution of water soluble general fertilizer during the summer months.

## Propagation

From ripe spores caught in sphagnum or peat moss and germinated under humid warm conditions. Also from leaf stems with a small section of root stock attached.

## Special Problems

Essentially pest-free. Excessive heat and dryness can destroy the plant.

*Phyllitis scolopendrium*

# PILEA

*Artillery Plant/Aluminum or
Watermelon Plant/Creeping
Charlie*

The various species of Pilea make excellent additions to any house plant collection.

## Origin

The genus Pilea is readily recognized in two of its more than 150 tropical species, namely Artillery Plant and Aluminum Plant. The genus is a member of the Nettle family (Urticaceae) and has a few nasty relatives such as Stinging Nettle.

## Description

Plants tend to become a bit straggly and weedy, so it is best to keep young plants coming along.

Artillery Plant, *Pilea microphylla* is a branchy plant that will reach about a foot in height. The graceful curving branches, covered with one-quarter inch oval shaped light green leaves give the plant a lush fern-like appearance. When kept in partial shade it produces small, inconspicuous flowers. When mature, these discharge puffs of pollen that are quite visible. It makes an attractive addition to a house plant collection by providing green trim in and around the other potted plants. Artillery Plant is native to the West Indies, Mexico and South America.

Creeping Charlie, *Pilea nummulariifolia*, found from the West Indies to Peru, is a tender perennial with creeping stems that root at the joints. While it will overhang the edges of a pot, it doesn't quite qualify as a hanging basket plant. The leaves are small and bright green. It is a good plant for dish gardens and terrariums.

Aluminum Plant sometimes called Watermelon, *Pilea cadierei* was discovered in Vietnam in the mid-thirties and introduced into France. It is a well branched, upright, bushy plant if kept pinch pruned while young. The bright green, quilted leaves are oval and about 5 inches long with rows of bright silver marks which account for the common name.

## Cultivation

Pilea should be located in a bright, semi-shade location with a temperature range of 15 to 21°C. (60 to 70°F.). Extra humidity should be provided by mist spraying the foliage with clear water and placing pots in trays or saucers containing crushed stone or pea gravel and filled with water. The bottom of the pot must be kept above the water level.

## Potting

The potting soil should be a rich well drained mixture such as equal parts rich loam, coarse builders' sand, peat moss and rotted or dried manure. Cover the drainage hole with an inch or so of broken shard or pea gravel.

## Watering

Plants should be watered regularly to keep the soil evenly moist.

## Feeding

During spring to late summer, feed the plants on a 10 day schedule with water soluble fertilizer.

## Propagation

Plants propagate readily by division, cuttings rooted in a glass of water, or in a pot of coarse moist sand which may be enclosed in a clear plastic bag to maintain humidity during rooting.

## Special Problems

This plant is essentially problem-free. Drafts and cold below 13°C. (55°F.) will destroy the plant. Control pests with malathion spray.

*Pilea cadierei*

# PITTOSPORUM tobira

*Mock-orange, Australian Laurel*

This makes a good tub plant or can be trained into a miniature tree.

## Origin

Genus Pittosporum, with about 100 species, is a member of the Pittosporum family (Pittosporaceae) and native to the old world tropics, especially Australia.

## Description

*Pittosporum tobira,* the favorite for pot culture, is native to China and Japan. It is a 6 to 10 foot evergreen shrub with shiny dark green, leathery leaves that grow to 4 inches. From May to summer, fragrant white to creamy-white flowers are produced in clusters. Variety 'Variegata' has leaves marked in white.

## Cultivation

Grow in good light, sun to semi-sun. Average room temperature is suitable. Lower winter temperature 13 to 16°C. (55 to 60°F.) is preferable.

## Potting

Use equal parts loam, builders' sand and peat moss. Place small pebbles over the drainage hole.

## Watering

Keep soil evenly moist. Less water is required during the rest period. Higher than normal room humidity is needed; mist spray foliage with clear water as often as possible and grow young plants over a humidity tray.

## Feeding

Use water soluble general fertilizer on a 14 day schedule during the growing and flowering period.

## Propagation

Use cuttings of half ripened wood taken in spring. Dip ends in rooting hormone powder and place in moist sand and vermiculite with humidity and warmth.

## Special Problems

Control spider mites and mealy bugs with malathion insecticide.

*Pittosporum tobira*

# PLATYCERIUM bifurcatum

*Staghorn Fern*

Ferns are grown primarily for the great beauty of their leaves. They are non-flowering plants and grow from spores rather than seeds. Nature has developed ferns in a wide variety of forms, shapes and sizes which vary from hair-like creeping stems with moss-like leaves, to tree ferns 40 feet or more in height.

## Origin

The Staghorn Fern is native to Australia, New Guinea through to Malaya and is a member of the Fern family (Polypodiaceae).

## Description

Staghorn Fern might be considered an abnormal genus with its epiphytic (air plant) nature and two distinct types of fronds. This is a tropical fern and is found on the trunks of trees and old plants where it often grows into enormous nests. The kidney-shaped brown fronds appear as rounded discs that fasten closely to the tree trunk or other support on which the fern is growing. The greyish dark green fertile, or spore bearing fronds, hang down and look like antlers. They will often reach 2 to 3 feet in length on a well grown specimen.

## Cultivation

The species *P. bifurcatum* (formerly called *alcicorne*) is the easiest one for home cultivation since it can take night temperatures in the 4 to 10°C. (40 to 50°F.) range. The plant enjoys a moist atmosphere so regular syringing with water is needed during the summer growing period. Since a modest rest is in order during the winter when the plant is indoors, it needs less humidity and syringing. Perfect drainage is a must at all times and for this reason, as well as for appearance, the fern is best grown vertically mounted on a board so that the antler-like fronds hang down.

## Potting

To plant, bore a 1-inch hole through a slab of bark covered wood or fern tree root, pack with sphagnum moss and place a substantial wad of the moss at the back of the board. This may be held in place with a piece of non-rusting aluminum window screening stapled firmly in place. Incorporate some bone meal and charcoal with the moss for food and drainage. Separate a young plant from the parent and hold in place with a wire hair pin until such time as the circular barren frond forms its own attachment to the board and moss. The plant also grows well in a hanging basket firmly packed with sphagnum moss, plus some bone meal and charcoal. A little extra moss may be added every second year. The circular barren fronds will completely cover the board or basket and there eventually will be a full complement of drooping antlers. The plant may be left undisturbed for years.

## Watering

Syringe the leaves frequently especially during the summer growing period.

*Platycerium bifurcatum*

## Feeding

From March to September use a water soluble general fertilizer solution at half strength on a weekly basis.

## Propagation

Propagate by removing offsets at any time—root in moist osmunda and keep humidity high.

## Special Problems

Essentially problem-free if mist spraying of the leaves is maintained.

142

# PLECTRANTHUS
*Prostrate Coleus*

These plants are seldom seen but certainly worth seeking out.

## Origin
Genus Plectranthus is a member of the Mint family (Labiatae). There are over 250 species native to tropical regions of the world.

## Description
*P. fruticosus* is an erect evergreen shrub growing to 3 feet or more. The 4-inch leaves are broadly ovate, hairy and serrated. Lots of erect flower spikes with pale blue flowers are borne from October into winter.
*P. oertendahlii,* sometimes called Prostrate Coleus, is a creeping trailing species suitable for ground cover or hanging baskets. The white marked foliage grows to 2½ inches and is somewhat circular. Flower spikes carry white to pinkish flowers.

## Cultivation
Grow in semi-sun to semi-shade in average room temperature on the cool side.

## Potting
Use a mixture of equal parts loam, builders' sand, peat moss and rotted or dried manure. Provide drainage with a layer of pebbles or pea gravel over the drainage hole. Repot when roots become compacted.

## Watering
Keep evenly moist. This plant will tolerate dry air.

## Feeding
Use water soluble general fertilizer on a 14 day schedule during the growing and flowering period.

## Propagation
From seeds sown in February or stem cuttings at any time, rooted in moist sand or vermiculite.

## Special Problems
Control white fly, mealy bug and aphids with malathion insecticide spray.

*Plectranthus oertendahlii*

143

# PODOCARPUS

*Southern Yew*

One method of escaping the instant synthetic Christmas tree syndrome is to grow an evergreen that will tolerate indoor conditions.

## Origin

The Podocarpus, a member of the Yew family (Taxaceae), is an evergreen tree native to the sub-tropical regions of Asia, Australia and South America.

## Description

*P. macrophyllus,* 'Maki,' the oriental species, is most commonly offered. It is native to Japan where it grows 50 to 60 feet high with horizontally spreading and drooping branches that are covered with narrow dark green glossy leaves in a dense spiral arrangement. The individual leaves are 3 to 4 inches long and at least $1/3$-inch wide. In the south, Podocarpus is grown as an evergreen shrub much the same way as Yew is used in landscape planting in the north.

*Podocarpus nivalis* forms a multi-branched shrub or small tree up to 15 feet with spreading branches. The dark green leaves are $1/2$ to $3/4$ inch in length. This species is native to New Zealand and Australia.

## Cultivation

A specimen may be grown in a 12 x 12-inch sturdy container to reach 6 feet in ten years and at no point be over 24 inches in diameter. Prune new growth to maintain shape and size. From mid-May to mid-September, the plant may occupy a semi-shaded spot on the patio. Inside in the winter, it should have a brightly lit spot in average room temperature and a humidity of at least 30%.

## Potting

Use a rich soil mixture of equal parts loam, coarse builders' sand, peat moss, rotted or dried manure or compost. Cover drainage holes in the container with at least one inch of pea gravel or broken shard. Repot young plants as soon as the roots fill the container. Hold the plant to final size by root pruning a slice from alternate sides every second year, and replacing the soil with the mixture discussed previously.

## Watering

Soak and allow to approach dryness before soaking again.

## Feeding

Use water soluble general fertilizer during the spring and summer growing periods.

## Propagation

Use cuttings of half ripened stems 4 to 6 inches in length dipped in rooting hormone powder then placed in moist sand. Enclose in a plastic bag and maintain a temperature of 21 to 24° C. (70 to 75° F.).

## Special Problems

Essentially none. Dust the foliage occasionally in the shower or use a moist soft cloth.

*Podocarpus nivalis*

144

# PODOCARPUS
*Southern Yew, Buddist Pine*

Grown as a tub plant, this makes a compact indoor shrub.

## Origin
Genus Polyscias, with over 70 species, and a member of the Ginseng family (Araliaceae), is native to tropical Asia.

## Description
*P. balfouriana*, Balfour Aralia, is the species most commonly used for pot and tub culture. In its native habitat of New Caladonia it is a 25 foot tree. As a tub plant it makes a compact shrub of 6 feet. Stems are pale green with dark stripes. The evergreen, 2 to 4-inch leaves are somewhat circular and scalloped. Variety 'Marginata' has white margined leaves.

## Cultivation
Grow in good light but out of direct sun. Average room temperature is suitable.

## Potting
Use a soil mixture of equal parts loam, coarse builders' sand, peat moss and rotted or dried manure or compost. Cover the drainage hole with a generous layer of pebbles or pea gravel.

## Watering
Keep evenly moist. This is a high humidity plant. Grow young plants over a humidity tray and frequent mist spraying of the foliage with clear water is required.

## Feeding
Use water soluble general fertilizer on a 14 day schedule during the summer growing period.

## Propagation
Use cuttings of mature wood in spring. Dip cut ends in rooting hormone powder and insert in moist sand or vermiculite. Maintain humidity and warmth.

## Special Problems
Control scale and red spider mites with malathion spray, especially in winter.

*Polyscias balfouriana*

145

# PRIMULA

*Fairy Primrose / Poison Primrose / Chinese Primrose*

*Primula malacoides*, Fairy Primrose, is an old-fashioned house plant that gives a note of cheer during winter and early spring. It must be grown in cool temperatures.

## Origin

Native to China, it was introduced into Europe around 1908. *Primula malacoides* is a member of the Primrose family (Primulaceae) which has 28 genera and over 320 species.

## Description

Fairy Primrose grows 8 to 20 inches high with pale green leaves and Hyacinth-like flower spikes with the flowers borne in tiers or whorls. The 3-inch oval-shaped leaves grow in rosettes from the base of the plant and are held on 3 to 6-inch stems. The flowers come in many shades of pink and lilac as well as glistening white. Individual flowers measure 3/8 to 1/2 inch across.

Other species grown as house plants include: *Primula obconica*, sometimes known as the Poison Primrose since many people are allergic to the foliage and develop a rash similar to that of poison ivy and *Primula sinensis*, the fringed Chinese Primrose introduced into Europe from Chinese gardens around 1820.

## Cultivation

Grown in medium intensity light. For an extended blooming period, remove faded flowers as they appear to prevent seed formation. If possible, move outdoors in the summer to a cool, semi-shaded location. Return the plants inside by the middle of September and grow in cool temperatures, the most desirable range being 16°C. (60°F.) by day and 7°C. (45°F.) by night.

Plants are normally discarded after flowering to be replaced by a new crop but it is possible in spring, after flowering, to transfer the plant to a rockery in a shaded location where it may continue to grow all summer. During late autumn if it is lifted and potted it should continue to grow and flower indoors as before.

## Potting

When seedlings are of sufficient size (3 leaves) prepare individual 2 to 3 inch pots using a rich potting mixture of equal parts sand, leafmould, peat moss and rotted or dried manure. Set the crown of the plant even with the soil. Do not allow young plants to become root bound. Move on to the next size pot as quickly as possible ending with a 5 or 6-inch pot.

## Watering

Primulas require a moist, well drained soil and must never be allowed to become dry.

## Feeding

Once plants are underway, supplementary feeding with water soluble general fertilizer may begin on a 10 to 14 day schedule.

## Propagation

Primrose seed is very fine and is usually sown between January and March in well drained shallow pans filled with a sieved mixture of equal parts builders' sand and leafmould. Fill the pan to within 1/8 inch of the top and sow the seeds thinly and evenly over the surface. Dust on a thin covering of the seed bed mixture, moisten thoroughly from the bottom and cover with a sheet of glass rather than plastic film. Germination takes up to 20 days at a temperature of 16°C. (60°F.). The glass should be removed upon germination. Keep the seed bed moist and in about two to three weeks the seedlings will be of sufficient size (3 leaves) to move to individual 2 to 3 inch pots using a rich potting mixture of equal parts builders' sand, leafmould, peat moss and rotted or dried manure. Care must be taken to set the crown of the plant even with the soil as too deep may cause rot while too shallow may cause toppling of the mature plant and necessitate staking.

## Special Problems

Red spider mites sometimes attack Primulas. If caught early enough, mist spraying with clear water should put an end to them. Severe infestations will require frequent spraying with malathion which will kill the adults but not the eggs. Give frequent sprayings to catch the young as they hatch before they are mature enough to lay a new batch of eggs. Use a suitable size carton placed on its side to hold a plant during spraying to help contain the over-spray.

Damp-off can be troublesome for young plants. Sterile soil and ventilation are good preventatives. Drench the soil with a proprietary solution of 8 Hydroxyquinoline Benzoate to control damp-off fungi.

*Primula malacoides*

# PUNICA granatum nana
*Dwarf Pomegranate*

A mystical plant long involved in Mediterranean culture from the time of ancient Egypt and Babylonia.

## Origin

Genus Punica, with two species, is the only genus of the Pomegranate family (Punicaceae).

## Description

Dwarf Promegranate, *Punica granatum nana,* is the usual species for pot culture. This plant is a dwarf compact shrub that can reach 6 feet. The deciduous leaves are bright green and from 3/4 to 1 1/2 inches in length. Young plants will produce one-inch red-orange flowers during summer. Several hybrids are available with larger, as well as double, flowers.

## Cultivation

Grow indoors in a sunny location in average room temperature. Out of doors in summer, grow in a sheltered sunny location. After leaf drop, store the plant in a light cool location where the temperature does not fall below 4°C. (40°F.).

## Potting

Use a mixture of loam, coarse builders' sand, peat moss and rotted or dried manure or compost. Provide drainage with a layer of pebbles or pea gravel over the drainage hole.

## Watering

Keep evenly moist; use less water during the winter rest. Average room humidity with occasional mist spraying with clear water is beneficial.

## Feeding

Apply water soluble general fertilizer on a 14 day schedule during the growing season, spring to autumn.

## Propagation

By seed. Also by hard wood cuttings in spring or soft wood cuttings in summer. Apply rooting hormone powder to the cut ends and insert in moist sand or vermiculite.

## Special Problems

Essentially trouble-free.

*Punica granatum nana*

# RHIPSALIS baccifera

*Mistletoe Cactus*

An epiphytic tree dwelling cactus is delightful in a hanging basket.

## Origin

Genus Rhipsalis is a member of the Cactus Family (Cactaceae). Species *R. baccifera* sometimes identified as *R. cassutha* is one of about 60 species. While Cacti are native to the Americas, Rhipsalis is an exception and is found in Africa and Ceylon.

## Description

Mistletoe Cactus was found growing on trees or rocks, hanging in many strands 3 to 30 feet in length. The cylindrical branching stems are about 1/4 inch in diameter. Stems are rarely spined and bristly only when young. In spring small white flowers are borne laterally along the stems and ripen into white mistletoe-like fruit bearing about 20 seeds.

## Cultivation

Grow in a semi-sunny location in average room temperature. A cooler winter temperature around 16°C. (60°F.) during the resting period is beneficial.

## Potting

Use a mixture of equal parts loam, coarse builders' sand and leafmould. Drainage is vital—use a generous amount of broken crock, pebbles or pea gravel over the drainage hole or at the bottom of the hanging basket. Repotting is rarely needed.

## Watering

Keep evenly moist during the summer growing period. In winter water only enough to prevent wrinkling of the stem tissues. Mist spraying with clear water is beneficial.

## Feeding

Use water soluble general fertilizer on a 14 day schedule during summer.

## Propagation

Readily from seeds or stem cuttings. Set cuttings aside for a week to form a callus over the cut end, then root in moist sand in bright light.

## Special Problems

Essentially trouble-free when properly grown. Excessive wetness may induce rot.

*Rhipsalis baccifera*

# RHOEO spathacea

*Moses-in-the-Cradle, Boat Lily*

Small white flowers are produced in a boat-shaped flower spathe.

## Origin

Genus Rhoeo, with only one species, is a member of the Spiderwort family (Commelinaceae) and native to the West Indies and Mexico.

## Description

*Rhoeo spathacea*, Moses-in-the-Cradle, is a short stemmed plant growing to one foot with crowded basal leaves that are lance shaped up to 12 inches long and 3 inches wide. The leaves are dark green above and purple below. Variety 'Vittata' has pale yellow, lengthwise stripes on the upper leaf surface.

## Cultivation

During summer grow in a semi-shady location. Use full sun in winter. Average room temperature is suitable.

## Potting

Use a mixture of loam, coarse builders' sand, peat moss and rotted or dried manure or compost. Cover the drainage hole with pebbles or pea gravel. Root growth is rapid; repot to larger size as soon as the root ball fills the container.

## Watering

Keep evenly moist with slightly less water over winter. Normal room humidity is acceptable. Mist spray leaves occasionally with clear water.

## Feeding

During the period March to August, fertilize on a 10 day schedule with water soluble general fertilizer.

## Propagation

Use basal side shoots 3 to 4 inches. Root in moist sand.

## Special Problems

Avoid excessive dryness. Control red spider mites with malathion insecticide.

*Rhoeo spathacea*

# ROSA
*Miniature Roses*

Rose enthusiasts can extend their gardening season by growing miniature roses in a cool sunny window. These potted plants are popular gifts at Easter and Mother's Day.

## Origin

Originally brought to Europe from China during the 1700's, the first mention of miniature roses in literature was in the early 1800's when Pom Pom de Paree *(Rosa semperflorens)*, with small double pink flowers, was widely sold as a pot plant in France. British rose gardeners used it extensively around 1850. After having disappeared by the turn of the century, miniature roses were rediscovered growing in window pots in the Swiss Alps. The discovery was made by Major Roulett around 1915. This plant *(Rosa chinensis minima)*, with rosy pink flowers, is considered a mutant of *Rosa semperflorens* and is now identified as *Rosa rouletti*.

## Description

Miniature roses grow from 6 to 15 inches high with individual 1/2 to 2-inch flowers that are duplicates of hybrid teas, except for size. Modern pot roses all trace lineage to *R. rouletti* and include such varieties as 'Rosina' (Josephine Wheatcroft), 1951, with small semi-double clear bright yellow flowers on a dwarf compact plant 8 to 12 inches. 'Coralin,' 1956, with double flowers, turkey red with an orange sheen on a 15-inch plant. 'Mr. Bluebird,' 1960, with small semi-double flowers, lavender blue in color grows about 15 inches. 'Starina,' 1965, grows to 10 inches with vivid orange scarlet double flowers. 'Tom Thumb,' 1936, the first of the modern miniatures, grows to 6 inches producing deep crimson flowers with a white base.

## Cultivation

Roses need a sunny location where the temperature will not exceed 21°C. (70°F. for any lengthy period. A night temperature of 15°C. (60°F.) produces the most robust plant. Normally, miniature roses drop their leaves and go dormant during late autumn and early winter. During this time, pot growth should be cut back one-half to two-thirds and the plant stored in a cool, frost-free place around 4°C. (40°F.). The plant may be returned to light and warmth in January to start new growth. Plants may be kept in active growth throughout the year by providing artificial lighting during autumn and winter. Use fluorescent lights and keep plants 6 to 8 inches below the bulbs. Schedule a 15 to 16 hour period of lighting for each day.

If you wish you may summer your plants outside. In late May the pots may be sunk to their rims in a sunny garden location. Watering and feeding must be maintained. In autumn the plant may be removed from the pot and all loose soil gently removed from the root ball. Return the plant to a fresh clean pot and firmly pack fresh potting soil around the roots, a small amount at a time. Prune back the stems one-half to two-thirds. Water thoroughly and place in a clear plastic bag until new growth is well underway.

## Potting

Soil is a critical factor for success. It should be a mixture of equal parts rich loam, coarse builders' sand, peat moss and rotted or dried manure. For each cubic foot of mix, incorporate one-quarter cup of 5-10-5 commercial fertilizer and one-quarter cup of lime to neutralize the mildly acidic nature of the peat moss. Roses thrive best in a pH range of 5.5 to 6.5. Add enough water to moisten the soil mixture and allow to stand two to three days before using. Use clay pots in preference to ceramic or plastic. Provide a generous layer of shard or pea gravel over the drainage hole for proper drainage. Repotting should be undertaken when the root ball completely fills the container or at the time when the plant is being reawakened from the rest period.

## Watering

Keep the soil evenly moist during periods of active growth and barely moist during the resting period. Miniature roses dislike dry atmosphere and high temperatures. Relative humidity should be maintained above 30%. Place the pots, above water level, in a deep humidity tray filled with crushed stones and water. Frequent mist spraying of the stems and leaves with clear water will also help to maintain proper humidity.

## Feeding

During the active growing and flowering period use water soluble general fertilizer on a 10 to 14 day schedule.

## Propagation

From seeds or stem cuttings taken during spring and early summer. Root in coarse moist sand or vermiculite.

## Special Problems

Faded flowers should be pruned away promptly so as to maintain a shapely plant. Hot dry conditions may encourage aphids and spider mites. Control these pests with humidity and regular spraying with malathion.

*Rosa rouletti*

# SAINTPAULIA

*African Violet*

Despite the common name, African Violet, this plant is in no way related to the viola (violet) family. It is a genus of the Gesneriad (Gesneriaceae) family of plants, along with Gloxinia, Achimenes, etc. Plants were first offered for sale in North America around 1925 and since that time the African Violet has become one of the best loved and most common flowering house plants. It is sometimes referred to as the friendly plant because of the ease with which it may be shared through propagation by leaf cuttings.

## Origin

African Violet (Saintpaulia) is a native of the Usambara Mountains of East Africa. It was discovered in 1892 by Baron Walter Von Saint Paul, the then governor of German East Africa and was introduced into Germany by his father. The name Saintpaulia was originated to identify the genus and to honor the discoverers.

## Description

This perennial plant has no main stem, growing as it does from a rosette shaped crown. The hairy, dark green, stemmed foliage of *Saintpaulia ionantha* is oblong in shape and somewhat pointed. The lavender flowers with their bright yellow centers are held above the foliage on flowering stems that branch into shorter stems carrying one flower each. There are 19 species of Saintpaulia and the many sports and mutations have resulted in an endless number of varieties; singles, doubles, frills, edged sometimes bicolored, in a range from white, pink, magenta, lavender to deep purple.

## Cultivation

The African Violet is considered to be a neutral daylight plant and while it does require a period of darkness each day, it is not too specific. They must be protected from lengthy exposure to direct sunlight. Outstanding heavy blooming plants are being grown the year round under artificial light with no daylight at all. Two 40-watt (48-inch) fluorescent lamps will give a growing area of four square feet. Proper distance from the light is around 12 inches which gives the light intensity of 400-foot-candles. Operation of the lights for 12 to 14 hours a day gives good year-round results.

Excessive light intensity causes the leaves to turn yellow. Too low a light level causes the leaves to be soft and long-stemmed and the plant refuses to bloom. The optimum day temperature is between 15 and 24°C. (60 to 75°F.) and the night temperature should not go below 15°C. (60°F), otherwise growth will be slow and the plants will not bloom as profusely. When plants are growing on a window-sill, they should be moved away at night or during severe weather, since window-sill temperatures are usually somewhat below middle of the room temperatures. While the African Violet will blossom indefinitely without rest, it does slow down in flower production in temperatures over 27°C. (80°F.) and, for this reason, many growers give their plants a rest during the hot summer months. African Violets have succeeded as house plants in North America more so than in Europe because the plant's temperature requirements closely match North America's home and apartment temperatures.

Humidity in the range of 40 to 60% is ideal and if your location is dry, you can overcome lack of air moisture by placing the pots in saucers or trays filled with water and enough gravel so that the bottoms of the pots are above water level. You may also mist or fog spray the plants with tepid water but never while exposed to direct sunlight.

High humidity can be maintained around new plants by enclosing pot and all in a clear polyethylene bag. This treatment is also useful for large plants during periods when they are unattended.

## Potting

African Violets will grow in a wide variety of loose, porous soils that give good drainage, thus an abundance of air in the soil for root growth. They are best served by a soil with high organic content since they have a fine root structure. They prosper in a soil of between 6.5 and 6.9 pH and with a 5-10-5 fertilizer.

Many African Violet troubles originate from the use of unsterilized loam (garden soil) and sand. If you are not using the convenient sterilized packages of African Violet soil now available at the grocery store as well as at the nursery, you should undertake the rather smelly job of soil sterilization. For this, place the loam and sand in a metal container and bake in the oven at 100 to 200°F. for one hour. Clay pots as well as drainage material that has had prior contact with soil should also be treated in this manner. Plastic pots will have to be scrubbed with hot, soapy water. After removal from the oven, cool and add enough water to moisten, then allow to stand for a couple of days before using.

A good friable potting soil mixture should be one part sterilized garden loam, one part builders' sand or vermiculite, one part peat moss, and one part well rotted compost or manure. Mix well and moisten slightly for ease of handling.

African Violets are not deep rooting and they will bloom in pots as small as 2½ inches. Thus with limited space, you can grow a fair collection in 3½-inch pots with a policy of raising young plants to take the place of those maturing from root restriction. Repotting should only be undertaken when a plant has overgrown its container. Avoid overpotting.

## Watering

Proper watering is considered by many to be the most important single factor for successful African Violet gardening. Only tepid or room temperature water should be used. It should be of drinking quality but if it is heavily chlorinated, it should either be boiled and cooled or allowed to stand open to the room for a few hours to allow the excess chlorine to dissipate.

Water from water softening processes should not be used. Rain water is ideal if it can be collected without the air pollutants we have these days.

A healthy African Violet should be given all the water it can use but never so much as to have the soil soggy for several hours since this will drown the fine roots. Keep the soil only slightly moist to the touch. Remember air in the soil is essential for a healthy root structure.

The best practice is to water alternately top and bottom to prevent accumulation of soluble fertilizer salts on the surface of the soil and subsequent damage to the stems touching the rim of the pot. A paper collar will keep the stems from touching. Water only with tepid water. Water that is cold will damage roots and cause spotting and streaking of the leaves through destruction of the green coloring matter, even though no water has touched the leaves.

There is no real objection to water reaching the leaves provided they are not chilled by cold water or exposed to the sun before they have become dry. Actually, the leaves may be dusted by washing with a fine mist of tepid water as well as by dry dusting with a soft camel hair brush.

## Feeding

During active growth, which can be essentially all year long, follow a program of supplementary feeding with a water soluble fertilizer every 10 to 14 days. Follow the manufacturers' directions and make certain the soil is moist before fertilizing. Some growers fertilize with every watering by using a solution at 1/10th the recommended strength.

## Propagation

While plants can be propagated from seeds, leaf cuttings and division of plants, the easiest and preferred method is leaf cutting. It is best to select young, husky leaves in the center of the plant since the mature outside leaves may be more difficult to root. Start off with fresh water

*Saintpaulia ionantha*

and a clean container. Cover the top with aluminum foil or insert a paper muffin cup. Give each leaf stem a clean cut with a razor blade (avoid pinching) and insert through slits in the foil or paper into the water. Should any of the leaves show signs of rot, remove the other leaves at once and transfer to a clean container and fresh water. Some growers change the water daily while others suggest blowing air into the water through a straw to provide aeration and to prevent stagnation. Roots form at the base of the leaf and the plantlet can then be potted. The mother leaf may be removed with a razor blade, cut and re-used as a cutting. It takes from five to eight months to produce a blooming size plant.

## Special Problems

To control pests use malathion spray.

153

# SANSEVIERIA trifasciata

*Snake Plant, Mother-in-Law's Tongue,*
*Bowstring Hemp*

*Sansevieria trifasciata laurentii*

Sansevieria, sometimes called Snake Plant, Mother-in-Law's Tongue or Bowstring Hemp, ranks with Aspidistra in its resilience to neglect. It makes an excellent subject for the beginner of indoor gardening.

## Origin

Named after the Prince of Sanseviero (Raimond de Sangro, born in Naples, 1710), this genus is a member of the Lily family (Liliaceae) and is native to India and tropical South Africa with well over fifty species identified and described. This genus continues to be an important crop for long, durable fiber, especially in India where it is known as Bowstring Hemp.

## Description

This tender, perennial plant has thick, creeping root stocks that produce clusters of 6 stemless leaves that grow up to 4 feet high. The thick leaves grow stiffly erect and are usually dark green with bands of greyish markings. Well grown mature plants send up tall flower stems and produce bracts of small whitish flowers, usually in spring. Flowering is somewhat irregular.

*Sansevieria trifasciata laurentii* is the best known species. Its leaves are striped golden yellow, lengthwise. The plant is a slow grower and the $2^1/_2$ inch spear-like leaves will eventually reach $2^1/_2$ to 3 feet. *Sansevieria trifasciata* 'Hahnii' is low growing with rosette-like clumps of dark green leaves mottled grey. Growing to 8 inches this nest-like species somewhat resembles a Bromeliad. It is often used in dish gardens and in combination with the taller varieties.

## Cultivation

While Sansevieria is a very tolerant plant, it thrives best in a light sunny window with average house humidity. It is usually grown indoors but there is no reason why it cannot be moved outside to the garden or patio in a sheltered location for the summer months. Care must be taken to provide gradual exposure to full sunshine, otherwise the foliage will be damaged from sunburn.

## Potting

Use a potting mixture of equal parts loam, coarse builders' sand and well decayed compost or rotted or dried manure. Add a small amount of lime to keep the soil slightly alkaline. Thorough drainage is important so use a generous layer of broken shard or pea gravel over the drainage hole. Repotting should only be undertaken when the underground root stock completely fills the pot and becomes so crowded that it starts to surface.

## Watering

Water regularly during the growing period March to September. Over winter, keep the soil on the dry side.

## Feeding

During the growing period feed with a water soluble fertilizer low in nitrogen.

## Propagation

Is usually achieved by division of the creeping root stalk. Three-inch sections of the leaves may also be used. Insert the cuttings half way into coarse moist sand and use bottom heat during the rooting period.

*Sansevieria trifasciata* 'Hahnii'

## Problems

This plant is essentially pest free; however, over-watering and too cool a location, under 15°C. (60°F.) can induce rot. In this event cut away the collapsed parts with a sharp knife, back to firm tissue, dust with sulphur and then improve the growing conditions.

# SAXIFRAGA sarmentosa

*Strawberry Geranium,*
*Strawberry Begonia*

*Saxifraga sarmentosa (stolonifera)*, with more than 200 years of cultivation, has been subjected to a lot of name calling: Strawberry Geranium, Strawberry Begonia, Aaron's Beard, Old Man's Beard, even Mother-of-Thousands and Creeping Sailor, because of the many plantlets borne on thread-like stems that are easily rooted in water or moist sand.

## Origin

This plant was originally introduced into England from China around 1770. It is a member of the Saxifrage family (Saxifragaceae).

## Description

*Saxifraga sarmentosa (stolonifera)* is a perennial plant growing to 9 inches with clustered, rounded leaves up to 4 inches across. The leaves have short red stems and are dark green with white veins with undersides of purplish-red. The main plant sends out long (up to 18 inches), slender thread-like runners, much like a strawberry plant, which bear attractive young plants at the tips. White flowers are usually borne, May to August, on a branching spike.

*S. sarmentosa* 'Tricolor' (Magic Carpet) has foliage marked creamy white with red variegations. It was introduced into England from Japan around 1860. Both plants are used in pots as well as hanging baskets.

## Cultivation

Locate plants in a light semi-sunny spot to maintain full leaf color, preferably where the temperature remains on the cool side, around 18°C. (65°F.) and even cooler over winter during the resting period, November to late January. Avoid crowding this plant in amongst others since it needs lots of fresh circulating air.

When placed outside for the summer, a sheltered location is necessary.

## Potting

Use a rich porous soil mixture such as equal parts rich loam, coarse builders' sand, peat moss and rotted or dried manure. Provide for drainage with a generous layer of pea gravel at the bottom of the pot.

## Watering

Keep evenly moist. Maintain 30 per cent humidity or higher. Frequent mist spraying with clear water is beneficial.

## Feeding

Feed regularly during the growing period, spring to autumn, on a two-week schedule with water soluble general fertilizer.

## Propagation

Propagation is readily achieved from rooted plantlets appearing at the tips of the trailing red runners. Plant several to a pot. Seed is also available from seed houses. Germination takes about 15 days.

## Special Problems

Soft growth resulting from high temperatures and low light may be attacked by aphids. Control with malathion spray and improve the plant's location.

*Saxifraga sarmentosa*

# SEDUM morganianum

*Burro Tail, Donkey's Tail*

Donkey's Tail is another useful succulent that makes an outstanding hanging basket plant.

## Origin

Sedum is a genus of the Stonecrop family (Crassulaceae). Species *Sedum morganianum*, Donkey's Tail, supposedly is a native of Mexico. It was first noted in the mid-1930s in the state of Vera Cruz.

## Description

Donkey's Tail is seen at its best in a hanging basket since the pendant branches often reach 3 feet in length and are covered with thick, sharply pointed, fleshy silver green leaves that completely and solidly encircle the branches. Clusters of small, pinkish red flowers rich in nectar, appear mid to late spring. They are rather inconspicuous and contribute little to the appearance of the plant.

## Cultivation

This plant doesn't require the blazing sun. In fact, it will show signs of sunburn if exposed to continuous summer sun, so hang it from the branch of a tree or from an overhang on the north or east side of the house. In winter it should hang inside in a sunny window with average room temperature and humidity.

## Potting

The potting soil should be one part coarse builders' sand, rich garden loam, peat moss and rotted or dried manure or compost. The addition of a little charcoal and hydrated lime will keep the soil sweet and ensure the calcium necessary for the full growth of the plant. Crushed egg shells are a satisfactory substitute if the lime is not available. If the mixture appears heavy, do not hesitate to add more sand, since porosity is a vital quality. Use a green plastic hanging basket with built-in saucer and cover the drainage hole with 2 inches of pea gravel or broken shard. This is not an easy plant to repot so move it into a 10 to 12-inch basket as early as possible. Here it may be maintained for many years with supplementary feeding and proper drainage.

## Watering

Do not add water after transplanting. Set the plant aside for a few days to enable damaged roots to heal. Then water only sparingly for thirty days or so. After the plant returns to a vigorous growing condition withhold water almost to the shriveling point then water heavily. Remember hanging plants dry out more rapidly than their earthbound neighbors.

## Feeding

During the growing period, spring to autumn, use a supplementary feeding of water soluble general fertilizer mixed to the manufacturer's instructions.

*Sedum morganianum*

## Propagation

From stem cuttings or individual leaves. Allow the cut ends to form a callus by drying in the shade for a few days. Carefully tie stem cuttings to a thin bamboo stake or a wire and insert the cutting about 1/4 inch into a pot of coarse builders' sand. Keep the sand only slightly moist. After a few weeks roots will have formed and the cutting may be planted in the dry soil mixture described under Potting.

## Special Problems

This plant is essentially trouble-free. Wet soggy conditions can destroy the plant.

# SENECIO
*German Ivy, Parlor Ivy / String-of-Beads*

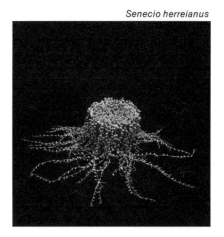
*Senecio herreianus*

Cascading plants for the window shelves and hanging basket.

## Origin

Genus Senecio of the Composite family (Compositae) has more than 2,000 species found in all parts of the world.

## Description

*S. mikanioides*, German Ivy or Parlor Ivy, is native to South Africa and is a tall, twining perennial with clusters of bright green, soft, ivy-like leaves (5 to 7 lobes) and small yellow flowers.
*S. herreianus* with slender succulent stems, 12 to 24 inches in length, creeps and cascades. The stems are covered with globular bright green leaves resembling small gooseberries.

This plant is commonly known as String-of-Beads. Since it is a succulent, winter treatment calls for coolness and little water. Otherwise, grow as for German Ivy as described below.

## Cultivation

Grow in a sunny to semi-sunny location in winter and shade to semi-shade during summer. While average room temperature is acceptable, 21°C. (70°F.) and below, coolness is a key to success as long as the area is frost-free.

## Potting

A rich soil mixture is required. Use equal parts loam, coarse builders' sand, peat moss, rotted or dried manure and leafmould. Incorporate a modicum of bone meal or ground limestone into the mix. Cover the drainage holes with a generous layer of small pebbles or pea gravel.

## Watering

Keep constantly moist, never allow the plant to become dry. Less water is needed during winter in cool locations. Above average humidity is desirable; use a humidity tray with frequent mist spraying with clear water especially in warm quarters.

## Feeding

From spring to August, apply water soluble general fertilizer every two weeks.

## Propagation

Any time of the year, root 3 to 4-inch terminal growth cuttings in moist sand or vermiculite.

## Special Problems

Excessive warmth and dry air will encourage attacks of red spider and scale with sudden leaf drop. Use insecticide malathion spray regularly, especially from autumn through to spring. With small plants, showering and washing the stems and leaves with water is very beneficial.

*Senecio mikanioides*

# SETCREASEA purpurea

*Purple Heart*

This plant was first described and classified as recently as 1955, although it had been in cultivation long before.

## Origin

Genus Setcreasea is a member of the Spiderwort family (Commelinaceae). There is only one species on record, *Setcreasea purpurea*, and it is native to Mexico.

## Description

Purple Heart makes an excellent plant for the apartment, especially in a hanging basket in a well lighted window where the leaves and stems develop their deepest color and soon cascade over the sides of the basket. The lance shaped leaves are 6 inches long and about 1¹/₄ inches wide and slightly hairy, giving a slight frost effect to the deep purple violet. It is closely related to Tradescantia (Wandering Jew) and is sometimes called Tradescantia in the trade. The short lived, small violet flowers appear at the ends of the cascading stems and they keep replacing themselves.

## Cultivation

The plant is tropical in nature and will thrive in average room temperature in a range of 18 to 21°C. (65 to 70°F.) with relative humidity around 30%. The beautiful deep violet color of the plant is dependent upon it having a bright light. Greenish foliage signals that more light is required. Regular pinch pruning is necessary to keep the plant shapely and within bounds.

During summer months and after frost, the plants may be placed outside and with sufficient rooted cuttings, a small edging may be planted along the walkway or the edge of the patio.

## Potting

Use a rich, well drained potting mixture such as equal parts loam, coarse builders' sand, peat moss and rotted or dried manure or compost. Ensure prompt drainage with a generous layer of pea gravel over the drainage hole. Plan to replace plants within two years from freshly rooted cuttings.

## Watering

Keep evenly moist.

## Feeding

Feed regularly with water soluble general fertilizer on a 10 to 14 day schedule during periods of active growth.

## Propagation

At any time of year from stem cuttings. Roots will form within two weeks in a jar of water and will be ready for potting shortly thereafter.

## Special Problems

Essentially pest-free.

*Setcreasea purpurea*

# SINNINGIA speciosa
*Gloxinia*

Now through the magic of electric light, the Gloxinia will blossom not only in the spring and summer but throughout the year. Anyone who is successful with African Violets (Saintpaulia) can find equal success and satisfaction with Gloxinias since the cultural requirements are much the same.

## Origin

Gloxinia is the commonly accepted name for *Sinningia* *speciosa*, which is the true botanical identification. It is native to the tropical Brazilian forest and grows from a tuber. Like the African Violet, Achimenes and Episcia, it is a member of the Gesneriad family (Gesneriaceae).

## Description

The large tubular flowers of the Gloxinia have a color range from light pink to the darkest purple. There are also ruffled whites, some with delicate tints while others are speckled and still others are spotted and netted. Probably the most spectacular are the vivid ruffled scarlets and reds that give a velvet-like sheen and appearance. The layers of large, oval leaves with a rich soft velvety texture, provide a complimentary background for the exotic flowers.

## Cultivation

Place plants in a south or east window where they will receive all the sun possible during the mid-winter months. At other times give plants good strong light shaded from direct sun. Gloxinias thrive in a night temperature of 18°C. (65°F.) and a day temperature of 21°C. (70°F.) with a relative humidity of 50 to 60%. The humidity problem may be helped by placing the plants in saucers or trays filled with stones and water. This will give evaporation and maintain the bottom of the pot above the water level.

Gloxinias may be grown year round and never see the light of day, by growing under lights. They need medium to high light intensity of 600-foot-candles for 16 to 18 hours a day. This means being kept within 4 inches of the fluorescent tubes in a two by 40 watt arrangement. They will grow and blossom with their tops 8 inches below the light (450-foot-candles) but stems will tend to be elongated and weak. If you use only daylight tubes instead of warm white be sure to mix approximately 10% incandescent light to maintain red light in proper balance for flowering.

Restrict the plant to one main shoot for best appearance and superior flowers. The secondary shoots can be allowed to grow to about 2 inches then carefully removed and transferred to vermiculite for rooting and development of new plants.

If the plant has produced an early crop of blooms in the spring, it may be cut back to just above the first pair of leaves and made to produce a second crop of flowers in 10 to 16 weeks. Following this, the plant should be given less and less water in preparation for the rest period.

After flowering the foliage should be kept growing until it yellows and dies back indicating that the tuber has become dormant. During this period less and less water is required. Remove all dead foliage and replant the tuber and store at 4 to 10°C. (45 to 50°F.) making certain the soil is kept only slightly moist. A Gloxinia will last many years if given rest periods.

## Potting

The instant way to begin a Gloxinia collection is to purchase potted plants or dormant tubers at your garden center. Plant one tuber to a 5 to 6-inch pot with the concave (indented) side of the tuber facing up. The potting soil must be fibrous, loose, well aerated and fast draining. A mixture of equal parts loam, coarse builders' sand, peat moss, rotted or dried manure or compost, plus a modicum of bone meal will give excellent results. If you plan to start Gloxinia gardening on a modest scale, you will probably find it more convenient to buy a small bag of African Violet potting soil now sold in most supermarkets. Make certain that the drainage hole of the pot is covered with pea gravel or broken crockery to prevent clogging and flooding of the roots. If there are no signs of growth at the time the tuber is planted, it may be kept in the basement or in a dark cupboard. The soil must be watered often enough to be kept only slightly moist. Growth may start at any time so the pot should be checked often for signs of new growth and leaves. Some tubers are slow to start and may extend their rest period up to three months or more. Once growth is started, place the plant in a south or east window where it will receive all the sun possible during the mid-winter months. At other times give the plant good strong light shaded from direct sun.

## Watering

Watering is best accomplished from below, as is the method used with African Violets. The water must be at room temperature. Make certain the soil is never waterlogged or that the pot stands in water for any extended length of time, otherwise some of the roots will die and result in failure of the flower buds to develop and bloom.

During the resting period, less water is required—keep only slightly moist.

## Feeding

Gloxinias make large plants and need regular nourishment in the form of a water soluble general fertilizer every 10 to 14 days.

## Propagation
### Leaf Method

It is possible to propagate Gloxinias from a leaf, as is the case with African Violets, or they may be grown from seed. When rooting a plant from a leaf, coarse builders' sand, vermiculite or peat moss may be used for the rooting medium. As soon as a tuber has formed at the base of the parent leaf it should be potted. Don't be surprised if it takes 6 months for the tuber to send up leaves.

### Seed Method

Gloxinias are readily raised from seed and flowering plants are possible within 220 days from germination which can vary between 10 to 30 days. The fresher the seed the faster it germinates. Seed over 12 months old is not of the best quality.

Prepare a seeding bed suitable for germination of the fine, dust-like seeds. One effective method is to place a small clay pot with the drainage hole cork tight into the center of a larger clay pot and fill the surrounding space with potting soil firm to within 1/2 inch of the rim. Maintain the rims of both pots at the same level. Moisten the soil and fill the center pot with water. Sow the seed on top of the soil and cover with a thin layer of milled sphagnum moss. Enclose the container in a clear plastic bag and keep out of direct sun. Uncover immediately at the first sign of germination.

The seedlings should be transplanted as soon as they are large enough to handle. The tuber starts to form underground as soon as germination occurs, so care must be exercised not to separate it from the top growth during transplanting. For a specimen plant, transplant seedlings directly to 5 to 6-inch pots.

## Special Problems

Soggy soil causes root rot. Dry air is mostly responsible for leaf curl. Aphids may be controlled with a malathion solution.

# SPARMANNIA africana

*African Hemp, Indoor Parlor Linden*

Sometimes called Indoor Parlor Linden, this evergreen plant makes an attractive winter flowering shrub.

## Origin

Genus Sparmannia, with less than five species, is a member of the Linden family (Tiliaceae). This genus was named to honor botanist Andreas Sparmannia (1747-1787).

## Description

*Sparmannia africana* is a showy evergreen shrub growing to 20 feet and is native to South Africa. The soft, hairy, light green, 5 to 6-inch foliage, has 3 to 7 lobes that are unequally toothed. The magnificent flowers borne in late winter are white with prominent yellow stamens.

## Cultivation

Grow in a light, airy location with all sun possible over winter and partial shade during the bright hot weather. Average room temperature is adequate and a temperature as low as 10°C. (50°F.) is beneficial during the October to December resting period. Pinch prune young shoots to encourage branching.

## Potting

Use a mixture of loam, coarse builders' sand, peat moss and rotted or dried manure or compost. Good drainage is essential. Use a generous layer of crock, pebbles or pea gravel over the drainage hole. Repotting should be undertaken in late spring after flowering and pruning.

## Watering

Keep evenly moist. Average room humidity is adequate.

## Feeding

During flowering and growing period, apply water soluble general fertilizer on a 14 day schedule.

## Propagation

From young shoots at any time of the year. Use rooting hormone powder on the cut ends before placing in moist sand or vermiculite. Provide humidity and heat for fast rooting. Mature plants are normally replaced every three or four years with fresh young plants.

## Special Problems

White fly, red spider and aphids can be controlled with regular spraying with malathion insecticide.

*Sparmannia africana*

160

# SPATHIPHYLLUM floribundum
*Spathe Flower*

Considered by many as the perfect apartment plant, Spathiphyllum is relatively undemanding regarding light, temperature and humidity. It produces attractive, evergreen foliage and interesting flowers.

## Origin

Native to tropical America, this plant is a member of the Arum or Calla family (Araceae) of which there are over 100 genera and 900 species including Philodendron, Monstera, Dieffenbachia, Calla Lily, etc. Genus Spathiphyllum has over 25 species.

## Description

*Spathiphyllum floribundum* is a native of Colombia and makes an outstanding pot plant. It grows about 12 inches high with rich green leaves that are held on short stems. The leaves are lance shaped, 6 inches long, 3 inches wide and grow in clumps from a thickened root stock. The calla-like flowers are produced in summer. The yellow-green, club-like, finger shaped flowering spike (spadix) has an attractive white petal-like branch (spathe) that is open and boat shaped. These long stemmed flowers are long lasting and may be used as cut flowers.

## Cultivation

This evergreen plant is very tolerant of light and will do well in semi-sunny, semi-shady to shady locations. It thrives in the average home temperature, but not below 16°C. (60°F.).

## Potting

Use a potting mixture of equal parts rich loam, coarse builders' sand, peat moss and leafmould. Ensure adequate drainage with a generous layer of broken shard or pea gravel over the drainage hole. Potting and repotting activity are best undertaken in early spring when the plant is sending out new shoots and preparing for active growth.

## Watering

It is best to keep the soil evenly moist throughout the year. During the winter resting period September to February, Spathiphyllum is very tolerant of the low humidity resulting from central heating. Mist spraying during the growing period, spring and summer, will improve the quality of foliage and flowers.

## Feeding

Fertilize only during spring and summer when the plant is in active growth. Use water soluble general fertilizer on a 14 day schedule.

## Propagation

Additional plants may be cultivated by division of the thickened root stock during spring and early summer. Pot up divisions using the soil mix discussed previously. Enclose in a clear plastic bag to maintain high humidity and place in a warm location around 21°C. (70°F.) to force the young plants into active root development. Plants may also be started from seed.

## Special Problems

This is essentially a durable, trouble-free plant.

*Spathiphyllum floribundum*

# STEPHANOTIS floribunda

*Madagascar Jasmine*

Among the indoor flowering plants, few have all the good qualities of Stephanotis. It is free flowering and has firm leathery leaves.

### Origin

Native to Madagascar, *Stephanotis floribunda* is a member of the Milkweed family (Asclepiadaceae) along with the well known, old fashioned plant Hoya.

### Description

This plant is a rampant woody climber that will rapidly reach 8 to 15 feet if not trained and pruned to shape. The glossy, dark green leaves are elliptic in shape with short leaf stems, and up to 3 inches long and 1$^1/_2$ inches wide. The outstanding feature of the plant is the waxy, fragrant, white flowers that are star shaped, about 2 inches across and borne on 1 to 1$^1/_2$ inch tubes. The flowers are widely used in bride's bouquets and Hawaiian leis, not only because of their beauty but the equally important exotic perfume. Flowers appear from spring through summer with the best production in June. *Stephanotis floribunda* is the species commonly grown.

### Cultivation

This plant requires good light such as found in an east or west window. Since it is from Madagascar it will tolerate heat but does best in a temperature around 18° C. (65°F.) and unlike many other tropicals, it doesn't require excessively high humidity — usually a reading around 30% is quite adequate. The resting period begins in late October lasting into January and only enough water should be given during this period to prevent shriveling of the leaves. A night temperature of 12 to 16°C. (55 to 60°F) is very beneficial during the rest period. Plants may be grown around a window or on a wire frame fashioned from heavy wire such as a coat hanger bent to shape. Soft pinch pruning will soon train the twisting stems into the desired shape.

### Potting

Use a mixture of equal parts rich loam, coarse builders' sand, peat moss, and rotted or dried manure or leafmould. Young plants should be repotted each year during February. Larger size plants may be kept in the same size pot for many years if top dressed and given supplementary feeding during periods of growth. Use a generous layer of drainage material, broken shard or pea gravel at the bottom of the pot.

### Watering

During the growing period March to September, water freely. In autumn start reducing the amount of water just enough to keep the soil barely moist during the resting period October into January.

### Feeding

Supplementary food should be given during periods of active growth— apply water soluble general fertilizer on a 10 to 14 day schedule.

*Stephanotis floribunda*

### Propagation

May be achieved from seeds that will germinate in about 30 days but is usually achieved from cuttings of half matured stems during spring and summer. Place cuttings in individual small pots filled with a mixture of builders' sand and peat moss. A temperature of 24 to 27°C. (75 to 80°F) is required during the 4 to 5 week rooting period. Use rooting hormone powder to shorten the rooting time. When roots fill the pot move the plants into larger sizes using the same potting soil as discussed previously. Prune back all growth at this time to encourage branching.

### Special Problems

This plant is much favored by mealy bugs and scale. Regular spraying with malathion will prevent trouble before it starts. Individual pests may be removed with a cotton swab moistened in rubbing alcohol.

High temperature during the resting period may bring on insect attacks as well as spindly growth.

# STRELITZIA reginae

*Bird-of-Paradise*

Bird-of-Paradise begins to show its exotic blooms around spring crocus time. It continues to blossom into early summer. The stout flower spikes with vivid blue and orange flowers are reminiscent of the shape and color of tropical birds in flight.

## Origin

Strelitzia is one of the six genera of the Banana family (Musaceae). It originates from South Africa's Cape of Good Hope. The name Strelitzia was given in honor of the family name of the wife of King George III.

## Description

Bird-of-Paradise is a trunkless curvaceous perennial that makes an outstanding and durable addition to any collection of potted plants. It has a character all its own and the leathery, grey-green, banana-like leaves don't shred in the wind like regular banana leaves. They grow on long stout stems and are about 18 inches long. The overall height of a mature plant is about 3 feet. *Strelitzia reginae* is the species best suited to pot culture.

## Cultivation

Grown indoors this plant needs bright light, with some protection from hot direct sun to prevent leaf burn. Plants summered out of doors are best located in broken shade. The roots of Strelitzia are exceptionally strong and will soon push a wooden container apart. Check the bindings regularly. A growing temperature of 15 to 21°C. (60 to 70°F.) is ideal except for the November/December rest period when a 10 to 12°C. (50 to 55°F.) temperature is preferred. Keep plants in an above 30% relative humidity.

Strelitzia is not a heavy bloomer and sometimes requires up to four years to start production, even from a good size division. The plant usually has to fill an 8 or 10-inch pot before giving any indication of blooming. Most of the flowers will be produced from spring into early mid-summer.

## Potting

When roots fill the pot or possibly have already burst the pot, repot to the next larger size using a potting mixture of equal parts loam, builders' sand, peat moss and compost or rotted or dried manure. Provide for easy drainage of excess water.

## Watering

Keep the soil evenly moist except during November and December resting period when the plant should be kept on the dry side.

## Feeding

During the active growing and flowering period, supplementary feeding should be given with water soluble general fertilizer as well as an ammonium sulphate solution made with one teaspoon of ammonium sulphate to one gallon of water.

*Strelitzia reginae*

## Propagation

The main method used for propagation is from suckers and divisions of old clumps. This is usually done in the spring and the new portions are kept warm and moist until rooting is well advanced. Bird-of-Paradise may be raised from seeds if given the right conditions of high temperature and bottom heat. Germination may require as much as 25 days or more.

## Special Problems

Pests seem to completely ignore this plant.

# STREPTOCARPUS
*Cape Primrose*

This curious stemless plant makes it a very unusual species to cultivate.

## Origin

Cape Primrose originated in South Africa and Madagascar (Malagasy Republic) and made its debut in England when it first blossomed at Kew Gardens in October, 1826 and was described as an interesting Gloxinia-like plant. In 1828 the genus was given the name Streptocarpus (twisted fruit) and the original plant was identified as species *rexii.* Thirty years later another species, *wendlandii,* made an appearance in England. It was unusual in that it had only one leaf, 2 to 4 feet long, lying on the ground and from it mid-rib flowers were borne on one foot high stems. This curiosity did much to revive interest in Cape Primrose, although it was not until 1887 that the first hybrids began to be noticed. Streptocarpus is a member of the Gesneriad family (Gesneriaceae).

## Description

Cape Primrose is a stemless plant with a cluster of medium green, glossy, waxy crowned leaves often as long as 15 inches and 4 inches wide. Today most amateur gardeners ignore the species and concentrate on the beautiful modern hybrids with flowers up to 4 inches across in shades of pink, red, blue, lilac and white.

## Cultivation

The plant requires conditions much the same as those for African Violets—early morning or late afternoon sun, moist roots and efficient drainage. It should be treated as a tender perennial that enjoys slightly cooler growing conditions than Gloxinias and African Violets. A reasonable humidity is also desirable, above 30% and as much as 50%. Flowering size plants take from 8 to 15 months to grow. Blooming will continue well into November and December in moderate temperatures around 21° C. (70° F.) and not lower than 13° C. (55° F.) at night.

## Potting

The recommended potting mixture for this plant is equal parts loam, sharp sand, peat moss and humus, (leafmould or well rotted manure). When the plants are young the texture of the potting mix should be fairly fine. Provide ample drainage at all times by using crushed stone or gravel to a fair depth over the drainage hole. When potting, avoid excessive handling of the soil and only gently firm with finger pressure. Final potting may take place in a 5 or 6-inch pot.

## Watering

Keep evenly moist.

## Feeding

Provide biweekly feedings whenever plants are actively growing with a water soluble general purpose fertilizer solution mixed to the manufacturer's instructions and apply only to well moistened soil to avoid burning the roots.

## Propagation

Propagation of any outstanding plants may be made by dividing plants with several crowns during spring repotting, or by rooting a portion of a completely mature leaf suspended with the tip in water or kept moist in moist sand until rooting and new growth begins.

The plant is not difficult to grow from seed and is usually raised by this method. The seeds are very small and care must be taken not to cover them too deeply. Seeds sown in autumn in a sterile medium such as vermiculite will take 15 to 21 days to germinate.

## Special Problems

This plant is essentially pest-free.

# SYNGONIUM podophyllum

*Arrowhead Vine, Goosefoot Plant*

The climbing and creeping nature of this plant makes it ideal for home decoration in hanging baskets or moss covered totem poles.

## Origin

Genus Syngonium is a member of the Arum or Calla family (Araceae). It has about 20 species all native to Central and South America.

## Description

While this genus is readily identified from other Arum plants because of its milky sap, young plants of the various genera are difficult to identify since the leaves rarely resemble those of the adult plant. Most species bear arrowhead shaped leaves often variegated in yellow, white and silver. Mature leaves become divided into finger-like lobes, 3, 5, sometimes as many as 8. Long leaf stems are the general rule. Principal species include:

*S. podophyllum* often called Nephthytis is native to Central America, Mexico to Panama. The glossy, medium green leaves are 12 inches in length with leaf stems up to 24 inches in length. Adult leaves may show 5 to 9 lobes. Several varieties are available with leaf variegations in silver, green or white. This is a useful plant for growing around the inside window frame or in a room divider plant box.

## Cultivation

Grow in a semi-sunny to shady location in average room temperature.

## Potting

Use a rich friable soil mixture of equal parts loam, builders' sand, peat moss and rotted or dried manure. Cover the drainage holes with pebbles or pea gravel. Repot in early spring and only when absolutely necessary.

## Watering

Keep the soil evenly moist at all times. Normal room humidity is adequate.

## Feeding

Feed on a 14 day schedule from late March to early September with water soluble general fertilizer.

## Propagation

Readily from cuttings at any time. Use moist coarse builders' sand.

## Special Problems

There are rarely any problems when properly grown.

*Syngonium podophyllum*

# THUNBERGIA alata

*Black-eyed Susan Vine*

One old-time favorite that has been returning to the scene after many years of absence is Thunbergia. You probably have seen and heard of it as the Black-eyed Susan Vine, so named because of the golden-yellow flowers with a dark purple spot, or eye, in the center. Many commercial plantings for hanging baskets use this plant drooping rather than climbing. This plant is a tender perennial and is readily raised from seed.

## Origin

Thunbergia is a member of the Acanthus family (Acanthaceae) and one of the many plants native to tropical Africa. It derived its name from Karl Peter Thunberg, a botany professor who died in 1828. The genus has about 75 species, most of which are climbers.

## Description

For indoor gardening one species and a variant are of interest: *T. alata*, a vine growing 4 to 6 feet with medium green leaves and flowers one inch in diameter, golden yellow with a dark spot.

Thunbergia 'White Wings' is a variant of *T. alata* with dark green leaves and pure white flowers up to 1½ inches across and no spot.

## Cultivation

Locate in a light sunny spot in average room temperature. After full flowering, plants should be cut back almost to the soil line and allowed to grow back for further blooms. Plants summered outside should be brought indoors before frost and located in a light, sunny location.

Rather than allowing your pots of vines to sprawl, consider a more disciplined approach with various shapes and styles of supports.

Pinch-pruning of the growing tips is the secret of forcing your will upon a growing vine. Consistent use of this technique will allow you to train small-leaved varieties into many shapes and forms. One of the most accessible supports is the ubiquitous wire coat hanger that may be bent and twisted into many interesting shapes once the wire hook has been cut away with pliers. Small mesh chicken wire is also very workable for shaping globes and for plant poles packed with sphagnum moss.

Poles of fern-tree root in 2-inch by 2-inch or 3-inch by 3-inch up to 4 feet in length are readily available, practically indestructible, and easy to work with for node-rooting vines. Wire, of course, is the natural for stem-twisting and leaf twining types.

Attaching a vine directly to a window frame will work for a period, but once the vine has to be removed for cleaning or protection, there is a real problem. This may be avoided by using a wire or very light wood frame trellis which will allow moving without disruption.

## Potting

Soil for potting and repotting should be a rich open texture such as equal parts rich loam, builders' sand, peat moss and rotted or dried manure. Provide for drainage with 2 or 3 inches of pea gravel at the bottom of the pot over the drainage holes.

*Thunbergia alata*

## Watering

Regular watering is required to keep the soil evenly moist. Maintain humidity at a minimum of 30%. This may be facilitated by placing the pot in a tray or dish that is filled with crushed stones and water. Keep the bottom of the pot above the water line. Frequent mist spraying of the foliage with clear water is also beneficial.

## Feeding

Supplementary feeding with water soluble general fertilizer solution should be given at two week intervals during periods of active growth.

## Propagation

Propagation is usually by seeds that germinate in about 10 days at room temperature. Firm young cuttings may be taken in winter or spring. Use a rooting hormone powder and root in moist sand or vermiculite.

## Special Problems

Control aphids and white flies with malathion spray.

# TOLMIEA menziesii

*Piggyback Plant*

This curious plant bears new plants on the back of old leaves, hence its common name Piggyback Plant.

## Origin

*Tolmiea menziesii* of the Saxifrage family (Saxifragaceae) is native to the North American West Coast, British Columbia to California.

## Description

This perennial plant has bright green, lightly haired leaves that grow in open rosette fashion to form mounds up to 12 inches high. The somewhat maple-leaf shaped leaves grow to about 5 inches in length and $3^1/2$ inches across and are notable for the growth of small plantlets that form at the base of the leaf at the juncture with the leaf stem.

In nature, these plantlets mature and fall off to take root in the surrounding soil. Piggyback plant produces a 6-inch flower spike that bears inconspicuous greenish colored flowers of no great interest.

## Cultivation

Locate plants in a light semi-sunny spot to maintain full leaf color, preferably where the temperature remains on the cool side, around 18° C. (65° F.) and even cooler over winter during the resting period, November to late January. Avoid crowding this plant in amongst others since it needs lots of fresh circulating air.

When placed outside for the summer a sheltered location is necessary.

## Potting

Use a rich porous soil mixture such as equal parts rich loam, coarse builders' sand, peat moss and rotted or dried manure. Provide for drainage with a generous layer of pea gravel at the bottom of the pot.

## Watering

Keep evenly moist. Maintain humidity at 30% or higher. Frequent mist spraying with clear water is beneficial.

## Feeding

Feed regularly during the growing period, spring to autumn, at two week intervals with water soluble general fertilizer.

## Propagation

Propagation is best achieved by pinning the plantlets to moist soil until they take root and are then severed from the parent plant.

## Special Problems

Soft growth resulting from high temperatures and low light may bring on an attack by aphids. Control with malathion spray and improve the location of the plant.

*Tolmiea menziesii*

167

# TRADESCANTIA and ZEBRINA
*Wandering Jew, Inch Plant*

The name Wandering Jew is commonly applied to a group of familiar trailing plants that are grown for their attractive foliage.

## Origin

Two genera of the Spiderwort family (Commelinaceae), Tradescantia and Zebrina, are commonly identified as Wandering Jew and sometimes Inch Plant. Both are native to tropical and sub-tropical America. The name Tradescantia originates from John Tradescant, a gardener to Charles I. The name Zebrina refers to stripes as on a zebra.

## Description

These tender indoor trailing plants are grown for their oval pointed leaves that are often variously striped. The long, succulent stems are sometimes branched and have prominent joints (nodes). Small flowers appear at the ends of the trailers usually from March to May. Principal species include: *Tradescantia albifloria,* a green foliage species from Brazil and Argentina. *T. albo-vittata* with blue-green leaves striped white. *T. blossfeldiana* from South America, bears loose clusters of small lavender flowers, trails rampantly and has leaves dark green above and dark purple below. *T. navicularis* from Peru has boat shaped purplish brown leaves and pink flowers. It is a slow grower.

*Zebrina pendula* from Mexico is the main species of Zebrina. The leaves are lance ovate with the under surface red-purple and the upper surface silvery white suffused purple. Variety 'Quadricolor' has leaves with a metallic green undertone, striped with white, green, red and rose.

## Cultivation

Locate plants in a sunny window; they will tolerate a bit of shade. Colors become more vivid in a south window. Normal room temperature is ideal and damage will occur if the temperature drops below 13° C. (55° F.). After hardening off, they may be summered outside during the frost-free months. Regular pinch pruning of all leaders will result in a bushy, well shaped plant.

## Potting

Use a potting mix of equal parts loam, coarse builders' sand, peat moss and rotted or dried manure. Normally, hanging containers of Wandering Jew are not repotted. The best practice is to have new plants in progress for a complete replacement. Plastic hanging containers with attached drip saucers are ideal for this plant. Make certain drainage holes are covered with shard or pea gravel.

## Watering

Keep evenly moist with tepid water. Average house humidity is suitable. Mist spraying with clear water is beneficial.

## Feeding

Feed weekly from March to September with water soluble general fertilizer.

## Propagation

Plants root readily from stem cuttings placed in a glass of water or moist sand. A well grown plant can provide many offsprings for friends and relatives.

## Special Problems

Excessive dryness can result in leaf damage and aphids. Spray with malathion.

*Tradescantia navicularis*

168

# TULIPA
*Tulip*

Tulips in bloom when the snow is piled high outside is the dream of almost every gardener.

## Origin

The tulip is a member of the Lily family (Liliaceae) and was introduced into Europe from Turkey, around 1555. Of the usually recognized 50 or more species, only a few are in general cultivation but these have given rise to thousands of varieties.

Speculation in tulips during the first half of the 17th century gave origin to the term "tulipomania." More bulbs than existed were sold, ownership was divided into shares and many bulbs where sold even before their origination. Individual bulbs were bought at a price of over $5,000. While Holland is still an important center for their culture, Holland, Michigan is a famous tulip-growing center in the United States.

## Description

Showy bell or funnel-shaped flowers, either single, double or wavy, in colors of deep purple, pale yellow, bright scarlet, and white, with shades in between, top this broad leaved plant. Of the many varieties available, the single and double early tulips make the best subjects for amateur forcing because they grow about 12 inches in height and thus are more manageable on the windowsill. In the singles, consider 'Bellona,' a pure golden yellow and 'Brilliant Star,' a bright scarlet. In the doubles look for 'Mme. Testout,' a deep rich pink and 'Schoonoord,' a pure white. For variety try the fascinating Parrot Tulip with its wavy fringed petals especially 'Fantasy' and 'Karel Doorman.' There are new developments and varieties almost yearly.

## Cultivation

After emergence of the flower buds, locate plants in full sun with a day temperature between 18 to 21°C. (65 to 70°F.) and between 13 to 16°C.) (55 to 60°F.) at night. Give the pot a quarter of a turn, clockwise, each day to maintain uniform and straight growth.

## Potting

### Planting

Purchase your bulbs as early in the fall as possible not only to get the best selection but to get planting completed during October. The best bulbs for forcing are plump, firm and free from blemishes. After purchase, store the bulbs in open paper bags in a cool dark spot until potting time in mid-October. Use a mixture of equal parts garden loam, builders' sand and peat moss and blend well. Don't add additional fertilizer as the size of the bulb has already determined the size of the plant and flower.

Anything that will hold soil may serve as a planter. However, there must be a drainage hole in the bottom. Porous containers such as clay pots should be soaked in water for at least a day.

Cover the drainage holes with pebbles or broken crockery. Fill the container with lightly compacted soil mixture to within two inches of the top. Place the bulbs (all of the same variety) on the soil as close together as possible without actually touching. You will note that the tulip bulbs have a flat side which should be planted facing the outside of the container. (This will cause the broad leaf of the tulip to droop over the rim.) Add more soil so that one inch of the tip of the bulb shows above the soil line which should be at least half an inch below the rim of the container to allow for proper watering. When the planting is completed, water the tulips by standing the containers in pans of water until the surface of the soil feels moist.

## Storing

For the next 8 to 12 weeks, store the bulbs at a temperature between 4 to 10°C. (40 to 50°F.) in the dark. The soil must always be kept moist. Storage may take place in a dark corner of a porch or shed or the containers may be completely buried in a trench in the garden. A cold frame or a window well is somewhat more convenient for retrieval when the ground is frozen hard. Lacking such facilities, you might be able to sneak a few pots into the main section of the refrigerator where the temperature is normally 4°C. (40°F.). If your refrigerator is the no-frost type, you may have to cover the pot with a plastic bag to avoid excessive drying.

## Forcing

Around the first of January, check the pots to determine whether root growth is showing through the drainage hole. If so, the pots may be moved to a cool dark room with a temperature around 10 to 13° C. (50 to 55° F.). As soon as the flower bud emerges from the neck of the bulb, the plant may be given more light gradually and it should bloom in about four weeks if kept at 13 to 16° C. (55 to 60° F.) at night and in full sun during the day.

## Watering

Constant moisture during the period when roots are forming and after growth begins is vitally necessary for bulbs. When leaves and flowers start into growth, severe drought, either in the soil or in the air, may cause buds to wither and die before opening.

## Feeding

No supplementary feeding is necessary.

## Propagation

Bulbs, once forced, cannot be forced a second time. If the plant is allowed to mature in the pot after blooming, the bulbs may be dried off and saved for planting out in the garden in autumn but don't expect optimum results.

## Special Problems

Grown properly, tulips are problem-free.

169

# VELTHEIMIA viridifolia

*Forest Lily*

A pretty house plant, usually in bloom at Christmas.

## Origin

Genus Veltheimia has five species and is a member of the Lily family (Liliacea). All are native to South Africa.

## Description

*Veltheima viridifolia*, Forest Lily, grows from a bulb. The basal leaves are strap shaped, wavy edged, green and about 12 inches long and 4 inches wide. A tall 24-inch flower spike is crowned with a cluster of 20 to 30 pinkish purple, tubular, drooping flowers.

## Cultivation

During autumn/winter growing and flowering period, keep the plant in full sun. Average room temperature is too warm for this plant; it requires coolness, preferably around 10°C. (50°F.). After flowering, keep the plant growing as long as possible since it is during this period that strength is recovered for flowering the next year. When the bulb goes dormant it may be left in the pot and stored on its side in a dark, cool, dry place.

## Potting

Use a rich fibrous mix of equal parts loam, coarse builders' sand, peat moss, rotted or dried manure and leafmould. Provide drainage with pebbles or pea gravel over the drainage hole. Plant one bulb to a pot that is 2 inches wider than the bulb. Planting period is September to November. Repot old bulbs each year during September.

## Watering

Water only slightly until growth starts, then soak thoroughly and continue full watering throughout the growing cycle. Normal humidity is suitable in a cool temperature.

## Feeding

When growth is underway use water soluble general fertilizer on a 14 day schedule. Continue until leaves fade and the bulb goes dormant.

## Propagation

From offsets that are several years old—separate from the parent bulb at time of repotting.

## Special Problems

High temperature will produce weak, soft growth and poor flowers. Control aphids with insecticide malathion spray.

*Veltheimia viridifolia*

# YUCCA aloifolia
*Spanish Bayonet*

A bold exotic specimen plant.

## Origin

Genus Yucca has about 40 species and is a member of the Agave family (Agavaceae). All are native to the warm regions of North America.

## Description

*Yucca aloifolia*, Spanish Bayonet, grows to 25 feet and may have a single or branched trunk. As older leaves die and are shed, the attractive rough trunk becomes exposed. Terminal growth appears in clusters of bright green, sharp pointed leaves up to 30 inches long and only 2¹/₂ inches wide. Variegated forms are also available.

## Cultivation

Grow in all possible light at normal room temperature during summer. In winter a resting temperature as low as 7° C. (45° F.) is desirable.

## Potting

Use a soil mixture of equal parts loam, coarse bulders' sand, peat moss and rotted or dried manure. Since drainage is critical, use a generous amount of pebbles or pea gravel at the bottom of the pot over the drainage hole.

## Watering

During summer soak and allow the soil to approach dryness before soaking again. Water very little during winter. This plant is tolerant of dry air.

## Feeding

Use water soluble general fertilizer on a 14 day schedule during spring and summer.

## Propagation

From seeds that take up to 50 days for germination; sometimes they stay dormant for a year. Also from offsets or stem cuttings that should be allowed to heal in the open for a few days before inserting in moist sand.

## Special Problems

Wet soggy conditions will induce rot.

*Yucca aloifolia*

# ZANTEDESCHIA
*Calla-Lily*

Grown as a pot plant, the common Calla-Lily *(Zantedeschia aethiopica)* gives a dramatic touch to the indoor garden during late winter and spring. Tubers that receive reasonable care will last for many years, some say fifty.

## Origin

Zantedeschia is a genus of the Arum or Calla family (Araceae). There are about nine species, all native to tropical Africa particularly swampy areas that become dry in summer.

## Description

Plants grow to about 36 inches in height from fleshy tubers. The lush, bright green, arrow shaped leaves are held erect on long fleshy stems. The small flowers are borne in clusters on an elongated club-like spike that is surrounded by a colored bract or spathe, a flower form that is typical of the Arum-Calla family.

Four species are commonly grown: *Z. aethiopica*, (the Calla used by florists), grows to 2½ feet with large smooth triangular leaves and a creamy white, trumpet shaped, pointed spathe that surrounds a bright yellow spadix. *Z. albo-maculata* has mottled green and white leaves and a pure white flower with a blotch of crimson at the base. *Z. rehmannii*, the pink or rose Calla, has light green and white dotted foliage and pink flowers a bit smaller than other species. It is a native of Natal. *Z. elliottiana*, the yellow Calla, has spotted green and white leaves, and deep lustrous yellow flowers that last about two weeks and become greenish with age.

## Cultivation

Grown as pot plants, the Callas should be planted in a 6-inch pot in a mixture of equal parts rich loam, rotted or dried manure and peat moss. Provide good drainage with small stones and pea gravel at the bottom of the pot. Plant the tuber so that it is covered with half an inch of soil. Moisten thoroughly and place aside in a cool spot, 16°C. (60°F.), for the formation of roots. During this period of three to four weeks, very little water should be added and may often be omitted entirely. As soon as top growth appears expose the plant to sunlight and a temperature of just under 21°C. (70°F.). Higher temperature promotes spindly growth. In about 10 to 12 weeks from planting, flower stocks will begin to appear and the plant should be kept in the sun.

Grown as house plants the tubers are normally planted in October. After flowering, and during the following June, the plant should be forced into rest by withholding water and placing the container on its side. In autumn the tubers should be replanted in fresh soil. Grown as a summer flowering plant, the dormant tubers are planted the same as above, but started in March or April. After frost, the plants may be transferred to the open ground or grown in pots sunk into the border or placed in a bright sunny window. In autumn, the plant is forced into rest and the tuber should be stored cool and dry over winter at 10°C. (50°F.) to be reawakened the following spring. Following the rest period the tuber should be removed from the old soil and cleaned.

## Potting

Plant in a 6-inch pot in a mixture of equal parts rich loam, rotted or dried manure and peat moss. Provide drainage with small stones and pea gravel at the bottom of the pot. Tuber should be planted so that it is covered with half an inch of soil.

*Zantedeschia aethiopica*

## Watering

During active growth, Calla needs lots of water, sometimes twice a day.

## Feeding

Supplementary feeding on a 10 day schedule with water soluble general fertilizer will promote lots of flowers.

## Propagation

Usually by division of the tubers and removal of off-shoots at the time of repotting. Seeds take up to 30 days to germinate in warm moist conditions, 21 to 27°C. (70 to 80°F.).

## Special Problems

Soft spots on tubers should be cut away with a sharp knife and the wounds dusted with sulphur.

# ZINGIBER officinale

*Ginger*

Reed-like in appearance with cane-like stems 3 feet or so high and long slender grass-like leaves of a soft green, Ginger makes a beautiful tropical pot plant for indoors or on the summer patio.

## Origin

*Zingiber officinale,* a member of the Ginger family, (Zingiberaceae), is a native of tropical South Asia. It was introduced into America by early Spanish explorers from plants brought to Europe by Marco Polo.

## Description

Ginger has reed-like stems and narrow, glossy leaves that give it a bamboo-like appearance. The plant grows from fleshy irregular roots (rhizomes) that are the source of ginger spice. Grown as a crop, the plant takes ten months from planting to harvest to develop the full pungency of the rhizome. Succulent young rhizomes used for candy ginger and oriental cooking are harvested somewhat earlier before the full pungency is developed.

## Cultivation

The plant does well in normal room temperatures in a semi-sunny location such as an east or west window. Maintain a higher than normal humidity by placing the pot on crushed stone in a humidity tray. During the frost-free months, plants may be summered on the patio or balcony. In autumn the plant will become dormant and the tops will wither. Plants should be set aside for rest in a cool, dry place until late January when new sprouts begin to appear.

## Potting

Use a rich potting soil composed of equal parts rich loam, coarse builders' sand, peat moss and rotted or dried manure or leafmould. Use a generous amount of pea gravel or shard over the drainage hole. Plant new tubers from January on in a pot of comparable size and move on to larger sizes as soon as the root ball fills the pot. Repot tubers taken from storage in fresh potting soil, annually.

## Watering

During active growth keep the potting soil evenly moist. Withhold water during the dormant resting period.

## Feeding

As soon as new shoots begin to show leaves, start supplementary feeding on a 10 to 14 day schedule with water soluble general fertilizer.

## Propagation

Divide tubers in early spring. Make certain each section has an active growing point.

## Special Problems

Essentially a trouble-free plant but poor drainage can induce rot.

*Zingiber officinale*

# ZYGOCACTUS truncatus

*Christmas Cactus, Crab*
*Cactus, Lobster Cactus*

Genus Zygocactus was introduced as a pot plant more than one hundred years ago and remains the most popular and widely grown member of the cactus family.

## Origin

Zygocactus is native to Brazil and a member of the Cactus family (Cactacea).

## Description

This plant grows in the high branches of the tropical forest and like its neighbors—Queen of the Night, Bromeliads, and Orchids—gets nourishment and moisture through aerial roots and the organic debris collected in the crotches of the trees it inhabits. Such plants are known as epiphytes (not parasites) since they merely live in the trees and not on the vital juices of their host.
Species *Zygocactus truncatus* (sometimes identified *Schlum-* *bergera truncata*) has drooping branches made up of short, leaf-like links giving a chain appearance. It is sometimes referred to as "crab" or "lobster" cactus because the individual leaf links give the appearance of a small clawed crab. However, since the bright fuchsia-like flowers found at the ends of the branches appear in December, the plant is more commonly identified as Christmas Cactus. The blooming period extends over the holiday season and often well into the spring. The long drooping branches make this plant ideal for hanging pots or baskets.

## Cultivation

Grow in a half sun, half shade location. After blooming, rest is a vital requirement for continued well being. Rarely is a cactus in active growth more than three or four months of the year. During the rest period give only enough water to prevent shriveling and do not force growth at this time. During the summer, hang plants outside in a filtered sun location. To ensure bloom by Christmas, the plant must have cool nights away from artificial light during autumn. A temperature range of 10 to 15° C. (55 to 60° F.) is required. Plants kept constantly at 21° C. (70° F.) and over rarely bloom. Hybridization has resulted in colors ranging from pink to red and mauve, and of course, white

## Potting

Contrary to popular belief, cacti do not thrive in sand alone, especially Christmas Cacti, which grow in nature in patches of decaying vegetation among branches. An ideal soil mix is three parts leafmould, one part builders' sand, one part well-rotted manure and one part good garden loam. Also, for each pot, include a teaspoon of bone meal but don't overdo this since this type of cactus enjoys acid rather than alkaline soil

## Watering

As with other cacti, water is a very important consideration. In general, these plants respond best when watered heavily at infrequent intervals. They should not be on the same watering schedule as other house plants. Constant dribs and drabs of water may eventually lead to the death of the plant. Err on the side of under watering until experience is gained. During the rest period give only enough water to prevent shriveling.

*Zygocactus truncatus*

## Feeding

Use water soluble general fertilizer during period of active growth on a two-week schedule.

## Propagation

The simplest and easiest method of propagating is by cuttings made at a joint, preferably in spring or summer. All cuttings should then be set aside on a shelf in a cool, dry location until a callus forms at the base, in one or two weeks. Then it may be placed in a pot of coarse, moist builders' sand until roots are formed, after which the plant may be planted in the soil mix discussed previously.

## Special Problems

This plant is essentially trouble-free.

# Part Two

# INDOOR GARDENING GUIDE

# Indoor Gardening Guide

# Potting Soil

Soil must do more than just hold a plant erect. Soil must provide suitable growing conditions for the roots so that the plant is well supplied with water and plant food. The soil must also drain freely of water to maintain circulation of air in the soil since a supply of oxygen for the roots is just as important as a supply of carbon dioxide for the leaves if optimum growth is to be achieved.

The best growing soil is one that drains freely while retaining some moisture and plant nourishment. Most plants will not grow in dense compacted soils and even if rootlets are able to penetrate such areas they soon die either from lack of oxygen around the soil particles or the build up of retained carbon dioxide generated from their own growth processes. Heavy garden soil in a pot may become so firmly compacted that even water has difficulty getting through it, let alone air, and the result may be a plant that is either too dry or waterlogged. An ideal soil mixture is one that is about two parts solids capable of holding one part each of water and air.

Most house plants grow well in soil-less growing mixes based on peat moss and builders' sand with food added as fertilizers or dried or rotted manure. These ingredients are thoroughly mixed then gradually moistened to develop a consistency that is easily handled. These mixes are easier to produce, store and are more uniform than soil-based mixes but watering and feeding can be more difficult. They require routine supplementary feeding with water soluble fertilizer solution especially during the growing season.

**Coarse builders' sand** is definitely not beach sand; it is the grade commonly used in the preparation of concrete. A small portion shaken in water in a bottle settles to give a clear solution.

**Peat moss,** as sold commercially, is a soft, light brown colored material. The water holding capacity of peat moss is its greatest asset and when incorporated into the potting mix it prevents rapid evaporation and provides for a proper exchange of air. The nitrogen content of peat moss is normally slow in availability due to its antiseptic nature. However, the introduction or inoculation with cellulose bacteria from rotted or dried manure hastens the release of this food. **Dehydrated or dried manure** is heat dried manure supplied in flakes. The heat processing destroys the weed seeds which may be present in rotted manure.

**Garden soil,** if used, should be mixed with builders' sand, peat moss and rotted or dried manure in equal proportions.

When garden soil is used it is important to sterilize it to get rid of harmful bacteria, insects and weed seeds. This may be accomplished by filling a roasting pan or stewing kettle with soil and covering with aluminum foil that has been liberally punctured with a fork or toothpick to allow the escape of moisture. Bake for 45 to 60 minutes in the oven at a temperature of 180°F. (82°C.) and be prepared to ventilate since the odor will be pungent. To sterilize lesser amounts, water may be added to the soil to make a slurry then brought to a boil on top of the stove. In both cases let the soil cool completely before use.

Soil sterilizing chemicals are available at large garden centers. This is a longer process and the treated soil must be thoroughly aerated after treatment to remove all residual chemicals. Processing could be carried out in the larger, heavier gauge plastic sacks.

Most house plants also grow well in John Innes seed and potting soil-based growing mixes. Four are widely available in the shops: John Innes seed (JIS) and John Innes Potting Nos. 1, 2 and 3. John Innes Potting mixes contain sterilized loam, peat and sand in the ratio 7:3:2 parts by volume. For each cubic yard of mix, the addition of 5 lb. of John Innes Base fertilizer and 1 lb. of chalk produces JIP1, double the fertilizer and chalk, JIP2 and triple them, JIP3. Most house plants, including many ferns, can be safely grown in JIP2 but, because this mix contains chalk, special ones should be used for lime-hating plants.

Store your supply of prepared soil-less mixes in large plastic bags so that they will remain evenly moist and be readily available for planting and repotting projects. Do not store soil-based mixes for more than one month—it is best to make them up as and when they are needed.

**Leafmould** may be substituted for dehydrated cow manure since it is also valuable as a gradual source of nitrogenous material as well as cellulose bacteria. Leafmould is easily prepared by collecting leaves in a circle of wire fencing. Keep them moist and turn them over occasionally during the summer months. Decay will proceed rapidly by collecting the softer leaves such as maple, birch and willow. White oak leaves take longer.

**Perlite** is volcanic rock that has been expanded by high temperature. It is used primarily for soil aeration. It has no absorptive qualities and is used by those who do not have access to coarse builders' sand. It is more expensive than sand.

**Vermiculite** is mineral mica that has been expanded by high heat. Because of its nature, it also provides drainage but unlike perlite it does hold moisture as does peat moss. It is more expensive than sand.

# Potting and Repotting

There is nothing complicated about planting in pots once you have assembled the proper materials: potting soil, crocking, pots, labels and plants. The term potting is usually applied to the first planting of seedlings and cuttings, whereas repotting refers to the transfer of a plant from one container to another usually because it has become root bound in the original pot.

Cuttings should be potted as soon as they have developed a strong set of roots. If the rooting has been taking place in water, a visible inspection is no trouble at all; if it has been rooting in a rooting medium, sand, vermiculite, etc., you may have to lift the cutting gently to determine rooting progress.

Seedlings should be potted when they are showing their third or fourth leaves over and above the original seedling leaves present at the time of germination. Repotting should occur when the root system has completely filled the container and is showing signs of becoming compacted with the result of weak top growth due to either lack of nutrients or insufficient drainage.

All pots and containers should be scrubbed clean whether they are wood, plastic, metal or clay. Clay is a naturally thirsty material and after cleaning should be submerged in water for 24 hours to prevent excessive moisture withdrawal from the potting mix.

The basic requirements of successful potting are a soil mix that will retain moisture and nutrients and a drainage system that rapidly drains away all excess water. Most authorities recommend a piece of crock, (broken clay pot) over the drainage hole to prevent blockage. While this is useful it is not necessarily adequate so add an additional one inch or so of small stones in the form of pea gravel which is readily available at large garden supply centers. Many recommend the addition of activated charcoal over the drainage material or a bit of sphagnum moss to prevent soil penetration. These steps are not absolutely necessary and of no particular value because if the soil mix

is not proper or the drainage material is inadequate there is no rescue with a bit of charcoal or sphagnum.

For seedlings and root cuttings fill the pot with moist potting soil to within half an inch of the rim of the pot since this space is necessary for ease of watering. Firm the soil gently into place with the fingers, then tap the pot

sharply on a bench or table top to ensure proper settling in. Make an adequate depression in the center of the soil and plant the seedling or rooted cutting at the same soil or rooting level to maintain the same amount of stem open to the air. Using the thumb and forefinger of each hand, press down near the stem of the plant to ensure

1. Gently remove plant from outgrown pot.

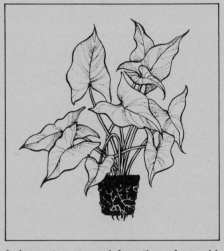

2. Inspect roots and free them from old soil.

3. In new pot, layer clay shards, coarse gravel, moss or charcoal and potting mixture. Firm plant into position.

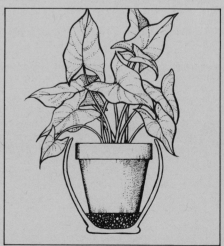

If you use a decorative container without drainage, double pot, with inside pot on layer of gravel.

firm soil in the region of the roots. Do not use the thumb around the edge of the soil like crimping pastry for pies as this compacts the soil in the wrong location. Water thoroughly by submerging the pot in a pan of tepid water to a depth just under the soil line. This will ensure thorough contact of the roots with the potting mix. Set aside to drain. Don't water again until there are signs of the soil drying out. This may be determined by poking a forefinger into the soil. Keep the plant in bright light out of direct sun. To ensure proper humidity and to mitigate wilting, the plant may be placed for a while in a clear plastic bag and closed with a fastener after blowing into it to give full distention. You now have a nursery/terrarium.

Once a plant has filled the container with roots it becomes necessary to undertake repotting. Young plants should be moved to the next size pot. Don't jump from a 3-inch to a 9-inch pot. Prepare the container as before and place the drainage material. Now turn the plant out of its pot by placing the left hand on top of the soil with the fingers straddling the main stem. Turn the plant upside down and try to remove the pot with the right hand. If it

doesn't budge, give the rim a sharp tap on the edge of a table or bench. If this doesn't work set the plant upright and run a thin, blunt knife or spatula around the inside between the soil and the pot and start over. When the plant is out of the pot inspect the roots for vitality and attempt to get rid of as much old soil as possible without disrupting the root system. A pointed pencil is useful for this. Measure the plant into the new pot keeping it at the same relative height as in the previous container. While holding it centered and in place with the left hand, start feeding in new potting mixture under and around the root system, firm gently as you proceed using your fingers or blunt pencil. The soil line should be half an inch below the rim of the pot after gentle firming. Firm the plant in position as described previously using the thumb and forefingers. Water thoroughly and set aside in bright light. Do not fertilize until the plant returns to active growth.

Eventually you will arrive at a finishing pot size 8, 10, 12 or 14 inches or more, either because there is no more space for a larger container or the plant is outgrowing the space available. At this time repotting will probably be re-

quired every two or three years. This is accomplished by removing the plant from the container as before. However, it may now be too tall to turn over. If this is the case, grasp the main trunk firmly, lift and tap the rim gently with a rubber hammer. Once the plant is removed set it upright and with the aid of a long, thin, sharp knife cut away a one or two inch slice of the root system on one side only. Return the plant to the container after checking the drainage hole and material. Fill the space provided by the removed slice with fresh potting mixture. Make an identification mark of the location so that you can work from the opposite side at the time of the next repotting. This root pruning not only allows the plant to continue in the same container with fresh soil but also brings about a dwarfing which is an important consideration for plants that tend to outgrow the living quarters.

Drainage is vital to pot culture. If you must use a water tight container for decorative or other reasons, double pot by first placing the plant in a proper pot that can be placed in the outside container which should have enough space at the bottom for an additional inch or two of pea gravel.

# Pots and Planters

Pots should complement the plant. The return of plants to room decoration requires that the pot be as attractive as the plant on display. The final selection remains with the individual. The choice and availability may run from hanging baskets, bird cages, copper pots, Venetian, Spanish or Mexican

pottery, wood or plastic tubs, soybean kegs, bean jars, crocks, etc.

Since porosity and drainage are vital to proper watering, the solution sometimes calls for double potting. Porous clay pots are still considered by many as the ideal container despite the fact that they dry out rapidly in warm

weather and high indoor temperatures and have a higher rate of breakage. The earth colors of unglazed clay pots, terra-cotta, tan, off-white and brown blend into any setting. Since the pots are porous they do exude moisture which usually leads to unsightly deposits that have to be scrubbed off

# Pots and Planters (continued)

from time to time to maintain top-notch appearance.

The standard clay pot was developed primarily for the florist and nursery trade and is usually as tall as the top diameter of the pot and sometimes higher which often results in a disproportionate container for the plant being displayed. They are usually available in 2 to 16-inch sizes. The standard fern or azalea pot is only three-quarters as high as the top diameter and thus gives a lower profile that is better for most plants. They are made in 4 to 14-inch sizes. Bulb pots or pans are also available and designed to give a height one-half of the diameter.

Non-porous pots in the form of plastic, rubber, glaze, glass, china, etc., have gradually gained acceptance to the extent that they are recommended as the best containers for apartment use where a low humidity and high temperature environment prevails. The absence of porosity means that moisture does not escape through the sides and thus less attention is required. The most ubiquitous non-porous container is, of course, what is now the common plastic pot available in dark green, white and red oxide. Shapes and sizes are the same as clay pots. The plastic pots are relatively unbreakable, light in weight and may be plunged in the summer garden beds. Plastic saucers supplied with these pots are waterproof and, unlike clay saucers, they protect furniture and floors from unsightly moisture rings.

Wooden containers are ideal for the larger specimens and small trees that are appearing more and more. Podocarpus and Citrus are examples of plants well suited to this type of pot. Wooden containers are available in four basic shapes: circular, hexagonal, square and rectangular. They are mostly natural wood in color but can be stained black or painted flat black with one of the modern latex paints. Such containers are normally constructed of hardwood or cedar and thus have a built-in decay resistant property along with moisture retention and high insulation value when moved onto the patio for the summer season. One drawback with the larger sizes is the requirement of a durable, unbreakable saucer or water catching tray to prevent damage to floors and rugs. Formed circular copper saucers as well as outside hard rubber are available for this purpose. Unfortunately, the hard rubber saucers are somewhat conspicuous because of the green color.

Growing plants in containers with no drainage hole is just too difficult a proposition. It can be done but is a risky business and a great deal more trouble. Faced with this situation resort to double potting by placing the plant in a conventional pot of a size that can be slipped into the jardinière or specially decorated container. With this treatment a regular inspection can be made to determine that all is well and the plant is not sitting in a pool of water which is deadly to the root system. For direct planting, such containers are best reserved for forcing Paperwhite Narcissus or growing the Umbrella Plant (*Cyperus alternifolius*) which just loves to sit in water.

Hanging containers are pretty much a part of the scene these days and are found in many forms—wire, clay, glaze and plastic. The drip and overflow from a hanging plant is the despair of many who don't have room in the shower or over the sink to take care of the chore. The newer plastic hanging containers have molded-in saucers that alleviate this problem once the proper volume of water per watering is determined.

# Watering

How much and how often to water is the despair of many indoor gardeners. Relax. It is almost impossible to over-water a plant assuming all the requirements of soil mixture and pot drainage have been given proper attention. However, soggy soil and puddles of water are fatal to most plants not native to the bogs and swamps. The importance of water for plants becomes obvious when you consider that the leafy parts are 70 to 85% water. Even the woody parts often contain as much as 50% moisture. Many plants have a degree of adaptability and survival despite exposure to excessive moisture or dryness. However, don't rely on this characteristic. The amount of water a plant receives is no less important than the light and temperature in which it is growing. Plants growing in soil constantly lose large amounts of water by transpiration (breathing) through the foliage and this water must be replaced through water absorbed by the root system. If water is unavailable the plant soon wilts and dies unless there is prompt remedial action.

While most people aspire to a rule of watering such as twice a week, once a week on Monday, there can be no overall rule that will apply to all situations. Each apartment, house and room is a variable environment. The only rule is to poke a finger into the soil to determine that moisture is always present. Anyone tending the plant soon develops a schedule to fit the growing conditions. It is impossible to over-water a plant at the time of watering. In fact, it should be completely soaked and allowed to drain. It is possible to over-water a plant by consistent additions of dribs and drabs of water that never thoroughly wet the root ball. All plants need water. How much and how often is determined not only by the plant but by the time of year—summer (growing), winter (resting), light exposure, room temperature and humidity. Keep checking the soil condition with a finger and you will soon establish your own rules.

Water should never be applied below the room temperature in which the plant is growing. It should be slightly warmer for best results. Cold water applied directly from the tap will not only cause trauma and shock to the root system but may cause death of the fine rootlets and subsequent root rot.

The amount of water vapor (humidity) in the air surrounding the plant is an important factor influencing the amount of water loss through transpiration from the leaves. Although excessive transpiration may not cause death, it is generally considered in-jurious to the well being of a plant and is one cause of brown burn spots on leaves and blasting of flower buds. The air in a room at 21°C. (70°F.) can hold considerably more moisture than one at 15°C. (60°F.). In other words, as temperature increases, the moisture holding capability also increases as does the drying capacity. During the winter, the cold air reaching the inside via doors and windows doesn't bring much water vapor into the room. Actually, when such air is heated it seeks moisture from the plants, furnishings and people present in the area. Most people are familiar with the term "relative humidity," which is expressed as a percentage. Fifty per cent relative humidity means the air is carrying fifty per cent of its moisture holding capacity at the existing temperature. Fortunately there is a wide selection of humidifiers on the market that can maintain the relative humidity of a room within a comfort zone for plants and people. A relative humidity in the 40 to 50% range is a boon for dry skin, irritated nose, throat and eyes as well as transpiring plant foliage.

Further boosts in humidity for luxuriant plant growth are frequent sprayings with clear water and wiping of both sides of the leaves with a soft wet cloth.

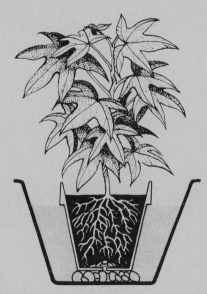

**WATERING PROBLEMS**

**1. If water runs right out bottom of pot, potting mixture has dried out and shrunk.**

**2. If water just sits on top of soil without draining, the soil mixture has caked.**

**3. The solution: prick over the potting mixture surface and soak the whole pot.**

# Feeding

All plant food must be in solution before it can be absorbed by the root tips to provide nourishment required for plant growth. Properly mixed and applied water soluble fertilizer gives a plant immediate access to the salts and chemicals required for growth. Use of granular fertilizers as well as decomposed organic material requires a longer period for results as they must be broken down to a form that is soluble in water before they can be utilized by the plant.

Take care not to overfeed your house plants. In general, plants in *active* growth and planted in a basic potting mixture need to be fed every 10 to 14 days. House plants growing in sand, vermiculite, peat moss or perlite need one-third to one-half strength fertilizer applied with every watering.

# Light

Probably no other factor plays a more important role in the growth of plants than does the visible portion of radiation, "light." It is the ultimate source of all energy stored by a plant in photosynthesis from which all forms of life, plant and otherwise, are directly and indirectly dependent. Without light, growth and all life would cease.

Photosynthesis is the term applied to the miraculous ability of green plants to manufacture food. The facts about this process may be summarized as follows:

Water supplied through the roots and carbon dioxide taken from the air are the raw materials used. Chlorophyl, the green pigment coloring of the plants, captures light energy which becomes stored in the carbohydrates that are formed by chemical reaction. Oxygen is liberated as a by-product of the process becoming the chief source of oxygen in the atmosphere. Thus plants of all types provide not only food but life-giving oxygen for all forms of life. The rate of photosynthesis is related to temperature and for every 6° C. (10° F.) temperature rise above the minimum growing temperature of about 10° C. (50° F.), the rate increases 2.2 to 2.6 times. However, once the temperature range of 13 to 18° C. (55 to 65° F.) is reached, photosynthesis is optimized and the rate begins to decline. Accordingly, this temperature may be considered the most effective for best growth. While photosynthesis is a process for storing radiant energy of light, it should be noted that very little of the radiant energy that falls upon plants is used in the process. Only the part absorbed can be used and this part consists only of visible red, yellow and blue-violet light. Even though 62 to 63% total sunlight energy is in the infrared (invisible heat rays), practically none is used in photosynthesis.

The composition of sunlight energy is: infrared 62 to 63%; visible 37%; ultraviolet .6%.

Since there is only a limited amount of sunlight in most homes, it is rather convenient that a great many plants grow by nature in partial sun. It is important to select plants whose light requirements can be met, otherwise they will sulk and eventually die. More often than not, light requirements for a plant will be given in terms of exposure. This can be misleading since the southern exposure (high intensity light) will only give maximum sun if it remains unobstructed by tall buildings or trees on the outside or curtains or window shades on the inside.

**Southern exposure** should provide sunlight almost all day and it is considered the most desirable since flowering plants may be grown directly in the window while foliage plants will still get enough light some distance away. Plants needing maximum sunlight include: Amaryllis, Bougainvillea, Geranium, Hibiscus, Croton, succulents (including cacti), Oleander, etc.

**Eastern exposure** (medium intensity light) receives strong, cool morning light for a few hours in the morning and a low intensity light for the remainder of the day. This is a partial sun location.

**Western exposure** also falls into this category. Plants that thrive in such locations include: African Violet, Gloxinia, Ivy, Bird-of-Paradise, Fuchsia, Gardenia, Norfolk Island Pine, Spider Plant, Wax Plant, etc.

**Northern exposure** (low intensity light) with bright sky light, no sunshine, is suitable for many foliage plants that will also tolerate interior locations for limited periods of time. During the short days of winter it is only common sense to use a location adjacent to an east window or to provide supplementary lighting. Flowering plants will not perform in a northern location. The foliage plants that will do reasonably well include: Australian Umbrella Tree, Monstera deliciosa, Begonia Rex, Aspidistra, Dracaena, Ivy, Fiddle Leaf Fig, Norfolk Island Pine, Philodendron, Rubber Plant, Snake Plant, Pothos, etc.

Most foliage plants will not tolerate extended periods of direct sun. The sunlight causes over-heating, rapid loss of moisture with eventual drying out of internal leaf tissues and death of such sections. This condition appears as brown patches of dead tissue on the leaf.

On the other hand, if a location is too dark, the plant will not receive sufficient light to manufacture enough food for growth. The leaves will become smaller and smaller and the plant may eventually die preceded by the browning and shedding of lower leaves.

The amount of indirect sunlight may be supplemented with light from incandescent light bulbs. They should be placed far enough away to prevent over-heating and eventual browning of

# Light (continued)

the foliage. Spot lights should be avoided and preference should be given to flood types that spread heat and light over a broader area.

Fluorescent light generates less heat than incandescent and seldom produces heat burn. With the proper use of light, plants may be grown and flowered in parts of the home that receive neither daylight nor sunlight.

The capability of plants for growing towards light is known as "phototropism." When light comes from one direction only, a plant will bend or grow towards the light source and thus must be turned regularly if it is to maintain upright growth.

Much experimentation has been recorded for planting, growing and harvesting of all types of plants under all types of artificial light, e.g. carbon, sodium, mercury, fluorescent and tungsten. It is indeed fortunate that of all the types tested, the two most familiar to us, fluorescents and incandescents, are the best for promoting plant growth. To grow flowering plants to maturity, balanced lighting is required and achieved with 25 watts of incandescent in proportion to 40 watts of fluorescent (cool white). To avoid possible over-heating by the incandescent portion, equal results can be achieved by using a fluorescent light combination of equal parts wide spectrum and cool white.

Foot-candles are the standard units for measuring the intensity of light, just as degrees measure temperature. If you want to take measurements you will probably find that the light meter for your photographic work has a scale for foot-candles. Don't worry if you don't have one, you can succeed without it. The outdoor light intensity on a clear summer day may be in excess of 10,000 foot-candles; on a dreary winter day, it may be as low as 500 foot-candles.

Plants may be roughly divided into three light groupings:

1. Low intensity (foliage plants), below 300 foot-candles. Most plants will fade away quite rapidly when intensity is below 50 foot-candles.
2. Medium intensity (African Violets, etc.), 300 to 700 foot-candles.
3. High intensity (seedlings, sunflower, Hibiscus, etc.), above 700 foot-candles. When light intensity is too high, leaf burn usually results. Just below this stage leaves will be lighter green due to the destruction of some of the green chlorophyl in the tissues. Substitution of one tube with one wide spectrum tube will give an even closer approximation of the light most beneficial for plant growth.

# House Plant Pests

A healthy house plant in the proper environment is rarely bothered by pests. Regular washing and mist spraying of the leaves is an easy and worthwhile preventative. With proper light, watering, feeding and air circulation, most plants develop a vigor that discourages the most persistent invasions. Prompt detection of trouble is half the battle and if care is taken to keep pests out of the house in the first place, you are well on the way to healthy happy plants. Develop a suspicious nature, and carefully inspect and decontaminate new acquisitions as well as plants returned indoors from summering in the garden. Always remember that insecticides and fungicides are poisons. Extreme care and full attention to the manufacturer's directions is not only efficient but prudent. Obviously such chemicals must always be out of the reach and access of children. If you have a sick or invaded plant, here are some of the things to look for:

**1.**

**Ants** spoil more than picnics. They are an indirect cause of plant damage by aphids. Aphids secrete a sweet sticky honeydew that is much loved by ants, so much so that ants maintain aphids as a farmer keeps cows and will often take their aphids along when new colonies are formed. Strict control of aphids and use of ant traps will take care of any ant problems.

**2.**

**Aphids**, commonly called plant lice, range in color from light green to blue-green, red and even black. They are about 1/16 of an inch, soft bodied, winged or wingless and tend to feed in colonies on leaves and stems. A few feed on roots especially when so positioned by ants. However, most suck sap from leaves or stems causing curling and distortion. Hardly a plant exists that is not subject to attack by one or more species of aphids. The honeydew excreted by aphids forms an ideal medium for black sooty mold which also detracts from the natural beauty of the plant. For control, wash the foliage, and spray with malathion.

**3.**

**Mealy Bugs** are sluggish, oval insects covered with white powdery fluff and are easy to see on the stems and leaves. The cottony clumps in leaf axils are the egg deposits. These are sucking insects that eventually devitalize the plant. Control can be achieved by washing and spraying with malathion. Individual bugs may be removed with a cotton swab moistened with rubbing alcohol.

**4.**

**Spider Mites**

Spider mites weave a fine white web on the underside of leaves where the small mites scurry about sucking sap from the leaves. Often damage is first notic-

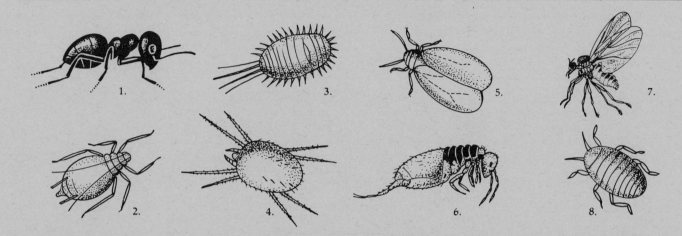

ed when the leaves turn pale yellow or reddish brown in spots on the top or underside of the leaves. Unchecked, spider mites can severely reduce plant vigor and in some cases kill the plant. Spider mites can range in color from off-white to green or red. They are oval shaped and not larger than 1/60th of an inch for the females and 1/80th of an inch for the males. Spider mites thrive in a warm, dry environment, thus frequent mist spraying of infected plants with clear water will help reduce the population. To control these pests, thoroughly cover all parts of the infected plants with an insecticide spray such as malathion. Follow the label directions carefully. Of the mites' natural predators, the ladybird is the best known.

**5.** ⎯⎯⎯⎯⎯⎯⎯⎯⎯⎯⎯⎯⎯⎯⎯⎯

**White Flies** are tiny insects closely related to aphids and scale insects. The adults are about 1/16 of an inch long with white powdery wings. Both larvae and adults damage plants by sucking sap from stem and leaves. Infected leaves will wilt, become pale, mottled or stippled and cause the plant to turn yellow and die. The insects may cause fruit and leaves to become covered with a black sooty mold. Leaves sometimes become sticky with honey dew. To control, spray with malathion.

**6.** ⎯⎯⎯⎯⎯⎯⎯⎯⎯⎯⎯⎯⎯⎯⎯⎯

**Springtails** are small (1/16 inch) wingless insects that jump like a flea but without the aid of powerful hind legs. Instead, springtails jump by means of a tail-like appendage. Although harmless nuisances that feed on decaying vegetable matter such as dead roots in the potted plant, they are readily controlled by applying a solution of malathion to the potting soil.

**7.** ⎯⎯⎯⎯⎯⎯⎯⎯⎯⎯⎯⎯⎯⎯⎯⎯

**Fungus Gnats**, small (1/8 inch), near-black insects are mostly a nuisance to have flying around the house plant. The harmless adults lay eggs on house plant soil which hatch into tiny white maggots that feed mostly on decaying organic matter such as dead roots. Eradicate by drenching the soil with a malathion solution.

**8.** ⎯⎯⎯⎯⎯⎯⎯⎯⎯⎯⎯⎯⎯⎯⎯⎯

**Scale Insects** barely move and adhere to the undersides of leaves and along the stems. They are less than 3/10 inch long and characterized by a waxy covering. They weaken plants by sucking the juices. Control with malathion spray or a swab of cotton on a toothpick dipped in rubbing alcohol.

# Plant Troubles

The adage "an ounce of prevention is worth a pound of cure" is never more true than in the case of house plants. When a plant is treated as an individual and given proper soil, pot size, light, temperature, humidity, water and prophylaxis in the growing area, a strong, healthy plant is assured. When conditions are less than ideal the plant develops symptoms that offer clue for corrective measures. A plant with highly developed symptoms is best destroyed as a weak, sickly plant becomes a liability and a ready source for insect and organism attacks to companion plants. Below is a chart giving symptoms and reasons for plant troubles.

(see over)

# Plant Troubles (continued)

## IDENTIFYING PLANT AILMENTS

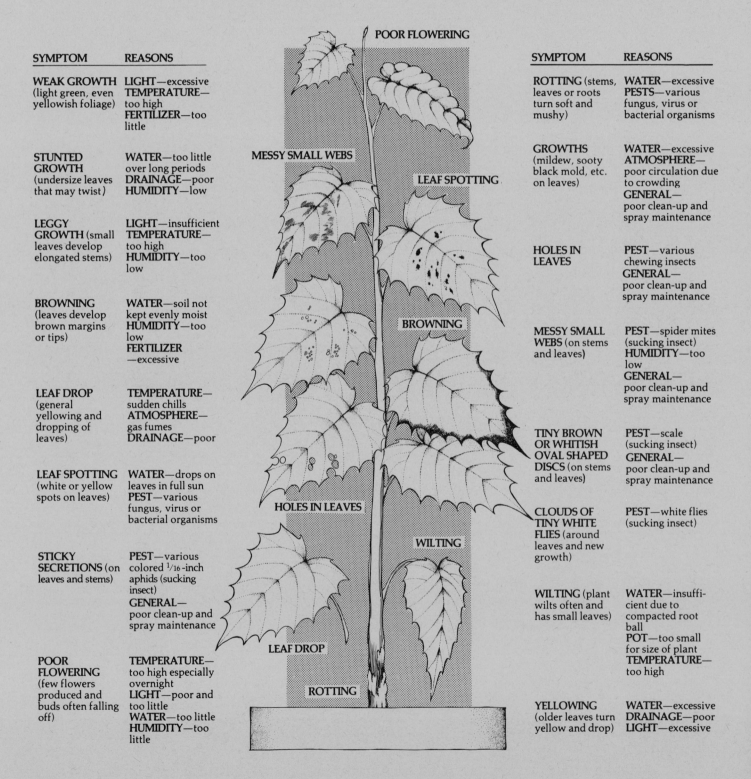

| SYMPTOM | REASONS |
|---|---|
| **WEAK GROWTH** (light green, even yellowish foliage) | **LIGHT**—excessive **TEMPERATURE**—too high **FERTILIZER**—too little |
| **STUNTED GROWTH** (undersize leaves that may twist) | **WATER**—too little over long periods **DRAINAGE**—poor **HUMIDITY**—low |
| **LEGGY GROWTH** (small leaves develop elongated stems) | **LIGHT**—insufficient **TEMPERATURE**—too high **HUMIDITY**—too low |
| **BROWNING** (leaves develop brown margins or tips) | **WATER**—soil not kept evenly moist **HUMIDITY**—too low **FERTILIZER**—excessive |
| **LEAF DROP** (general yellowing and dropping of leaves) | **TEMPERATURE**—sudden chills **ATMOSPHERE**—gas fumes **DRAINAGE**—poor |
| **LEAF SPOTTING** (white or yellow spots on leaves) | **WATER**—drops on leaves in full sun **PEST**—various fungus, virus or bacterial organisms |
| **STICKY SECRETIONS** (on leaves and stems) | **PEST**—various colored 1/16-inch aphids (sucking insect) **GENERAL**—poor clean-up and spray maintenance |
| **POOR FLOWERING** (few flowers produced and buds often falling off) | **TEMPERATURE**—too high especially overnight **LIGHT**—poor and too little **WATER**—too little **HUMIDITY**—too little |

Diagram labels: POOR FLOWERING, MESSY SMALL WEBS, LEAF SPOTTING, BROWNING, HOLES IN LEAVES, WILTING, LEAF DROP, ROTTING

| SYMPTOM | REASONS |
|---|---|
| **ROTTING** (stems, leaves or roots turn soft and mushy) | **WATER**—excessive **PESTS**—various fungus, virus or bacterial organisms |
| **GROWTHS** (mildew, sooty black mold, etc. on leaves) | **WATER**—excessive **ATMOSPHERE**—poor circulation due to crowding **GENERAL**—poor clean-up and spray maintenance |
| **HOLES IN LEAVES** | **PEST**—various chewing insects **GENERAL**—poor clean-up and spray maintenance |
| **MESSY SMALL WEBS** (on stems and leaves) | **PEST**—spider mites (sucking insect) **HUMIDITY**—too low **GENERAL**—poor clean-up and spray maintenance |
| **TINY BROWN OR WHITISH OVAL SHAPED DISCS** (on stems and leaves) | **PEST**—scale (sucking insect) **GENERAL**—poor clean-up and spray maintenance |
| **CLOUDS OF TINY WHITE FLIES** (around leaves and new growth) | **PEST**—white flies (sucking insect) |
| **WILTING** (plant wilts often and has small leaves) | **WATER**—insufficient due to compacted root ball **POT**—too small for size of plant **TEMPERATURE**—too high |
| **YELLOWING** (older leaves turn yellow and drop) | **WATER**—excessive **DRAINAGE**—poor **LIGHT**—excessive |

# Propagation

The reproduction of favorite plants to share with friends or to replace older plants that have begun to look a bit scraggly and less than best is not so much a challenge as the next logical step for maintaining top-notch indoor house plants.

Fortunately, plants have evolved protected with two basic methods of reproduction or survival:

Sexual, from seeds produced by the flower parts when male pollen fertilizes the female ovule. Some plants are self-fertilizing while others have male and female parts on separate plants as is the case with palms.

Asexual, from vegetative parts of the plant when a leaf or a bit of stem or root may, under proper conditions, develop a new root system and a new plant. Asexual propagation includes cuttings, stolons, offsets, runners, suckers, division, air-layering, grafts, etc.

## SEXUAL PROPAGATION
### SEEDS

If this is the first attempt to grow seedlings, start small and try only a few varieties for experience.

Containers can vary from wooden flats, aluminum foil loaf tins, cut off milk cartons, to sleek plastic seed trays available from the garden center. Whichever is used, make an adequate number of drainage holes in the bottom of the container. Compressed peat pots are ideal. They are a complete sterile growing unit that combines the functions of a pot and a potting soil. When water is applied to the pellet it expands to 1¾ inches in diameter and 2 inches high. Sow three or four seeds to an expanded pellet, then thin to one seedling.

Seeds may also be sown in a commercial sterile medium such as milled sphagnum moss, vermiculite and perlite, or you may prepare your own soil mixture by mixing equal parts coarse builders' sand, peat moss and garden soil. Such a mixture gives a loose friable medium that will accommodate the tiny hair roots of the seedlings. This mixture should be sterilized before planting by using a commercial drench or you may sterilize it in the kitchen oven by filling a roaster pan or a large kettle with the soil mixture, covering with aluminum foil which has been punctured in several places to allow the steam to escape. Bake in a 180°F. oven for 40 to 60 minutes. Cool and mix thoroughly before use. This treatment destroys weed seeds, insects and fungus that can cause damp-off in seedlings. Damp-off causes young seedlings to shrivel and collapse at the soil line. Spores of the disease are usually present in all soils and the conditions for germination of seeds are equally favorable to the growth of the fungus in unsterilized soil.

To proceed with planting, assemble the containers, soil mix, identification labels and the seeds. Fill the containers or flats with the soil mix to within half an inch of the top and place the container in a tub containing about 2 inches of water. Soak until the top of the soil is wet. Remove from the water and drain thoroughly. This will help to gently compact the soil mixture and the seeds may now be sown.

Fine seeds should never be covered and it is easier to broadcast them over the surface than to attempt planting in rows. The seeds should be pressed firmly onto the surface of the mix, using the fingertips.

Water again by placing the container in the tub and allowing moisture to show at the top. Remove, drain and cover with glass or clear plastic wrap. Plastic bags are very useful for this purpose. Covering helps maintain a condition of high humidity during germination but all coverings must be removed as soon as tiny shoots appear.

Place in a bright window or 6 to 8 inches under fluorescent lights. Temperature requirements are in the range of 16 to 18°C. (60 to 65°F.). Keep a daily check on the planting to ensure the soil remains moist.

The first set of leaves to appear are the seedling leaves, the second set are the true leaves and at this time supplementary feeding with diluted liquid fertilizer at a strength for seedlings as recommended by the manufacturer may begin.

When the seedlings are half an inch high, with several pairs of leaves, they are ready to be transplanted into a regular soil mixture. Each plant should be lifted with a pencil or a wooden label as gently as possible to keep the roots intact. Plant two inches apart in individual pots, pressed peat pots or in flats. (If peat pellets have been used seedlings may be moved to regular pots without any root disturbance as soon as roots penetrate the outside of the pellet.) Water with a fine spray and place in full light. Avoid direct sunlight for the first few days. Sturdy compact plants need lots of light, otherwise they will become leggy and weak.

## ASEXUAL PROPAGATION
### CUTTINGS

The rooting medium can be coarse builders' sand, vermiculite, or peat moss alone or in mixture. It is essential that the medium remain damp and provide thorough aeration as well. Containers can be anything that holds 3 or 4 inches of rooting medium and have drainage holes. For bottom heat there are a variety of trays on the market with a small heating cable inside. Except for succulents, high humidity must be maintained to prevent wilting. A clear plastic bag is excellent for this purpose. Cuttings should always be located in bright light out of direct sun. As soon as a generous supply of roots have formed, individual rooted cuttings should be moved into individual 3-inch pots with the appropriate soil mixture for the plant. Gradually move on to larger size pots as soon as the root ball occupies the available space. Freshly potted cuttings should be kept in sheltered light for the first few days. Commercial rooting hormone chemical is a great boon for the indoor gardener. It is available at most garden supply outlets under various trademarks. Scissors are not suitable for taking cuttings since they tend to crush as they cut. Use a very sharp knife, razor blade or razor-blade knife.

### Soft Wood Cuttings

Soft wood cuttings are taken after the first flush of spring growth of shrub-like plants that eventually produce woody stems. Such cuttings are usually 3 to 5 inches of flexible, semi-mature terminal growth. These require trimming to just below a leaf node as well as partial trimming of very large leaves. With rooting hormone and bottom heat of 24 to 27°C. (75 to 80°F.) rooting will occur in thirty days or so. Humidity is maintained by enclosing in clear plastic. *(see over)*

# Propagation (continued)

## Soft Wood Cuttings

**1. Choose a non-flowering, flexible shoot. You may need to trim very large leaves.**

**2. Brush or dip the cut end into rooting hormone, and put it in a small pot of sandy compost.**

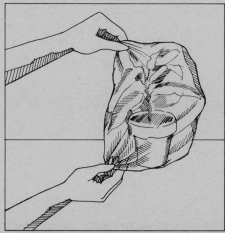

**3. Cover pot and plant with clear plastic to maintain humidity.**

## Herbaceous or Soft Tissue Stem Cuttings

This covers a wide range of house plants. Many will root in a glass of plain water with a bit of activated charcoal to reduce stagnation. Roots produced in this manner are usually brittle and coarse with very few hair roots. Such rooted cuttings require gentle handling to avoid damage to the roots at the time of transplanting. However, this method is widely used for one or two cuttings. Stronger rooted cuttings are produced with rooting hormone and the regular coarse builders' sand or vermiculite rooting medium. Cuttings should be 3 to 4 inches in length.

## Leaf Cutting

**Remove a healthy mature leaf and cut veins that stand out on underside. Place leaf underside down in rooting medium. Weight with small pebbles. Roots will form at cut points.**

## Leaf Cutting

Leaf cutting is a common method for propagating African Violets and Begonias. Leaves with stems attached may be rooted in water or inserted in a rooting medium. Full leaves or pieces of leaves with the major veins cut may be rooted in coarse builders' sand or vermiculite medium either by insertion or by pinning the leaves to the top of the medium.

## OTHER METHODS OF ASEXUAL PROPAGATION

### Air-Layering

This method is a popular technique for propagation of tropical and subtropical plants that have outgrown the ceiling space. This is achieved by selecting a spot 6 to 12 inches from the top of the plant and making a sloped cut about half way through the stem with a sharp knife. Using a brush, dust the upper part of the cut with hormone powder. Wedge the cut open with a small pebble or toothpick and cover the area with two handfuls of moist peat or sphagnum moss (sphagnum is easier to handle). Hold the moss in place with a square of clear plastic film wrapped around the rooting medium and tied close to the top and bottom of the moss ball. In approximately thirty days roots will completely fill the moss ball and become visible through the clear plastic. When this occurs cut away from the main stem just below the moss root ball. Remove the plastic and plant the root ball in the appropriate soil mix for the plant. Keep moist and sheltered from hot sun for a week or so until the roots strengthen.

### Suckers

These are leafy shoots produced from adventitious buds at the summit of underground parts of plants. Such shoots can be cut away with a sharp knife with a portion of the root intact, trimmed back, and placed in the propagation bed for further root development.

### Stolons and Runners

These are branches that grow downwards and produce roots when contact is made with soil. When completely rooted such growth can be separated from the parent plant and planted to grow into an independent plant. These may also be treated as stem cuttings.

## Air-Layering

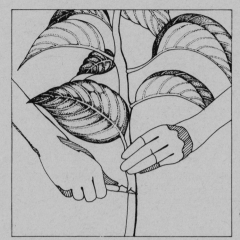

**1. 6 to 12 inches from top of plant, make a diagonal cut halfway through the stem.**

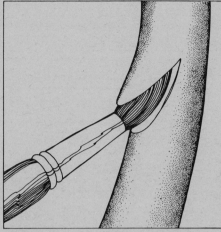

**2. Brush the upper part of the cut with hormone powder.**

**3. Wedge open the cut with a pebble or toothpick. Cover with moss and wrap with plastic.**

**4. Roots will show through plastic. Unwrap and sever root ball. Plant in appropriate soil.**

### Offsets (Offshoots)
These are short lateral branches or stolons produced near the base of plants, a form of natural propagation. They usually take root and make clumps of new plants. They can be cut away with a sharp knife and planted to form a new plant.

### Spores
Spores are asexual, usually one celled, reproductive bodies of flowerless plants (ferns, mosses, mushrooms). The basic difference between spores and seeds is that they contain no embryo. While reproduction of plants from spores is not dependent on sex as in flowering plants, the process is akin to it.

The black or brown spots of many ferns produce thousands of spores. When these alight or are caught on moist surfaces (e.g. moist chopped sphagnum moss) they germinate to produce small plant bodies (prothallia) which develop sex organs (male— antheridia and female—archegonia) and these in turn develop sex elements (gametes) which fuse. The fusion body then develops into the plant, in this instance a fern plant. Moist, humid conditions are required for successful propagation by spores. Chopped sphagnum moss is a normal rooting medium.

### Bulbils
Bulbils are small bulb-like structures usually borne in leaf axils (i.e., Tiger Lily), or among or in place of flowers as well as in other unusual places. These may be harvested and started in a rooting medium or potting soil.

### Bulblets
Bulblets are the small bulb-like structures that form underground around the bulb and root structure of the mother plant. These may be harvested and planted to produce new plants.

### Bulbs
Bulbs are made up of closely packed, fleshy scales attached to a comparatively small base part of solid tissue. Tulips and onions have continuous scales, while those of lilies are separate and leaf-like. Individual scales, with a portion of base attached, can be planted to propagate mature bulbs in the course of time.

### Corms
These are the enlarged bases of herbaceous stems. They consist of one or several internodes that serve as a storage of food materials. A corm differs from a bulb in being solid rather than bud-like and differs from tubers by being mainly upright or nearly so. Corms usually produce one to three new corms above the old one which shrivels and dies.

### Cormels
Cormels are little subsidiary corms (called spawn) that are often developed between the old and new corms. Cormels may be collected and planted to grow into large corms in two or three years.

### Tubers
These are usually swollen roots as with Begonias, Dahlias, Sweet Potato, etc. or they may be swollen stems as is the case with Jerusalem Artichoke and the potato.

For example, Tuberous Begonias can be propagated by dividing the tubers. The best procedure is to place the tubers in damp peat moss in a warm location until new growth commences and then divide the tuber into sections (with a sharp knife) with at least one sprout. Before planting, the cut surfaces should be dusted with sulphur to prevent decay while roots and new growth get underway.

### Rhizomes
Rhizomes are thickened shoots that grow underground or along the soil surface producing roots from the underside and leaves or shoots above ground. The Bearded Iris is the most familiar of such plants. Rhizome scales are produced by some of the Gesneria, i.e., Achimenes, Gloxinia, etc. These scales may be scraped away and planted individually.

# Terrarium

Recently gardening in bottles has been hailed as a new discovery. Actually the discovery of the terrarium was around 1830 and is credited to Dr. Nathaniel Ward, a British medical man by training and a botanist by avocation. The discovery was made during a casual walk through the woods when grasses and small ferns were discovered growing in a discarded glass bottle. A few years of experimenting by Dr. Ward and others during which plants in sealed bottles were sent on sea voyages for as long as eight months, led to a publication of the findings and subsequent popularity of covered glass gardens or Wardian Cases. This, in turn, led to a successful expansion of tea and rubber plantations. For the first time, 20,000 tea plants were successfully delivered to the Himalayas by this technique.

Planting your own bottle garden is one way to relieve mid-winter boredom. The first consideration should be location since a terrarium should not be in direct hot sunlight. Bright light, yes, even fluorescent light, but not direct sunshine—otherwise you may end up with over-heated and cooked plants. Flowering plants such as African Violets and variegated foliage plants need the brightest light, while ferns and green foliage can take lower intensities. When you decide on the location, consider the size and shape of the glass container that will suit the room. Keeping the décor in mind, search the attic, the storage room or the garage for a suitable container—possibly an old aquarium of clear glass with a cover or an opening that may be covered. If the search is fruitless you will be able to purchase a container designed or at least selected for bottle gardens. Choose a container with a large enough opening to accommodate your hand. Smaller openings will require specially designed scoops, tongs, hooks and pruners on long wire or chopstick handles that will fit into the bottle to allow for planting as well as maintenance.

Your purchase should also include: drainage material—this may be pea gravel, aquarium gravel or clear glass marbles or beads; drainage material cover—fiberglass window screening can be used to separate the soil from the drainage material which otherwise would soon become soil clogged (pieces of old nylon stockings can be used for this purpose); potting soil—this is sold commercially for house plants and is usually sterile. It is important to use sterile material since fungi and mould thrive in enclosed environments and they will destroy the garden; perlite—this is expanded volcanic rock with no food value. It provides aeration and drainage. If it is not available use coarse grit instead; peat moss—this provides moisture retention without waterlogging; sand—a coarse builders' grade complements the soil mixture and further aids drainage and soil aeration; charcoal—the activated horticultural type absorbs impurities as they develop.

You are now ready to prepare the bottle garden for planting:

1. Wash and thoroughly dry the inside of the container and try to keep the inside clean during the addition of the various materials. Form a funnel out of heavy kraft paper, long enough to reach the bottom of the container.

2. Mix three parts of drainage material to one part of activated charcoal and use enough to give a depth of 1 to 4 inches below the planting soil.

3. Fit the drainage material cover on top of the drainage material. Try to keep the edges neat and attractive.

4. Add planting mixture that is made of two parts potting soil, one part peat moss, one perlite or grit and one builders' sand, plus a little activated charcoal. Mix thoroughly and moisten with water for ease of handling. Place the drainage cover by pouring small portions through the paper funnel. It is important to note that the planting bed now completed should be no higher than about one-quarter the total height of the container. This gives the best appearance and allows head room for the plants.

5. With the soil in place you are ready to begin planting. It is best to concentrate on miniature, small size plants. Avoid over-planting. One plant by itself can make an attractive planting.

Small plants may be found in supermarkets, department and chain stores, nurseries and florists. Select small healthy specimens. When you bring them home, wash the leaves thoroughly with a tepid mild soap solution to remove all pests. Let the leaves dry and soak the root ball before removing from the pots. Carefully remove as much of the loose potting soil as possible before planting in the bottle garden. Make a suitable depression in the new planting location, place the plant and firm into place. Water slowly and carefully with room temperature water until the soil turns evenly dark. Put the terrarium in its permanent location and close the top with a cork, glass or the cover provided. Once the terrarium is planted and water-enclosed, a rain cycle is established by the plants taking in moisture through the roots and bringing out water vapor through their leaves. As the vapor builds up it condenses on the inside of the glass and returns to the soil. If a time arrives when there is no condensation then add water. If there is too much condensation, remove the cover for a few hours to reduce the amount of moisture. Once the bottle is established it can go on for months, even years, unattended.

6. Maintenance-remove all dead leaves promptly. If insects become a problem use a general purpose, indoor insecticide supplied in a spray can. Smudges on the inside glass surface may be removed with a small piece of sponge or towelling attached to the end of a chopstick. Fertilize monthly, only during periods of active growth, using a half strength water soluble general fertilizer solution.

Some of the plants that do well in bottle gardens include: Ajuga (Bugle Weed), Adiantum (Air Fern), Buxus (Japanese Boxwood), Episcia (Flame Violet), Hedera helix (Ivy), Helxine soleirolii (Baby Tears), Chamaerdorea elegans (Parlour Plant), Oxalis, Pilea microphylla (Artillery Plant), Saintpaulia (African Violet), Sansevieria trifosciata hahnii (Bird's Nest Snake Plant), Streptocarpus (Cape Primrose), plus many others.

# Dish gardening

Frustrated gardeners who have no landscape to design and mold, find that dish gardening gives some scope for their landscape expression. A dish garden can vary in size from a nut bowl to a large brandy snifter, to any space available, either by purchase of specialized containers or those you can make with wood or plastic. In general, a dish garden should allow for at least 4 inches of soil and have a drainage hole. Growing in dead end containers is possible but the extra care hardly justifies such selections. While small containers can only at best give a crowded collection of plant shapes in balance, a large rectangular container allows for the creation of a miniature landscape. In due course, plants outgrow their space and must be removed and given individual pots to grow on to a grander size.

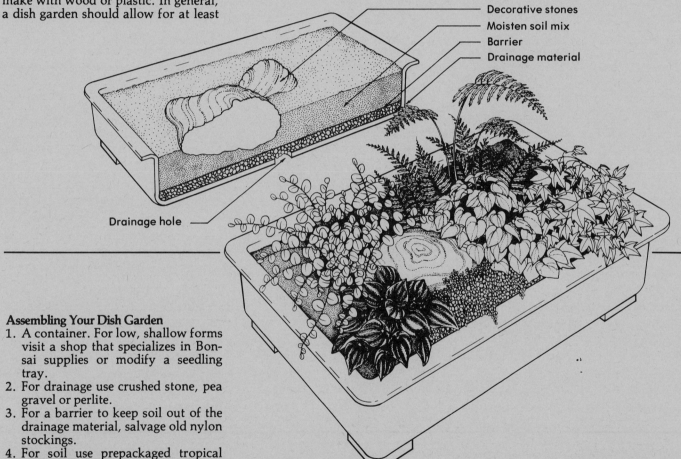

Decorative stones
Moisten soil mix
Barrier
Drainage material

Drainage hole

### Assembling Your Dish Garden

1. A container. For low, shallow forms visit a shop that specializes in Bonsai supplies or modify a seedling tray.
2. For drainage use crushed stone, pea gravel or perlite.
3. For a barrier to keep soil out of the drainage material, salvage old nylon stockings.
4. For soil use prepackaged tropical soil mix and add extra coarse builders' sand or perlite to open up the texture.
5. For small plants visit the nursery or the supermarket where there is an extensive supply of young plants in 2½-inch pots. Most are well suited for dish gardens in their youth. Remember cacti and succulents are particularly slow growing.
6. Search out a few small rocks or pieces of decayed wood or branches to include in scale to add interest to the landscape.

Having assembled all the materials, start off by making sure your container has holes. Cover the bottom with about one inch of drainage material. Cover the drainage material with a single layer of nylon stocking fabric. Next add moistened soil mix to within half an inch of the rim of the container. Then proceed with the planting and design.

Watering is critical especially if you have chosen a container with no drainage holes. In any event water should be applied at the base of each plant. Experience will determine how much and how often. Locate the plant in a semi-sunny location and remember it is portable so can be used as a centerpiece on the dining table or on the coffee table in the living room for brief periods.

# Bonsai

Bonsai is more than just a dwarf plant in an ornamental container. It is a definite art form that interprets nature in miniature to the oriental taste. It requires an understanding of the fully mature tree or shrub as it appears in nature. The technique of Bonsai requires not only skilful pruning and trimming but will often require changing the plant's shape by hanging weights on the ends of the branches. While it is somewhat startling and to a degree unbelievable to see a Bonsai 300 years old, it must be remembered that age is not really the name of this hobby, it is the appearance of age that counts.

Influenced by the early Chinese art, the Japanese have been practicing Bonsai for over 800 years. This activity relates to their great interest in nature and appreciation of shape and line—in short, the oriental art form. Around the end of the 19th century, a technique was evolved whereby the shape of a plant could be changed by wrapping copper wire on branches and trunks and bending to the desired shape. No. 8 wire is quite heavy and two strands are usually used for shaping and training trunks. Lighter gauges (10, 12, 16, etc.)

are used for the lighter growth. It is reported that trees which were distorted and stunted through natural conditions of altitude, wind or seashore were collected and potted for this hobby. As the supply from this source dwindled, conifers were grown

Cascade

Raft

Windswept

# Bonsai (continued)

in containers from seeds or cuttings and this method gave good looking, small scale trees for planting in ornamental containers. Eventually training and control of growth was undertaken to simulate the gnarled and weathered specimens once available in nature and thus Bonsai was originated. While Bonsai are basically outdoor plants, usually evergreen, needle bearing types, there are some species that will adapt to indoor culture even for apartments. Included in this group are Gardenia, Azalea, Hawthorne, some Hollies, Bamboos and Citrus, so be sure to inquire about any plant you purchase or receive. The outside Bonsai should not be kept inside more than a few days at a time. When indoors, all Bonsai should be positioned in bright light with good ventilation but away from direct sunlight and heat (hot air or otherwise) that might over-heat the container and soil.

Watering a Bonsai must not be neglected for any great length of time. A daily watering from top or bottom will usually suffice. Too much water can be as damaging as not enough. Misting and washing the foliage will help humidify and remove any pests.

Shaping by pinching and nipping of buds is carried out in spring to early summer and heavy pruning that is needed should also be done at this time. Wiring of stems and branches to persuade the tree to a particular shape should be undertaken during periods of active growth when tissues are more pliable. For additional persuasion, hang small weights on the ends of the branches.

Roughly about every two years the plant will need repotting. You must check this by lifting the plant out of the container and inspecting the roots. If they are packed firmly in the shape of the container with very little soil showing, then repotting should be undertaken. Remove about one-third of the root ball by trimming and return to the same container making certain that the drainage holes are free—a piece of broken pottery or wire mesh may be used for this purpose. Refill the container with a soil mixture of equal parts sharp builders' sand, peat moss and good garden loam. Firm around the roots. Water and keep the plant in a shaded protected location for a few days to allow new root growth to get underway.

Bonsai should not be fed with dry fertilizer or manure. Use only the water soluble types and err on the over-dilution side. The best time to fertilize is when new growth is showing. Remember you don't create Bonsai by undernourishing the plant. Keep it healthy.

To grown good healthy plants, outdoor Bonsai should be wintered cold so as not to force unseasonal growth and to allow the plant a normal rest period. Place the plants on a 4-inch bed of gravel in a coldframe and pack straw around and over the container. Cover the frame with a loose fitting window sash or plastic film so that light is not excluded and some air circulation is maintained. Gradually rehabilitate the plants in the spring by uncovering during the day and protecting at night until the hard frost has passed and there is no danger of freezing the root ball and cracking the ornamental container.

For vacation care, get acquainted with another Bonsai devotee and reciprocate. As an alternative, in the summer, bury the containers to their rims in a section of the garden that receives only northern sun. Excessive dryness and moisture may result in death of the plant.

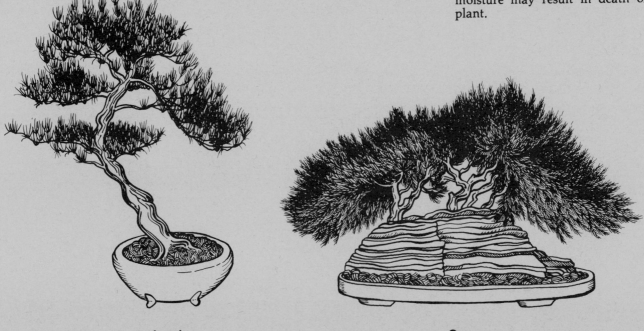

Leaning

Group

## Tools for bonsai cultivation

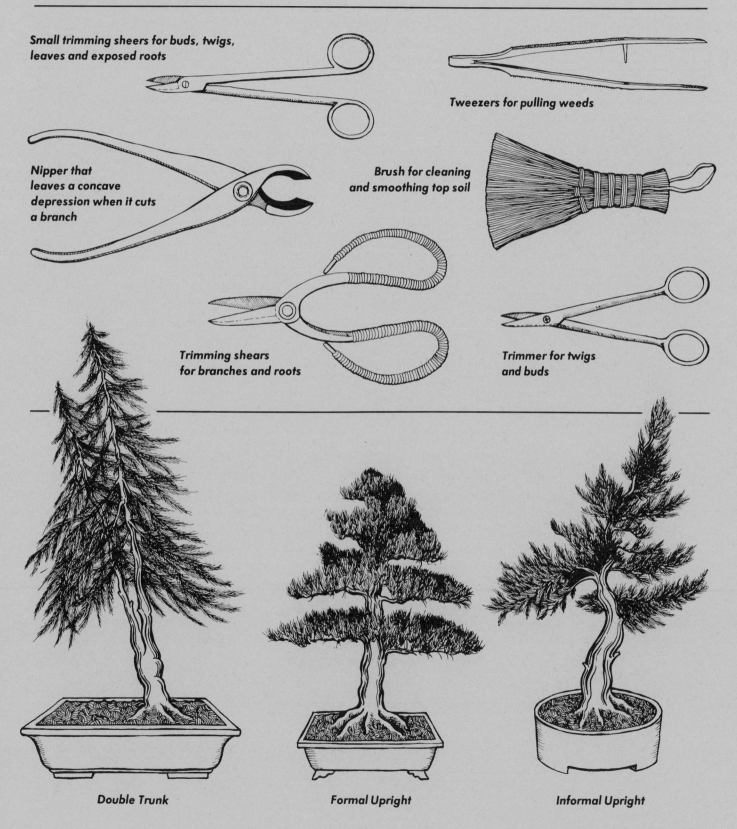

Small trimming sheers for buds, twigs, leaves and exposed roots

Tweezers for pulling weeds

Nipper that leaves a concave depression when it cuts a branch

Brush for cleaning and smoothing top soil

Trimming shears for branches and roots

Trimmer for twigs and buds

**Double Trunk**

**Formal Upright**

**Informal Upright**

# Kitchen Herb Garden

Man has used plants through the centuries for food, shelter and medicine. Almost all books on plants published from the 14th to the middle of the 18th century were mainly written from the medicinal viewpoint and were called "herbals." The wisdom of the ancients is reaffirmed today with modern scientists now re-evaluating many of the old time herbals and searching jungles and other remote areas seeking native remedies.

Broadly speaking, a herb may be annual, bi-annual or perennial. It is usually considered to be a plant with aromatic or healing properties. Herbs with flavor add a dash of elegance and sophistication to the plainest foods. A pinch here and a sprinkling there can elevate a meal to an experience.

Herbs are a delight to grow since most need only two things: a soil that is not overly rich, and sunshine. Most can be grown indoors. Herbs are hardy, easy to grow plants despite their delicate flavor. They prosper in a well drained alkaline soil but are remarkably tolerant of less than ideal conditions. If the soil is too rich, they may have large leaves but poor fragrance and flavor. Most require water regularly but will sulk if left standing in it. Although sun is basic for most, there are a few, such as parsley and mint, that will do well in light shade. The best time to harvest herbs is when the plant's aromatic oils are highest during the sunny morning hours. Tender leaves may be cut as soon as plants are well established. With flowering varieties, blooms and leaves are harvested together just as the buds begin to break.

**Sweet Basil** is an annual 1 to 2 feet tall, with leaves of varying shades of green and purple and tiny white flowers. It is a spicy herb with a slight peppery taste that may be used in salads, vinegars, sauces, vegetable dishes (especially fresh sliced tomatoes) and stuffings. Grow it as a potted plant or in the garden border. It repels flies and mosquitoes. Pinch prune for bushier plants. Harvest before flowering.

**Chives** are perennials which grow in grass-like clumps two feet tall. The leaves are tubular and the flowers are a lavender color. They have a mild onion flavor and can be used in soups, salads, omelets, soufflés, and in sour cream for baked potatoes. The clumps make attractive ornamental plantings anywhere in the garden. They are probably the easiest plant to grow in the kitchen herb garden. The plant may be grown from seeds. Divide the clumps in autumn and pot for use during the winter.

**Dill** is an annual growing 3 to 4 feet tall with lace-like green leaves which add a delicate flavor to meat dishes (notably lamb), salads and fish. The seeds have a slightly bitter taste that enhance sauces and home made breads. Stems and seeds are widely used in pickling. The plant also makes a nice background plant. Grow it from seeds and make repeated sowings for a lasting supply. Harvest the leaves as the flowers begin to open. The brown flat seeds should be harvested as they ripen.

While it is a delight to use freshly picked herbs, they can be prepared for later use by drying the leaves and flowers. Herbs can be dried by spreading the cuttings on a flat surface to permit free circulation of air. A window screen is ideal for this purpose. When the leaves are crisp and dry, strip them from the stems and store in air-tight containers. Decorative glass containers for storage add a nice touch in the kitchen. Herbs may also be dried by hanging small bunches in an area where there is no sunlight or dust. Small amounts can be dried in the oven with the door open under close watch and never above 150°F. (66°C.).

Just before use, remove the required amount and crush on a cutting board or in a small mortar.

A second storage method for many herbs, especially chives, dill, tarragon, basil, etc. is freezing. Harvest and wash the herbs as for drying, but leave the foliage on the stems. Bunch together and tie, and holding the tail of the string, blanch the bunches in boiling unsalted water for 50 seconds. Cool immediately in ice water, then remove the leaves from the stems and wrap in freezer bags or foil for immediate freezing. Keep the batches small for easy retrieval.

You can obtain a wide selection of herb seeds from most mail order seed houses.

**Sweet Marjoram** is a perennial in mild climates but to be safe winter a rooted cutting inside. It is a bushy plant one to two feet tall, with grey/green leaves and purplish pink flowers. It is a sweet spicy herb that complements stuffed or sautéed mushrooms, salads, vinegars, meats, sauces and wine marinades. It makes an attractive container plant and may be used throughout the garden as well. Grow from seeds or cuttings and locate where it will receive plenty of sun.

**Mint** is a perennial growing 1 to 3 feet tall. Spearmint, peppermint, orange mint, golden apple mint, all have purplish flowers with leaf color ranging from dark green, to green streaked with purple and yellow. It is used as a garnish for foods and drinks. Crushed leaves add zing to coleslaw and vegetables. It is often used for teas. Use mint in sauces for lamb and veal and garnish fruit salads and lemonades with it for a refreshing flavor. It will do well as a container plant and is ideal as a ground cover for banks. Grown from seeds or cuttings, it will do well in sun or shade. Keep the flower spikes cut before they go to seed.

**Oregano** is sometimes called "pizza herb," and is a perennial about 2½ feet tall. It has medium size, oval green leaves and purplish pink flowers. This pungent relative of sweet marjoram is used fresh or dried on meat and vegetable dishes, salads and sauces (especially tomato). The plant does well in a container and lends itself to use as a ground cover for banks. It may be grown from seeds or root division.

*(see over)*

199

**Parsley** is a biennial plant grown from seed that has been soaked at least 24 hours or from transplanted potted plants from the nursery. It grows 6 to 12 inches tall and the glossy dark green leaves may be finely curled, triple curled or plain. The plant has a refreshing fragrance and is widely used as a garnish on salads, meats, seafoods and for dressing some vegetables. It is a good seasoner alone or with chives and onions. It makes an ideal edging for walks and flower beds and is an attractive indoor plant.

**Rosemary**, often called "queen of the herbs", has been used for 3,000 years and signifies remembrance. It is a perennial and perfectly hardy when grown outside. It is shrub-like, growing up to 24 inches with grey-green oblong leaves. It has a slightly bitter taste and is excellant in stuffings, especially poultry, and baked fish stuffings. It is often used in herb breads and baking powder biscuits. Start from seeds sown indoors or cuttings and keep it pruned to encourage growth.

**Sage** is a hardy perennial that will grow 4 to 6 feet tall. The foliage is grey-green and bears spikes of pale blue flowers that make it an attractive addition to the garden. Sprinkle on chicken, lamb and roasts or use in the stuffing. It can be trained as a hedge and makes a useful ground cover. Grow from soaked seeds or transplants. It likes a dry sunny spot and needs frequent pinch pruning to direct the growth. Each spring prune back to about 6 inches.

**Thyme**, the herb of courage, is a perennial ground cover that grows 8 to 12 inches high with pink and lilac flowers. The clove-like flavor enhances stews, gumbo, chowders and cooked vegetables. It is often used in sauces for turkey and fish. Grow the plant from seeds or cuttings in dry soil with lots of sun. Thin plants to 8 to 12 inches apart and clip the tops when in full bloom. One plant to a pot will suffice in the kitchen.

# Window Salad Garden

With the soaring prices of green groceries, every little bit raised will be an economic contribution as well as a gastronomic treat.

Among the vegetables to consider for the window salad garden are: lettuce, radishes, mustard, garlic sprouts, parsley, chives, onion sprouts, cress and bean sprouts.

For those fortunate enough to have a growing under lights setup, there is no problem since these plants fall into the 300 to 400 foot-candle range on an 8 to 10 hour day. For most people it is a matter of selecting the brightest, coolest window location.

Gardening may be undertaken in any container that allows for 4 to 6 inches of soil with ample drainage holes so that the soil never stays wet, only moist.

An ideal soil mixture is equal parts coarse builders' peat moss and well rotted compost manure. Commercial potting soil can also be used. If it seems a bit muddy when wet add a generous amount of perlite or grit to ensure proper aeration of the soil and roots.

Once growth is underway, start supplementary feeding with water soluble general fertilizer on a ten day schedule, half strength at first, then gradually to full strength to the manufacturer's directions.

In general, a program of successive plantings should be followed for a continuing supply of greens.

**Cress,** garden cress, pepper cress or upland cress as opposed to watercress, is a fast growing salad plant that may be clipped when only one inch or so high. With careful cutting it will send up new growth for further harvest. Sow the seed thickly, about ¼ inch deep. Look for germination in a few days. Make successive sowings 10 to 14 days apart. Cress is a cool weather plant that grows quickly and soon passes its prime. It has a pungent, peppery taste, is rich in vitamins and makes a fine addition to most salads.

**Lettuce** is best confined to the leaf type such as Tom Thumb or dwarf cos like Little Gem. You will probably harvest when the plants are 4 to 5 inches high, using the complete plant, roots and all. For this reason alone, successive sowings are a must. Take care that the seed is only slightly covered since light is necessary for lettuce seed germination. Sow fairly thickly and cover with glass or clear plastic until germination occurs. Germination takes 6 to 8 days and the first thinning harvest can be as early as three weeks. Green lettuce leaves are an excellent source of Vitamin A and a good source of Vitamin B.

**Radishes** are a good source of vitamin C and are easy to grow. Plant the seeds about ½ inch deep—germination will take place in 4 to 6 days. Plant only the early varieties such as Cherry Belle and thin to 1 inch as soon as possible. Wash and use the thinnings in a salad. The crop matures in 3 to 4 weeks.

**Parsley,** usually considered a garnish, is a vegetable in its own right and one of the best sources of Vitamin A and when used uncooked it is also an excellent source of Vitamin C. This plant is a biennial and usually lives over winter outside but produces little new growth. By sowing seed indoors in spring and autumn, parsely can be picked all year-round. The seed takes 2 to 4 weeks to germinate and 70 days or so before you can start harvesting, so it is necessary to plan ahead for this salad plant. Being such a valuable source of vitamins, it should be used chopped or whole in salads and in cooking as frequently as possible. It is such a decorative plant that it can be grown outside in a hanging basket so it can be moved inside during late autumn.

**Mustard greens** will do well under lights as well as on the windowsill. You can grow a pot in about 4 weeks that should give more greens for the salad than lettuce. Substitute vermiculite in the soil mix in place of peat moss.

**Chives** are often offered in the supermarket in 2 x 2 inch plastic pots. The only way to succeed with these is to immediately turn the plant out of the pot and soak it in tepid water for several hours. Then tease it apart to individual plants that may be planted six or so to a 4-inch pot. Grow on the cool side.

**Garlic sprouts** provide a source for a mild garlic taste. Separate a garlic clove into individual cloves and plant four or so in a 4-inch pot. Place half in, half out of the soil with the pointed end up.

**Shallot sprouts,** the pièce de résistance in French cooking, may be obtained in the same manner as garlic sprouts by planting onion sets.

**Onion sprouts** can be obtained by hanging a small mesh bag of onions from the kitchen pot rack. From February on, there is a plentiful supply of green sprouts for the salad and won ton soup.

**Bean sprouts,** one of the chief fresh vegetables in the diet of most oriental populations, can be grown with ease to round out the winter salad garden. You can grow these without soil, plant food or lights. The best known beans used for this purpose are soya beans and mung beans. Of the two, soya bean sprouts are by far the most nutritious. Start with 2 ounces of dried beans and a two cup, wide mouth jar. Wash the beans thoroughly in a strainer and place in the jar. Cover with room temperature water. In 12 hours they will have swollen to triple their size. Tie a cloth over the mouth of the jar, invert the jar and drain. It is preferable to rinse thoroughly and drain every four hours to wash away putrefactive bacteria and molds as well as to change the air in the jar or you can rinse in fresh water and drain daily. Within 4 to 5 days the sprouts will be fully developed. The edible portion is the sprout with or without the attached cotyledons (embryo leaves). Separate the sprouts when they are about ⅛ inch in diameter and 3 inches long. For highest vitamin content use fresh and uncooked as an addition to a salad. If cooked, use little or no water.

# Artificial Lighting

If you don't have a sunroom or greenhouse and have run out of windowsills there is always the basement where you can garden as effectively as in any greenhouse. Growing plants under artificial light opens up a new gardening world that can make any room, light or dark, downstairs, upstairs, even a closet, a green thumb delight.

A wide variety of plants, exotic and otherwise, can be grown in the basement and it will serve for many special functions as well such as a place to root cuttings, force bulbs, maintain special plants indoors during winter and a place to start seedlings for transplanting outdoors in the spring.

Since the beginning of time, light has played a major role in plant growth but the effect of light remains one of the most complicated questions in plant study today.

While photosynthesis is the plant's process for storing the radiant energy of sunlight in the form of carbohydrates (sugars), it should be noted that very little of the radiant energy that falls on plants is utilized in the process; that only the part absorbed can be used and that this part consists only of visible red, yellow and blue-violet. Even though 62 to 63% of total sunlight energy is in the infra red (invisible heat rays) practically none is used in photosynthesis. Sunlight energy also has about 37% in the visible spector and about 0.6% in the ultraviolet.

The visible or white light is a mixture of colors; the red portion causes plants to grow tall and leggy, while the blue-violet portion promotes low stocky growth. A proper balance of colors produces plants of normal growth and shape. Much experimentation has been recorded for the planting, growing and harvesting of all types of plants under all types of artificial light, e.g. carbon, sodium, mercury, fluorescent and tungsten. It is indeed fortunate that of all the types tested, the two most familiar, fluorescence and incandescence, are the best for promoting plant growth.

To grow plants to maturity, balanced lighting is recommended and is achieved with 25 watts of incandescent in proportion to 40 watts of fluorescent. However, for short periods, such as for growing seedlings for planting out in

## TABLE I

2/40 watt fluorescents with 12 inch reflector

| | | Distance From Lamps | Approx. Foot-Candles |
|---|---|---|---|
| High Intensity | | 1" | 1000 |
| | | 2" | 800 |
| | | 3" | 700 |
| Medium Intensity | | 4" | 600 |
| | | 5" | 550 |
| | | 6" | 500 |
| | | 7" | 450 |
| | | 8" | 400 |
| | | 9" | 390 |
| | | 10" | 360 |
| | | 11" | 325 |
| | | 12" | 300 |
| Low Intensity | | 18" | 225 |

## TABLE II

| | |
|---|---|
| Germinating Seeds: | 10 lamp watts/sq. ft. of growing area 6" to 8" from seed bed |
| Seedlings: Mature leafy house plants | 10-15 watts at 12" to 15" |
| Mature flowering plants and vegetables | 15-20 watts at 12" to 15" |

the border, either type will do, with fluorescent being preferred due to its shape and coolness which reduces the chance of cooking seedlings. It is also preferable since flowers are not being produced at that particular time.

"Foot-Candles" is the standard unit for measuring the intensity of light, just as degrees measure temperature. If you want to take measurements, you will probably find that the light meter for your photographic work has a scale for foot-candles. Don't go out and buy one for this project, since you can succeed without it. The light intensity on a clear summer day may be in excess of 10,000 foot-candles; on a dreary winter day, it may be as low as 500 foot-candles.

Plants may be roughly divided into three light groupings:

1. Low intensity (foliage plants).
2. Medium intensity (African Violets).
3. High intensity (seedlings, sunflowers, hibiscus, etc.).

Basing the basement garden on two new 40 watt fluorescents with a 12-inch reflector, the following table will give some guidance for position of the groups. The center 12 inches of a 4 foot fluorescent lamp produces the most intense light, closest to daylight, particularly from lamps designated standard, cool-white. Measurements reported in Table 1 are from the center of two tubes. Special wide spectrum fluorescent lamps are available that give the total balance of light in each lamp for growing plants. The standard lamp is designed primarily for the propagation and growth of low energy indoor plants that grow in shade or semi-sun. The wide spectrum lamp is designed for the growth of plants that normally grow in full sunlight and require high energy, such as roses, tomatoes, cucumbers, etc.

While the rated life of the wide spectrum lamps is 18,000 hours, the effective life for the plant growth is 5,100 hours or about one year on a 14 hour per day operating period. Required light intensity with these lamps is shown in Table II. To determine watts per square foot of growing area, multiply the width by the length of the growing area and divide this figure (square feet of growing area) into the rated wattage of the lamp.

An important factor in the timing of plant maturity is the length of days and nights. In temperate regions, plants growing out of doors are exposed to alternate light and darkness. Day length varies from 15 hours in summer to 9 hours in winter. It is known that growth and development of plants is markedly influenced by the length of day. For example, Chrysanthemum and Poinsettia will flower with short days (long nights). Since a regulated lighting period is desirable, an automatic on/off plug-in, time switch is a good investment for controlling power cost as well as the health of the plants. Reportedly, tomatoes, for instance, are injured and finally killed in any day length over 19 hours.

The response of plants to length of day period of illumination has been called "photoperiodism," and plants may be grouped as being short day (10 to 13 hours of light), long day (14 to 18 hours), and indeterminant (12 to 18 hours).

Short day plants include Christmas Begonias, Chrysanthemums, Gardenias, some Orchids, Poinsettias.

Long day plants include Calceolaria, China Asters, Coreopsis, Dahlias, Lettuce, Nasturtiums, Philodendron, annuals, seedlings and cuttings.

Indeterminant day plants include: African Violets, Begonias, Coleus, Geraniums, Gloxinias, Tomatoes.

# Hydroponics

Many terms have been used to describe this method of growing plants: hydroponics, chemical gardening, soilless gardening, sand culture, hydroculture, gravel culture, sawdust culture.

Hydroponics had its first glimmer in the late 17th century when studies were conducted to determine whether water or soil was responsible for plant growth. By the middle of the 19th century, plants were being grown successfully in chemical solutions. Until the 1930's soil-less plant culture was mostly a laboratory technique until Dr. William Gericke demonstrated it was possible to grow plants on a large scale using the "hydroponic" procedure. Experiments begun on Wake Island in 1938 proved the advantages of this type of farming and dramatic use was made of this during the Second World War to supply fresh green vegetables to American troops stationed in isolated, arid locations.

The success of hydroponics relies on the nutrient solution and the following three conditions:

**Light**—All plants need sunlight, some more than others.

**Heat**—For optimum results, warm season plants require a night temperature of 16°C. (60°F.) and a day temperature of 21°C. (70°F.). Cool season plants prosper in a 10°C. (50°F.) climate at night and 21°C. (70°F.) during the day.

**Air**—It provides carbon dioxide for the leaves and oxygen for the roots.

There are two basic systems of chemical gardening:

## WATER CULTURE

Here the root system is in direct contact with a large volume of nutrient solution. This requires a tank or trough of water-tight construction that will accommodate 6, 12 or 18 inches of solution. The trough may be as long as the space available but is usually 24 to 30 inches wide for ease of maintenance. A rigid frame wading pool could be adapted for this purpose.

Supply root anchorage by covering the tank with ½ inch wire mesh tray, 3 to 6 inches deep, filled with excelsior and hardwood sawdust, coarse sand or other decay resistant material. For aeration, leave an air space between the bottom of the planting tray and the surface of the solution. If this proves inadequate, use an aquarium type air pump to push air directly into the solution. The planting tray should be raised a few inches several times a day to permit air circulation.

*(see over)*

# Hydroponics (continued)

## AGGREGATE CULTURE

Plants are grown in sand, gravel or other inert materials (aggregates). The planting container is flooded with nutrient solution, which is then drained away and collected for recycling.

This method is referred to as the "slop method" and has the advantage of providing excellent root aeration as the solution drains away and fresh air moves in. Apartment cultivators can use—singly or in combination—sand, gravel, wood chips, sawdust, perlite, vermiculite, glass/plastic beads or foam chips to make their gardens grow. Most of these materials are available from building supply and garden stores.

Don't let the aggregate dry out or the roots of the plants will perish. It may be necessary to recycle the nutrient solutions several times a day.

With very small installations the problem may be overcome by using the "drip method," wherein nutrient solution is constantly dripping on the pseudosoil from a suitable reservoir. Both types of chemical gardens call for fresh nutrient solution every two weeks and a flushing of the root system with clear water to prevent excessive build up of salts. Balcony farmers with a small spread and a watering can may prefer to by-pass the recycling system. Gardeners who don't collect the nutrient flow-through can use almost any kind of container for the aggregate, as long as suitable drainage is provided to prevent stagnation and smothering of the roots. Even heavy duty plastic bags, filled with sand or sawdust and punctured at the bottom to allow for seepage, can produce a rewarding crop. Old mop buckets, plastic pails, even dishpans, fill the bill as efficiently as window box containers and custom built planters.

Up to now, assembling the waterproof containers, tubes, reservoirs and the weighing and mixing of the basic chemicals and trace elements has been a bit of a chore except for the handy person. Today this is no longer a deterrent or excuse since commercial growing kits are available that have all the pieces professionally designed and produced, even to a "slave" that constantly circulates the nutrient solution with proper aeration.

However you garden, it is the nutrient solution that counts. The mixture of chemical salts and water reaches the plant through the root system and this applies to gardens grown in either tanks or aggregate.

Mineral elements for plants are usually grouped into two categories:

(1) The essential elements nitrogen, phosphorus, potassium, calcium, magnesium and iron.

(2) Trace elements equally essential, boron, manganese, copper and zinc.

With so many formulas for nutrient solutions in existence, novice gardeners should look for ready-mix chemicals in the proper proportions. These are found in the water soluble fertilizer section of the garden store. Examine the label to be sure the trace elements are included. Since nutrient solutions destroy metals, they should be stored in glass-lined, plastic-lined or asphalt coated containers.

This is a typical mix-it-yourself nutrient mixture as recommended by the U.S. Department of Agriculture.

| | |
|---|---|
| Monocalcium Phosphate | —4 oz. |
| Magnesium Sulphate | —6 oz. |
| Potassium Nitrate | —9 oz. |
| Ammonium Sulphate | —1½ oz. |
| Calcium Sulphate | —7 oz. |
| Iron Sulphate | —¼ tsp. |

Use commercial grades rather than reaction grades and the trace nutrients of manganese, boron, zinc and copper will be present automatically. Carefully mix all ingredients and crush any large crystals to powder. Store in a dry glass jar with a screw on lid. Use a level teaspoon of the mixture per gallon (132 oz.) or a slightly heaping teaspoon per Imperial gallon (160 oz.).

The relative acidity of the nutrient solution is more critical than that encountered in the open garden and should be checked to keep it within a 5.5 to 6.5 pH range, which is slightly acid and acceptable to most plants. Look for chemicals at garden supply stores, pharmacies and laboratory supply houses.

Deficiencies in the plant nutrients will be signaled by the plant as follows:

| Deficient Chemical | Symptoms |
|---|---|
| Nitrogen | Small, light green leaves, weak stalks, lower leaves lighter than the upper ones. |
| Phosphorous | Lower leaves show yellow between the veins, dark green foliage, purplish color on the leaves. |
| Potassium | Mottled lower leaves, marginal browning. |
| Iron | Severe yellowing develops between the veins of the upper leaves of the plant. |
| Calcium | Feeding roots, tips of shoots and leaves die. |
| Magnesium | Leaves appear nettled and even the smallest veins remain green when foliage yellows. |
| Sulphur | Veins are lighter than the rest of the leaf. |
| Boron | Tips of shoots die. Leaves and stems thicken and become brittle. |

# Greenhouse gardening

The favorite green fantasy of most gardeners is "a garden anywhere—any time". Fortunately we live in a time when this dream is within the grasp of the dedicated without having to move South. Gardening in winter is no longer in the exclusive domain of the wealthy.

The home owner who can spare as little as 6 x 10 feet of ground is well on the way to gardening the year-round. The economy of a lean-to greenhouse attached to an existing building becomes obvious in view of the fact that one side already exists and the cost of extending heat and water is minimized.

If possible, a greenhouse should have a southern exposure, second and third best are southeast and southwest. However, don't despair if the only exposure available is north since foliage plants grow well without direct sun and if there is full light, open sky, African Violets and Orchids do well.

The inclusion of a bank of fluorescent lights allows for the growing of sun-loving plants under such circumstances. For the amateur the attached lean-to offers the most advantages since it is so readily accessible from the living quarters, which means it is easier to tend and usually more often shared by the rest of the family. With a detached separate greenhouse it becomes a matter of bundling up on the cold blustery days of winter to reach the house and this can dampen the enthusiasm of the most avid gardener especially if it becomes necessary to shovel a path through the snow as well.

In these days of instant everything, it is gratifying that the greenhouse has not been overlooked and it is possible to obtain prefabricated greenhouses in many shapes and sizes (lean-to, free-standing, straight eave, curved eave) and basically of durable aluminum for installation on a masonry wall or in a glass-to-the-ground style for the most growing space. There are even window greenhouses that can fit almost every size window. This can be the best answer for the apartment or rented premises.

With proper design, a greenhouse can be almost self-operating, at least during vacation absence.

Such situations require:

1. Automatic ventilation controlled by thermostat.
2. Automatic humidity controlled by humidistat.
3. Automatic watering by time clock, solenoid valves and weighted, spaghetti size hoses leading to each and every plant.
4. Automatic air circulation, continuous, or by time clock control.

There are many suppliers of greenhouses and operating equipment and their advertising is readily accessible in any gardening magazine. The starting point for a greenhouse venture is to request literature and price lists from several suppliers.

# Decorating with plants

It is now possible to live with plants year round even without an atrium or greenhouse. The introduction, and in some instances the reintroduction, of many sturdy foliage plants, with their low light requirements, has resulted in architectural planning of plants in the interior environment as well as a reawakening of plant use in vintage homes and apartments.

The increased use of picture windows, room dividers, planter boxes and alcoves, really leaves the home and apartment dweller with very little excuse not to get with it especially in view of the readily available plant material in department stores, supermarkets and nurseries. Lack of potting soil is not even a legitimate excuse for doing nothing, since it also is available where plants are sold and in sizes convenient for the city and cliff dwelling gardener.

Consider a plant as a piece of living art and you will be well on your way to selecting a specimen plant to suit your decor and personality. Decorators consider that a properly selected plant can do more for a room than an additional piece of furniture. While many specimens can grow to 15 feet or so, most can be stabilized at a height of 5 to 7 feet with the dwarfing that results from confinement of the root system in smaller size containers.

Always use plants in decor with full respect of their own architectural form and dramatic impact. Try not to locate specimens against over-patterned wallcoverings. Properly placed night lighting can give an exciting plus to any specimen from the resulting highlights and shadows.

Thirty years ago, the Philodendron was the durable mainstay for indoor plants in difficult locations, along with Ficus, the rubber plant. *Philodendron cordatum* growing up bark or a pressed fern stick with its shiny heart shaped leaves was about the only species available a few years ago. But today, you can readily make selections from 18 to 24 species of Philodendron off the shelf, so to speak. There are at least 250 known varieties of Philodendron, so look for a wider and wider selection. The natural habitat of this plant is the tropical high jungles of Central and South America. Most, but not all varieties are climbers and in their native habitat they climb right up to the tree tops. The leaves of these plants cover a wide range of shapes and sizes and, with their durability and low light requirements, they are naturals for difficult locations.

In general, it may be stated that foliage plants now outnumber flowering plants in the inside environment, even considering the proliferation of African Violets.

As more and more people realize that plants may be grown indoors without direct sun, they have become venturesome and planters of 14 to 20 inches in diameter displaying specimen plants are often the one and only focal point in a decor and often take as much space as the largest single piece of furniture in the room.

The main point to remember when using plants in the decoration is that they are not fixed like walls, rugs and draperies and can be moved to suit a special mood or effect if only for the interval of a party. The mobility of plants in pots cannot be over-emphasized and this quality is often under-used for creating special, dramatic effects for the duration of a special occasion. A plant will not suffer unduly from being moved out of its acclimatized location for two or three days.

When landscaping your room with specimen plants keep in mind that the plant should suit the decor and the other elements in the room. The container should complement the plant as well as the surroundings. Some of the dramatic plants used in room landscaping include: *Abutilon, Auraucaria excelsa, Bambusa multiplex, Beaucarnea recurvata, Cactus, Ficus elastica, Ficus lyrata, Ficus benjamina, Howea forsteriana, Musa cavendishii, Rhapis excelsa, Yucca aloifolia.*

While such plants may be grown from cuttings for small size plants, immediate effects can only be achieved by purchasing specimen sizes which cost substantially more but no more than an additional piece of furniture.

Basic rules for trouble-free cultivation of plants for interior decoration are relatively simple:

1. The potting soil should be loose, friable and capable of holding moisture but never becoming soggy. A mixture of equal parts garden loam, builders' sand, peat moss and rotted or dried manure is the optimum. With care you can also achieve fine results from the mixture sold commercially in supermarkets and nurseries; however, it is usually best to add more sand or perlite.
2. The container must have a drainage hole that is covered with a generous layer of crushed stone, broken crock, or pea gravel.
3. Water should be used at room temperature.
4. Don't allow the pot to sit in a saucer or container of water for more than thirty minutes.
5. Always check the soil before watering by feeling the texture and degree of moisture. Never let it become totally dry.
6. In general, the smaller size pots may require water twice a week while the larger ones will find once a week adequate. However, this can vary depending on the condition in the room. During winter, usually less water is required.
7. Feed only well established plants during their growing season with water soluble fertilizer, mixed and applied to the manufacturer's instructions.
8. Keep the plants out of cold drafts and don't close them in between drapes and the window where they may be chilled on cold nights.
9. Humidity around plants may be increased by filling trays or large plant saucers with crushed stone and water and placing the plants on top with the bottoms above the water level.
10. Clean the leaves regularly by using a soft cloth dampened with warm water.
11. Temperatures of 13°C. (55°F.) minimum and 21 to 22°C. (70 to 72°F.) max. are considered ideal.
12. Avoid scorched leaves and overheated pots by shading from direct sun.
13. Deflect hot air from radiators and vents away from plants.
14. If pests or diseases do develop, treat them immediately.
15. Apply common sense and you will get many years of enjoyment out of your living decorations.

# Holiday Gift Plants

For many years the **Poinsettia** plant has occupied a special spot in the heart at Christmas time. Many consider it to be a difficult plant since it will drop its leaves if given sudden chills, kept in drafts or not kept moist. However, given the attention it requires along with the recent hybrids, it will give satisfaction over the holiday and often well into late winter. While it was in the grower's greenhouse, the Poinsettia was grown at a 16° C. (60° F.) night temperature and a 18 to 21° C. (65 to 70° F.) day temperature. Accordingly, when the plant arrives swathed in tissue paper and green wrapping, try to duplicate the grower's conditions along with bright light. Wilting must be avoided by keeping the soil evenly moist.

Potted **Chrysanthemum** is the work horse of the potted plant industry of holiday gift givers. Bear in mind that by nature, it is autumn blooming, it thrives in the cooler temperatures around 18° C. (65° F.) and in bright light. With all its beautiful foliage it really needs a lot of water—check as often as twice a day. Keep it moist but don't allow it to stand in water more than fifteen minutes.

**Azalea** is probably the most beautiful of the gift plants and in some ways has become the most expensive. The plants are grown at about 16° C. (60° F.) in the grower's greenhouse, so be sure to keep your gift plant in a bright cool location. They are usually grown in peat or peat with a small amount of soil, thus careful watering is required. Check moistness often to prevent foliage drop. One useful method for watering is to submerge the plant in a bucket of water at room temperature and leave it until air bubbles cease to arise in the water.

**Jerusalem Cherry** and **Ornamental Peppers**, the former with scarlet berries about half an inch in diameter and the Pepper with its miniature hot red-peppers that may be eaten, belong to the same family. Keep the plants in a cool bright location around 18° C. (65° F.). Water daily and give a thorough soaking at least once a week. Both plants will shed their leaves rather dramatically if subjected to drafts or leaking gas, even from the pilot.

**Cyclamen** has a spectacular beauty that is a little difficult to maintain since the plant is normally grown at 10 to 16° C. (50 to 60° F.). Keep cool in good light and well moistened. You will note that the plant is growing from a corm (bulb) that is half in, half out of the soil of the pot. Watering is best accomplished by partial submersion of the pot for a brief period.

The bright brick-red flowers of **Kalanchoe** are being seen more and more at Christmas time. This plant has made a fantastic comeback as a holiday gift. It is a succulent from South America and is best grown in bright light at 18° C. (65° F.) Don't over-water, keep on the dry side, just moist, never soggy.

Potted **Oranges**, **Lemons**, or **Limes**, will probably reach you with ripe fruit, green fruit and more often than not with heady perfumed blossoms, which of course makes them a unique gift. The plants like it cool 18° C. (65° F.) with some sun. Keep the soil moist soaking regularly. Err on the dry side.

**Easter Lily**, the symbol of Easter and purity, usually arrives with at least one white funnel-shaped flower in full bloom and several buds. Keep the plant in full sun at about 18° C. (65° F.) when not on display. Keep the soil evenly moist and well drained. For recycling keep the plant green for as long as possible after flowering. Fertilize with water soluble fertilizer (low in phosphorous) on a 14-day schedule.

# Vacation Care

When you plan a vacation, also plan to have your plants receive the proper care and attention they deserve. The ideal solution is to have a neighbor come in to water and care for your plants. Failing this, there are several methods, depending on the length of your absence, for maintaining a supply of water for your plants.

## Automatic Watering

There is now on the market an automatic watering aid which consists of a clay probe body and a plastic tube top. The body is filled with water, inserted in the soil and the connecting plastic tubing is placed in a container of water at a higher level than the plant. The capillary action allows the water to flow through when the soil becomes dry. This system can be used for very long periods providing the water supply is adequate.

## Wicking

Another method of automatic watering uses porous threads or wicks drawn through the drainage holes of the pot. The lower ends then hang in a container of water.

## Plastic Enclosure

A certain degree of moisture can be achieved by enclosing your plants in clear plastic bags thereby creating a terrarium effect.

## Bathroom

Some indoor gardeners place all their plants together on porous water-soaked bricks positioned in a few inches of water in the bath tub; however, the lighting in most bathrooms is not adequate and it is best to experiment first before relying on this method.

# Part Three

# APPENDIX

# GLOSSARY

## Acid Soil
Soil may be acid (sour), alkaline (sweet), or neutral. The degree of acidity or alkalinity of soil affects the availability of some of the minerals which plants need for growth.

## Aeration
Most plants must have air around their roots. Waterlogged or compacted soil causes plants to suffer through lack of air (oxygen).

## Air Layering
A form of propagation. The most successful method for air layering is to cut a slit in the stem and, keeping the cut open with a matchstick or small pebble or some other material, cover with moist sphagnum moss and wrap the moss with plastic.

## Alkaline Soil
This is the opposite of acid soil. Extreme alkalinity is injurious to most plants. Moderately alkaline soil is needed by many plants, especially those of the Pea family (Leguminosea).

## Alternate
Parts of a plant (e.g. leaves) placed singularly at different heights on the stem of the plant.

## Ammonium Sulphate
A 20% nitrogen fertilizer used to add nitrogen to soil as a plant food and to maintain a moderately acid soil condition.

## Annual
Grows in one season from seed to maturity and then dies.

## Anther
Part of stamen which bears pollen.

## Aquatic Plants
Plants which live in water or very wet soils.

## Areole
A spine-bearing spot on a cacti stem sometimes raised, sometimes sunken.

## Armed
Has defensive spines, thorns, prickles or barbs.

## Asexual
Without sex. Asexual propagation is propagation of plants by use of cuttings, by air layering or by division.

## Axil
Upper angle such as made at the juncture of a leaf stem to the main stem.

## Ball (Root Ball)
The round mass of roots and soil that fill the pot.

## Basal
At the bottom or lower end.

## Basal Rot
A disease which attacks the bottom (or base) of certain bulbs.

## Biennial
Grows in two seasons from seed to maturity and then dies.

## Bisexual
Both sexes present in the same flower (stamen and pistil).

## Blade
The broad part of a leaf or flower petal.

211

## Bone Meal

A slow acting fertilizer made from the bones of animals. It contains approximately 1 to 2% nitrogen and 25% phosphorous. Bone meal takes a long time to decompose and becomes plant food if used in conjunction with humus.

## Bract

A specialized leaf, often colored, and sometimes confused with the flower (e.g. the bract of the Poinsettia).

## Broadcast

To scatter or spread widely.

## Broad Leaved Evergreens

Plants, trees and shrubs that retain their foliage during the winter but are not conifers, e.g. Azaleas (Rhododendrons).

## Builders' Sand

A grade of clean, coarse sand commonly used in the building trades in the preparation of mortar and cement.

## Bulb

An underground thickened stem with scales as in a Lily.

## Bulbil (Bulblet)

A small bulb offset from the mother plant.

## Bush

A thick shrub with no defined trunk.

## Callus

New tissue that covers and protects cut or bruised tissue.

## Calyx

Leaf-like parts forming the outer protective envelope of the flower.

## Campanulate

Bell shaped.

## Carnivorous

Literally meat-eating in plants, i.e., insectivorous.

## Cold Frame

A frame which is enclosed and covered with clear glass or plastic and is used to start plants.

## Compost

Decomposed vegetable matter. Useful in potting mixes as garden loam but it must be screened and sterilized.

## Compound

Similar parts in pairs or more.

## Conifers

Trees and shrubs with needles and bearing cones.

## Corm

A bulb-like part as in crocus.

## Cormel

A small offset corm from the mother corm.

## Creeping

A trailing part that takes root throughout its length.

## Crown

The bottom of the plant where stems and roots meet.

## Cultivar

A term used to describe a plant (cultivated variety) maintained only in cultivation; a selection with clearly distinguishing features that may be reproduced sexually or asexually.

## Cutting(s)

To cut off part of a plant in order to start new plants.

## Damp-off

A serious fungus condition which affects young seedlings at the soil level.

## Deciduous

Shedding all leaves annually.

## Dentate

Toothed.

## Division

A form of propagation.

## Dormant

The period when a plant is in a resting stage after the end of a cycle of growth. Most plants, with a few exceptions, have their dormant periods in the winter.

## Elliptic

Oval with narrowed end.

## Epiphyte

A plant growing on another for support only.

## Evergreen

A plant that remains green at all times by shedding only a few leaves at a time and over an extended period.

## Family

Botanical term to indicate grouping of plants according to their similarity and resemblance, especially in the floral reproductive parts.

## Fertilizer

Used to encourage growth in plants. May be organic (from nature) or commercial (from inorganic chemicals).

## Fetid

Stinking, disagreeable odor.

## Flat

Shallow box or other container with drainage holes used to sow seeds or plant seedlings.

## Force (Forcing)

To induce a plant to reach maturity out of its normal season.

## Frond

Leaf of a fern or palm.

## Fungicide

Used to destroy or control diseases.

## Genus

The main subdivision of a plant family. Each genus is further divided into species, then varieties or cultivars.

## Germination

The point at which a seed sprouts.

## Habit

Mode of growth.

## Habitat

Natural home.

## Half-hardy

Plants that can take some normal winter temperatures.

## Hardening-off

Conditioning plants which have been grown indoors to enable them to grow outdoors by gradually exposing them to colder temperature and bright light.

## Hardy

Plants that are adapted to cold winter temperatures of an area.

## Heating Cable

An electric cable used to provide heat to the underside (bottom) of a propagating table or bench.

## Herb

A plant used for flavoring, medicinal purposes or fragrance.

## Hormone, Rooting

A chemical used for hastening root development in a cutting.

## Humus

Partially decayed plant or animal matter. Humus provides nutrients, holds moisture, separates soil particles and improves the condition of soil.

## Hybrid

A plant resulting from cross-pollination of two or more different species of plants.

## Hydroponics

Growing plants without the aid of soil in a nutrient solution.

## Imbricate

Overlapping like tiles or fish scales.

## Inorganic

Fertilizers which are produced chemically. Often identified numerically, e.g. 10-6-4, which means 10% nitrogen, 6% phosphoric acid and 4% potash.

**Insecticide**
Chemical or organic material used to kill insects.

**Internode**
Part of stem between one leaf node and the next.

**Lateral**
On, at, or from, the side.

**Latex**
Milky sap of some plants.

**Leader**
The central trunk of a tree, shrub or plant from which side branches develop.

**Leaflet**
One division of a compound leaf.

**Leafmould**
Partially decayed leaves used in potting mixture: must be screeened and sterilized.

**Leaf Stalk**
A petiole; the stalk of a leaf by which it is connected to a plant's main branch or stem.

**Lime**
Is added to soil to reduce acidity.

**Loam**
A soil that is composed of clay, silt and sand. A rich loam contains organic matter.

**Manure (Rotted or dried Manure)**
Used to enrich soil.

**Mid-rib**
The continuation of the leaf stem forming the main rib of the leaf.

**Mutant**
Different from the parent, often visibly.

**Nitrogen**
Nitrogen is a major plant food either organic or inorganic. It is essential to leaf growth.

**Node**
The point on a stem where the leaf is attached.

**Nutrient Solution**
Contains all the foods needed for plant growth as used in hydroponics.

**Obtuse**
Blunt, not pointed.

**Organic**
Animal or plant matter.

**Ovate**
Egg shaped.

**Palmate**
Divided in open hand-like fashion.

**Peat Moss**
Partially or wholly decayed plant parts. It is used in potting mixture because of its water holding capacity. Long-term it will supply nitrogen to the plant.

**Perennial**
Living for more than three seasons.

**Perlite**
Expanded volcanic rock used primarily for soil aeration. It supplies no nutrients and doesn't hold moisture. It may be used in place of sand.

**Petiole**
The stalk of a leaf which attaches it to the plant's main stem or branch.

**Phosphate**
A salt of phosphoric acid that stimulates root formation and seed production.

**Pinch (Pinch Prune)**
To remove the young new tip (or terminal) growth of a stem to stimulate branching and bushiness.

**Pistil**
Female reproductive parts of a flower.

**Plant Foods**
Usually composed of three elements: nitrogen, potash and phosphate, and used to encourage growth in plants.

**Plunge**
To place a pot up to its rim in soil (outdoors), or in water to moisten the plant's soil.

**Potash**
An oxide of potassium that enhances flower, fruit and seed production.

**Pot Bound**
When roots of a plant fill the pot to the point that the plant is unable to progress further.

**Potting**
To place plants, rooted cuttings, bulbs, in specially prepared pots.

**Pricking Out**
To remove tiny seedlings very carefully.

**Propagation**
To grow additional plants either from seed, cuttings, air layering, division.

**Prostrate**
Flat to the ground.

**Pseudobulb**
Bulb form stems of some orchids.

**Repellents, Insect**
Substance which drives insects away.

**Repotting**
To move plant from one container to another.

**Rest Period**
Period of inactivity in plant growth.

**Rhizome**
A thick, fleshy root-like stem which occurs underground or creeps along the surface of the soil. New plants and roots come from the joints.

**Root Ball**
The round mass of roots and soil that fill the pot.

**Rooting Hormone**
A chemical used to hasten root development in a cutting.

**Rooting Media**
Material such as sphagnum moss, builders' sand, vermiculite, perlite, in which cuttings are placed.

**Root Pruning**
Cutting of roots to keep plant within bounds.

**Rosette**
A cluster of leaves radiating symmetrically from a central stem.

**Runner**
A trailing shoot that takes root at the nodes.

**Sand, Builders'**
A grade of clean, coarse sand commonly used in the building trades in the preparation of mortar and cement.

**Scald, Leaf**
Bleaching of the leaves of plants caused by too much exposure to sun.

**Scape**
A leafless stem that bears flowers.

**Scurfy**
Scaly.

**Sepal**
A part of the calyx.

**Shallow Rooted**
Plants whose roots are close to the surface of the earth.

**Shrub**
A woody plant divided into stems at the ground.

**Simple Leaf**
A leaf which has only one blade attached to the main leaf stalk.

**Spadix**
A thick fleshy flower spike, usually enclosed in a spathe.

**Spathe**
A bract surrounding a spadix.

**Species**

Term which is used to designate a major subdivision in a plant family.

**Sphagnum**

Bog mosses dried and used as a planting medium.

**Spike**

An elongated cluster of flowers on the flower stem.

**Spine**

A sharp woody part arising from a stem of a leaf, etc.

**Spreading**

Extending horizontally.

**Spur**

One or more of the petals of a flower forming a tube-like structure.

**Staking**

To fasten stems or flowers to sticks or supports to hold them erect.

**Stamen**

Male reproductive parts of a flower.

**Sterilization**

To destroy insects, diseases, weed seeds in soil by use of steam, heat or chemicals.

**Stolon**

A horizontal root stem that produces a new plant from the tip.

**Succulent**

Plants which have special water storing properties.

**Sulphate of Ammonia**

A nitrogenous fertilizer (20% nitrogen) used to add nitrogen to soil as a plant food and used where moderate acid conditions are required.

**Syringe**

A rubber bulb used for wetting foliage.

**Tender**

Unable to survive cold.

**Tendril**

A thread-like growth by which a plant clings for support.

**Terminal**

At the tip.

**Terrestrial**

On the ground.

**Top Dressing**

To add fresh soil mixture to top of soil.

**Trauma**

Condition arising from a disturbance or change in light, heat or water.

**Tuber**

A swollen underground stem or root from which bulbs are borne.

**Tuberous-Rooted**

Growing from a tuber, e.g. tuberous-rooted Begonia.

**Variety**

A subdivision in a plant family used to designate a natural variation in a species.

**Vermiculite**

Mineral mica expanded by high heat. A sterile planting medium used for rooting cuttings. It is frequently combined with loam and peat moss as a substitute for sand. It has capacity for holding moisture.

**Whorl**

Ring of three or more leaves or flowers.

# CREDITS

**Editor :** Anna Ozvoldik
**Design :** Wayne Chen
**Photographer :** Marc Cramer
**Illustrator :** Carmen Jensen

We gratefully acknowledge the assistance of Mr. André Champagne, Director of the
Montreal Botanical Garden and the cooperation of his staff in the selection and preparation
of the majority of house plants photographed for this book.


Back Cover: Home interior photo
© Larry D. Gordon/The Image Bank of Canada

# INDEX